Societal Impact on Aging Series

Series Editor

K. Warner Schaie, PhD
Director, Gerontology Center
College of Health and Human Development
The Pennsylvania State University
University Park, PA

K. Warner Schaie, PhD, is an Evan Pugh Professor of Human Development and Psychology and Director of the Gerontology Center at the Pennsylvania State University. He has previously held professional appointments at the University of Nebraska, West Virginia University, and the University of Southern California. Dr. Schaie received his BA from the University of California–Berkeley, and his MS and PhD degrees from the University of Washington, all in psychology. He is the author or editor of 22 books and over 150 journal articles and chapters related to the study of human aging. Dr. Schaie is the recipient of the Distinguished Scientific Contributions Award of the American Psychological Association and of the Robert W. Kleemeier Award for Distinguished Research Contributions from the Gerontological Society of America.

Carmi Schooler, PhD, is Acting Chief of the Laboratory of Socio-environmental Studies of the Intra-mural Research Program of the National Institute of Mental Health. He received his BA from Hamilton College in 1954 and his PhD in social psychology from New York University in 1959, after which he began in his present laboratory. Throughout his career he has been actively involved in the experimental–psychological investigation of the social–psychological and cognitive aspects of schizophrenia. His more recent experimental–psychological research has also examined cognitive functioning in the elderly.

His sociological research, which has been published in both books and the major sociological journals, centers on social-structural and cultural determinants of normal and abnormal psychological functioning throughout the life span. Much of this research has focused on the psychological effects of occupational conditions. Other sociological interests include the theoretical and methodological examination of such concepts as coping, self-esteem, and environmental complexity, as well as empirical studies on the effects of social structure and culture on both the nature and symptoms of mental illness and the functioning of and attitudes toward the elderly.

Impact of Work on Older Adults

K. Warner Schaie
Carmi Schooler

Editors

SP **Springer Publishing Company**

HD
6279
I43
1998

Springer Publishing Company, Inc.
536 Broadway
New York, NY 10012–3955

Cover design by Margaret Dunin
Acquisitions Editor: Helvi Gold
Production Editor: Pamela Lankas

98 99 00 01 02 / 5 4 3 2 1

Library of Congress Cataloging-in-Publication Data

Impact of work on older adults / K. Warner Schaie, Carmi Schooler, Editors.
    P.   cm. — (Societal impact on aging series)
   Includes bibliographical references and indexes.
   ISBN 0-8261-9920-8
   1. Aged—Employment—Social aspects—Congresses. 2. Aged—Employment—Psychological aspects—Congresses. 3. Retirement—Congresses. I. Schaie, K. Warner (Klaus Warner), 1928– . II. Schooler, Carmi. III. Series.
   [DNLM: 1. Aged—psychology—congresses. 2. Work—psychology—congresses. 3. Job Satisfaction—in old age—congresses. 4. Retirement—in old age—congresses. 5. Cross-Cultural Comparison—congresses.
   6. Quality of Life—congresses. WT 145 I34 1997]
   HD6279.I43   1997
   306.3'61—dc21
   DNLM/DLC
   for Library of Congress   97-24103
                                               CIP

Contents

Contributors

Leslie Caplan, PhD
Section on Socio-Environmental
   Studies
National Institutes of Mental
   Health
Bethesda, MD 20892

David J. Ekerdt, PhD
Gerontology Center
University of Kansas
Lawrence, KS 66160-7117

James L. Farr, PhD
The Pennsylvania State University
Department of Psychology
University Park, PA 16802

Mark D. Hayward, PhD
The Pennsylvania State University
Department of Sociology
University Park, PA 16802

James S. House, PhD
Department of Sociology and
   Survey Research Center
Institute for Social Research
The University of Michigan
Ann Arbor, MI 48106-1248

Ann Howard, PhD
Leadership Research Institute
   and Development Dimensions
   International
Tenafly, NJ 07670

William J. Hoyer, PhD
Department of Psychology
Syracuse University
Syracuse, NY 13244-2340

F. Thomas Juster, PhD
Institute for Social Research
The University of Michigan
Ann Arbor, MI 48106-1248

Arne L. Kalleberg, PhD
Department of Sociology
University of North Carolina
Chapel Hill, NC 27599

Stephanie R. Klein, MS
The Pennsylvania State
   University
Department of Psychology
University Park, PA 16802

Victor W. Marshall, PhD
University of Toronto
Institute for Human
  Development, Life Course and
  Aging
Toronto, Ontario
Canada M5T 3J1

Gary Oates, PhD
Section on Socio-Environmantal
  Studies
National Institutes of Mental
  Health
Bethesda, MD 20892

Matilda White Riley, ScD
Senior Social Scientist
National Institute on Aging
National Institutes of Health
Bethesda, MD 20892

Aage Sørensen, PhD
Department of Sociology
Harvard University
Cambridge, MA 02138

Gerald A. Straka, PhD
Institute for Interdisciplinary
  Research on Aging
University Bremen
D-28334 Bremen
Germany

Harvey L. Sterns, PhD
Department of Psychology and
  Institute for Life-span
  Development and Gerontology
The University of Akron
Akron, OH 44235

Paul E. Tesluk, PhD
Tulane University
Department of Psychology
New Orleans, LA 70118-5698

Chikako Usui, PhD
University of Missouri at
    St. Louis
Department of Sociology
St. Louis, MO 63121-4499

Peter Warr, PhD
University of Sheffield
Institute of Work Psychology
Sheffield S10 2TN
England

Preface

This is the 10th volume in a series on the broad topic of the "Societal Impact on Aging." The first five volumes of this series were published by Erlbaum Associates under the series title "Social Structure and Aging." The present volume is the fifth published under the Springer Publishing Company imprint. It is the edited proceedings of a conference held at the Pennsylvania State University, October 16–17, 1995.

The series of Penn State Gerontology Center conferences originated from the deliberations of a subcommittee of the Committee on Life Course Perspectives of the Social Science Research Council, chaired by Matilda White Riley in the early 1980s. That subcommittee was charged with developing an agenda and mechanisms that would serve to encourage communication between scientists who study societal structures that might affect the aging of individuals and those scientists who are concerned with the possible effects of contextual influences on individual aging. The committee proposed a series of conferences that would systematically explore the interfaces between social structures and behavior, and, in particular, would identify mechanisms through which society influences adult development. When the second editor was named director of the Penn State Gerontology Center, he was able to implement this conference program as one of the center's major activities.

The previous nine volumes in this series have dealt with the societal impact on aging in psychological processes (Schaie & Schooler, 1989); age structuring in comparative perspective (Kertzer & Schaie, 1989); self-directedness and efficacy over the life span (Rodin, Schooler, & Schaie, 1990); aging, health behaviors, and health outcomes (Schaie, Blazer, & House, 1992); caregiving in families (Zarit, Pearlin, & Schaie, 1993); aging in historical perspective (Schaie & Achenbaum, 1993); adult intergenerational relations (Bengtson, Schaie, & Burton, 1995); older adults' decision making and the law (Smyer, Schaie, & Kapp, 1996); and the impact of social structures on decision making in the elderly (Willis, Schaie, & Hayward, 1997).

The strategy for each of these volumes has been to commission six reviews on three major topics by established subject-matter specialists who have credibility in aging research. We then invited two formal discussants for each chapter—usually one drawn from the writer's discipline and one from a neighboring discipline. This format seems to provide a suitable antidote against the perpetuation of parochial orthodoxies as well as to make certain that questions are raised with respect to the validity of iconoclastic departures in new directions.

To focus the conference, the editors chose three topics of broad interest to gerontologists. Social and behavioral scientists with a demonstrated track record were then selected and asked to interact with those interested in theory building within a multidisciplinary context.

The purpose of the conference reported in this volume was to examine the mechanisms through which the workplace impacts the older individual as well as to examine the effects of retirement as constituting the loss of this stimulating influence. It has become clear that the meaningful nature of work and the stimulation provided by the workplace have a major impact on maintaining cognitive functions as well as providing viable social roles for persons past midlife. Thus the work place may be conceptualized also as a major social support system, one that allows for natural nonfamilial interpersonal contacts and communication. Nevertheless, the workplace may also be the source of increasing stress as older workers try to maintain accustomed roles when lowered energy levels and response speed may affect their productivity.

Changing demographics bring into question previous assumptions on the timing and circumstances of giving up these roles through retirement. With the baby boomers being followed by smaller cohorts, we can expect the average age of the workforce to continue rising into the early part of the 21st century. Attributes of the workplace that either support or reduce the productivity of older workers therefore assume increasing importance.

If the workplace is seen as a major influence in maintaining competent cognitive and interpersonal functioning in individuals, then it also becomes important to consider the effects on a person's functional effectiveness when he or she leaves the world of work. Although there is only a limited literature on what we know about the impact of the workplace prior to retirement, conceptualizations of mechanisms are needed to help understand the vast individual differences in postretirement adjustment and intellectual functioning. Because retirement practices, attitudes about retirement, and retirement consequences are often unique to a particular society, we decided to include in this volume a comparative analysis of the cognitive and social impact of retirement in the exemplar case of Japan.

The volume begins with an examination of the impact of work on older persons. The first chapter explicates the seminal model of Kohn and Schooler and addresses the manner in which jobs affect older workers, and, in turn, how older workers transform characteristics of the job and of the organization. These issues are investigated by a broad review of relevant psychological and sociological research. Western societies have far less structured ways of dealing with older workers (other than retirement and pension structures) than is the case in other societies. Chapter 4 therefore presents a cross-cultural view by presenting a case study of how older workers are treated within the Japanese context. Transforming the roles of older workers and transitioning them toward retirement by systematic outplacement activities are considered.

The second topic in this volume deals with the effects of the workplace on the older worker. The first chapter in this section focuses on workplace norms and examines how such norms influence the roles assigned to the older worker as well as the expectations as to when and under what circumstances workers are expected to retire from the workplace. These matters are expanded further in the second chapter, which examines the organizational structure of the workplace and the role of the older worker within a systems framework. In this context, supervisor/management evaluation and reinforcement of older workers are also considered.

The third topic is concerned with noncognitive influences in the workplace. Here we first consider career trajectories and the older workers, using economic models to show that somewhat different consequences for the duration and nature of work may be expected depending on the particular labor market model to which a given job conforms. This chapter also discusses the nature of work and the responsibilities of people in different positions of the work-related social hierarchy toward the end of their occupational careers. As a final topic, a systematic examination of the role of work is provided that shows its effect on well-being and mental health.

Our emphasis on understanding the impact of broad societal trends affecting the welfare of individuals and their development into old age brought together scientists interested in individual development, the organizational structures of work, economics, as well as social policy. A formal epilogue tries to draw the lessons these interdisciplinary deliberations seemed to suggest. It is hoped that the resultant interplay of views from various disciplines contributes to our theoretical understanding of basic issues in the impact of work on older persons and provides an in-depth review of the literature that can inform policy development and practice.

We are grateful for the financial support of the conference that led to this volume, which was provided by Conference Grant AG 09787-05 from the National Institute on Aging, and by additional support from the Vice-President for Research and Dean of the Graduate School of The Pennsylvania State University. We are also grateful to Judy Hall and Alvin Hall for handling the conference logistics, to Anna Shuey for coordinating the manuscript preparation, and to Joan Houtz for preparing the indexes.

K. Warner Schaie

REFERENCES

Bengtson, V. L., Schaie, K. W., & Burton, L. (1995). *Adult intergenerational relations: Effects of societal changes.* New York: Springer Publishing Co.

Kertzer, D., & Schaie, K. W. (1989). *Age structuring in comparative perspective.* Hillsdale, NJ: Erlbaum.

Rodin, J., Schooler, C., & Schaie, K. W. (1990). *Self-directedness and efficacy: Causes and effects throughout the life course.* Hillsdale, NJ: Erlbaum.

Schaie, K. W., & Achenbaum, W. A. (1993). *Societal impact on aging: Historical perspectives.* New York: Springer Publishing Co.

Schaie, K. W., House, & Blazer, D. J., (1992). *Aging, health behaviors, and health outcomes.* Hillsdale, NJ: Erlbaum.

Schaie, K. W., & Schooler, C. (1989). *Social structure and aging: Psychological processes.* Hillsdale, NJ: Erlbaum.

Smyer, M., Schaie, K. W., & Kapp, M. B. (1996). *Older adults' decision-making and the law.* New York: Springer Publishing Co.

Willis, S. L., Schaie, K. W., & Hayward, M. (1997). *Societal mechanisms for maintaining competence in old age.* New York: Springer Publishing Co.

Zarit, S. H., Pearlin, L., & Schaie, K. W. (1993). *Social structure and caregiving: Family and cross-national perspectives.* Hillsdale, NJ: Erlbaum.

CHAPTER 1

Aging and Work: An Overview

Carmi Schooler, Leslie Caplan, and Gary Oates

This book follows the general theme of the previous Pennsylvania State University conferences designed to promote interaction among the various social sciences and those disciplines specifically concerned with investigating individual differences in human aging processes. The topic of this book is the impact of the workplace on elderly individuals and of elderly individuals on the workplace. Its aim is to go beyond an account of how and how much the elderly and work-place affect each other to an examination of the mechanisms through which cultural and social structural factors mediate these efforts.

The two disciplines being brought together in this are sociology and psychology. Areas in both disciplines share a common interest in issues of aging. Nevertheless, sociologists and psychologists are each often unaware of the theoretical approaches and of empirical findings in the other discipline that are directly relevant to their own research and that are generally important for understanding what happens as we grow older. The other chapters in this volume will detail some of the most recent findings and theoretical conceptualizatons in each discipline about how social structure and culture affect the way work and the elderly mutually impact each other. In this introductory chapter, we will try to furnish an appropriate background by providing a brief overview of findings and conceptualizations that have already appeared in the sociological and psychological literatures.

SOCIOLOGY, AGING, AND WORK

Perhaps the most thorough conceptualizations and literature integrations in the sociology of aging have come from Matilda Riley's "aging and society" approach, as exemplified in her work and that of her colleagues from the Program on Age and Structural Change (e.g., Riley, 1987; Riley, Johnson, & Foner, 1972; Riley & Riley, 1994). Among Riley's concerns are the social, structural, and psychological effects of historically based differences in cohort size, longevity and life experience. She sees as "peculiarly sociological in . . . (her) conceptual framework . . . the interplay between the two dynamisms: aging of individuals in successive cohorts and changing age structures of society. Each dynamism is distinct; neither is reducible to the other. Each has its own tempo" (Riley, Foner, & Waring, 1988, p. 245).

Several overarching principles emerge from her conceptualization:

1. *Principle of cohort differences in aging* "Because each cohort is born at a particular date, it lives through a unique segment of historical time and confronts its own particular sequence of social and environmental events and changes. . . . [B]ecause society changes, people in different cohorts age in different ways. The aging process is altered by social change." (Riley, 1987, p. 4).

2. *Principle of cohort influence on social change* "Because members of successive cohorts age in new ways, they contribute to changes in the social structure" (Riley, 1987, p. 4).

3. *Principle of asynchrony* "Aging and social change, though they are interdependent, are not synchronized with one another. . . . Within each cohort, people moving along the axis of the life course are born and die according to a rhythm set by the approximate current length of the human lifetime. In contrast, social change moves with no comparable rhythm or periodicity" (Riley, 1987, p. 5).

4. *Dialectic between aging and social change* Although not explicitly so identified by Riley, a fourth principle can be derived by considering the joint implications of the first two principles listed
previously—the dialectic between aging and social change. There
is "a continuing interplay—energized by cohort flow—between
individual aging and social change. . . . In response to social
change, millions of individuals in a cohort begin to develop age-
typical patterns and regularities of behavior. . . . These behavior
patterns then become defined as age-appropriate norms and rules,
are reinforced by 'authorities,' and thereby become institutionalized in the structure of society. . . . In turn, these changes in age
norms and social structure redirect age-related behaviors" (Riley,
1987, p. 4).

Riley's principles and concerns are directly applicable to understanding recent empirical sociological and sociodemographic findings
germane to issues of work and aging. The relevance to issues of work and
the elderly of Riley's view concerning the importance of differences in
cohort size and longevity is exemplified by how such demographic differences affect the potential numbers of older individuals in the workforce. Primarily as a consequence of significant declines in fertility and
mortality levels in recent years, the population of the United States has
been aging so rapidly that its aging will be "one of the most important
social phenomena of the next half century" (Preston & Martin, 1994).
The percentage of the North American population aged 65 and over rose
from 8.7% in 1955 to 12.5% in 1990, and is projected to rise to 18.5%
by the year 2025 (see Preston & Martin, 1994, Table 1.1, p. 2). Shifts in
the age composition of the U.S. labor force mirror those of the population, as members of the aging baby boom generation are being supplanted
in the labor force by a declining percentage of younger individuals (see
Crawley, 1992; Jessup, 1989; Longman, 1988; Mor-Barak & Tynan,
1993). The proportion of the U.S. labor force aged 18–34 has been declining since the early 1980s. This trend is likely to continue at least to the
end of this century (Crawley, 1992; Mor-Barak & Tynan, 1993).

The relative scarcity of younger workers should presumably have made
employers more willing to use older workers, hence increasing these older
workers' market value and encouraging them to keep working. There has
been, instead, a remarkable trend toward earlier retirement, particularly

among older men. In 1900, two out of every three American men aged 65 and older participated in the paid labor force. This proportion plunged to approximately 46% in 1950 and to 19% in 1980.

This somewhat incongruous trend toward early retirement seems to be rooted in the profound shift in norms regarding the economic activity among older individuals that the industrial revolution induced. As such, it is an example of one of Riley's principles—the principle of cohort differences in aging. Retirement of older workers from the preindustrial era productive sector, dominated by small-scale agricultural production and self-employment, was rare. However, the shift to large, technology-intensive production requiring a more highly skilled and educated labor force resulted in the placement of a premium on younger workers. Older workers received palpable signals that cessation of their paid labor force activity would be preferable (DeViney & O'Rand, 1988; Mor-Barak & Tynan, 1993; Schrank & Waring, 1989). Another of Riley's principles—the effect of cohort experience on social change—is exemplified by how the experience of early retirement and increased longevity were factors leading to the development of the Social Security system.

Recently, societal and institutional signals regarding the continued labor force participation of older workers have become progressively more age-neutral. This shift has occurred in tandem with growing concerns about the tremendous economic burden of early retirement to society and, to a lesser degree, with concerns about anticipated shortages of younger workers (Schrank & Waring, 1989). The apparent asynchrony between established norms of early retirement deriving from earlier socioeconomic conditions and newer pressures toward longer workforce participation originating from limitations in society's financial resources and demographic changes limiting the potential number of younger workers illustrates another of Riley's principles—the asynchrony of aging and social change.

Among the first signs that American social institutions are beginning to view longer workforce participation more favorably was the Age Discrimination in Employment Act of 1967. This act proscribed arbitrary discrimination on the basis of age and sought to assist employers in overcoming problems arising from the employment of older workers (Levine, 1988). In addition, mandatory retirement rules, once applicable to nearly one-half of all American workers, have now been eliminated via legislation for the vast majority of the American labor force

(Quinn & Burkhauser, 1994). Although the overall structure of the Social Security program continues to encourage earlier retirement (Quinn & Burkhauser, 1994; Schrank & Waring, 1989), the most recent modifications to the amount of Social Security benefits collected by retirees have also been designed to reduce disincentives to prolonged labor force participation. Private employer pension plans, which had often provided an even greater incentive for early retirement than the Social Security program, have now ceased expanding and may even be declining (Quinn & Burkhauser, 1994).

The shifts toward age neutrality notwithstanding, retirement at age 65 has emerged as the "normative threshold" in American society (see Ekerdt, chapter 7 of this volume), and early retirement patterns among men may have reset the transition period back an additional 10 years (DeViney & O'Rand, 1988). In addition to the disincentives to prolonged employment within Social Security and private employer pension plans, norms discouraging late retirement are often enforced by age-biased organizational policies (Schrank & Waring, 1989) predicated on the assumption, often embraced by older workers themselves, that older workers are more costly and less productive.

All in all, seen from the perspective of Riley's sociological principles, the change earlier in the century, resulting from the full implementation of the industrial revolution, to relatively early retirement is an example of how changes in the social structure can lead to cohort differences in the behavior of older adults. The development of a Social Security system supporting relatively early retirement exemplifies her principle of cohort influence on social change. The continuing tendency toward early retirement in the face of societal changes that would seem to encourage longer labor force participation is an example of Riley's principle of asynchrony between aging and social change. This complex picture of the mutual effects of the aging experience of individual members of successive cohorts and the social structures of which they are a part provides an excellent example of the dialectic between changes in the aging experience of different cohorts and social change, which is at the core of Riley's conceptualization. (For a discussion of the theoretical and empirical reasons why changes in social structures may affect the functioning and behavior of individuals more rapidly than such individual changes affect the nature of social structures, see Schooler, 1994).

PSYCHOLOGY, AGING, AND WORK

The sociological approach to issues of work and the elderly tends to assume that the elderly react to the social–structurally determined conditions of their environments in much the same manner as do other adults. In contrast, much of the psychological approach to the elderly has focused on possible differences between the ways that they and younger people react to environmental demands. Thus the major theoretical conceptualizations and research findings in the psychological literature relevant to issues of aging and work center on the possible *distinctiveness* of the older worker in two major areas: (1) abilities and skills that may be relevant to job performance, (2) attitudinal and motivational variables such as job satisfaction and worker commitment. Nevertheless, many of Riley's principles are, as we will see, relevant to interpretations of findings in these areas as well.

Abilities and Skills

Much of the research in this area is based on the assumption that age-related differences in job performance are not the result of age per se, but of age-related differences in abilities and skills (see Salthouse & Maurer, 1996, for a thorough exposition of this assumption). Therefore, most studies focus on decrements in abilities and skills that may accrue with age. However, any discussion of age-related decrements in cognitive functioning must acknowledge the high degree of heterogeneity demonstrated in the literature. There are two major types of heterogeneity. The first involves differences among skills and abilities in the degree to which they are susceptible to age-related impairment. For example, older people are more likely to demonstrate age-related decrements in tasks that rely heavily on fluid intelligence (i.e., problem-solving and inductive skills originally believed to be relatively "culture-free") than in tasks that rely heavily on crystallized intelligence (i.e., knowledge acquired through cultural experience; see Horn, 1980; Horn & Cattell, 1967; Schaie, 1996b, for further discussions of this distinction). The second type of heterogeneity results from the marked differences among individuals in the degree to which they demonstrate age-related decline (e.g., Schaie, 1996a). These differences among individuals can be attributed, at least in part, to a variety of variables: life or occupational complexity (e.g.,

Arbuckle, Gold, & Andres, 1986; Hultsch, Hammer, & Small, 1993; Kohn & Schooler, 1983; Schaie, 1996b), educational level (e.g., Arbuckle et al.,), cohort (e.g., Schaie, 1989), and physical health (e.g., Hertzog, Schaie, & Gribbin, 1978; Hultsch, et al., 1993).

In addition, we must keep in mind the fact that most studies of age differences in abilities and skills have been conducted with cross-sectional designs. Therefore, any age differences observed may be due either to aging per se or to cohort differences. To the extent that experiences of cohorts have changed in relevant variables, such as exposure to technology early in life, or even in educational levels, such experiences will appear in these studies as age effects.

In this section, one should keep these caveats in mind as we examine three major questions. First, to what extent do people demonstrate age-related decrements in abilities and skills that may be relevant to job performance? Second, because age and job tenure are frequently correlated, older workers may face particular problems with obsolescence. Because it is plausible that obsolescence may be remedied by training, we examine the literature on age differences in training effectiveness. Third, aside from training programs specifically designed to enhance occupationally relevant skills and abilities, to what extent do the occupational conditions that individuals experience and the nature of the tasks they do during their work lives affect their cognitive functioning as they grow older?

Age Differences in Basic Abilities and Skills

The literature on cognition and aging suggests that two aspects of cognitive functioning are particularly vulnerable to aging effects. First, a number of researchers have demonstrated that mental or cognitive speed tends to decrease with age (e.g., Cerella, 1985; Salthouse, 1982, 1985; Waugh & Barr, 1980). Second, many authors have suggested that the functioning of working memory (i.e., one's ability to keep information "in mind" while engaging in higher level tasks such as language comprehension, reasoning, and problem solving) also tends to decrease with age, although the exact nature of the decrement is subject to dispute (Craik, 1983; Craik & Rabinowitz, 1984; Hasher & Zacks, 1988). Both cognitive speed and working memory are critical to the performance of cognitive tasks, particularly complex ones. Age-related decrements in these two aspects of cognitive functioning may not be independent; for example, a number of authors (e.g., Salthouse, 1991) have suggested that much of the age differences in working memory can be accounted for by age differences in cognitive speed.

Interestingly, however, older people's performance on psychometric and laboratory tasks may lead to severe underestimates of their "real-life" competencies (Rabbitt, 1977; Salthouse, 1990), including those involved in job performance. This discrepancy is consistent with the fact that although age-related decrements are the norm in laboratory and psychometric investigations, studies of the effects of age on job performance generally reveal no effects of age (see meta-analyses by McEvoy & Cascio, 1989; Waldman & Avolio, 1986), although the nature of the age effect can depend on factors such as the nature of the job (Warr, 1994).

There are many plausible reasons for this apparent contradiction (see Salthouse, 1990; Salthouse & Maurer, 1996, for more complete discussions than are possible here, particularly regarding methodological issues). One possibility is that in many areas, expertise or compensatory mechanisms acquired over years of experience may be used to compensate for age-related declines in basic abilities or skills (e.g., Charness, 1981a, 1981b, 1989; Salthouse, 1984). Such an explanation is consistent with Avolio, Waldman, and McDaniel's (1990) finding that experience was a better predictor than age of job performance. Nevertheless, laboratory studies rarely find that expertise eliminates age-related decrements completely. Yet another possibility is that laboratory and psychometric tasks are more likely to push people to their "cognitive limits" (which are presumably age related; see Kliegl, Smith, & Baltes, 1986) than are highly practiced job-related tasks with which people are very familiar. A third possibility is the likelihood that older individuals who are encountering noticeable cognitive declines may have left the workforce. In addition, as we shall see, the general tenor of the evidence suggests that older individuals tend to be more motivated and satisfied with their jobs than younger ones, and it is possible that this motivational difference leads them to dedicate a higher proportion of their potential to doing their jobs well. In any case, the reasons underlying the discrepancy between older adults' performances in laboratory and work settings are not fully understood.

Age Differences in the Effectiveness of Training

Although older people may not be at a major disadvantage when it comes to jobs that change relatively little over time, such jobs are becoming more and more rare. Instead, as the rate of technological change has increased over recent years, workers have found themselves more and more pressed to acquire new skills in an effort to keep up. The longer a worker remains in a job, the more likely he or she is to require training. Therefore, it is important to consider whether older workers are as likely as younger workers to benefit from training designed to combat obsolescence.

Older individuals can certainly benefit from training on cognitive tasks. For example, Willis and Schaie (1986) have shown impressively that older adults not only benefit from basic abilities training, but they also demonstrate appropriate skill-related transfer. However, studies that have focused on training tasks that are more similar to those one might encounter on the job have yielded mixed results. In the area of computer skills, a number of authors have shown that older people can acquire the skills; however, they are slower, tend to need more help, and make more errors on post-tests (e.g., Czaja & Sharit, 1993; Elias, Elias, Robbins, & Gage, 1981).

These findings suggest that younger and older adults may differ in the types of training procedures that are optimal for them. Such differences may exist in many aspects of computer-related training, for example, training materials (Caplan & Schooler, 1990; for related findings, see also Lipman & Caplan, 1992) and the social context of training (Zandri & Charness, 1989). In addition, age differences may be more apparent for some kinds of computer systems than for others (Egan & Gomez, 1985). Although investigations of age differences in the effectiveness of training techniques are relatively uncommon, findings such as these suggest that organizations that are serious about maintaining high levels of skill for both younger and older workers may need to consider tailoring their training techniques (or using multiple techniques) to accomplish this goal.

Continuing Impact of Occupational Conditions on the Cognitive Functioning of the Elderly

As noted in the earlier discussion of sources of heterogeneity, there is evidence that complex environmental conditions that foster learning and require the application of problem-solving skills exert a salutary effect on the intellectual functioning of older individuals still in the workforce (for a fuller review, see Schooler, 1990). This tendency holds true for occupational conditions. Thus, Miller, Slomczynski, and Kohn (1985) found that in both Poland and the United States the degree to which substantively complex work increases intellectual flexibility remains constant across the life span. What differs with age is the substantive complexity of the work people do. In both countries, the work of older adults is less substantively complex. Avolio and Waldman (1990) also found that the positive intellectual effects of job complexity are not affected by age. In addition, they found some evidence of less age-related decline among people doing complex clerical work than among those in other occupational categories.

Perhaps even more striking are findings that complex occupational conditions may decrease the risk of memory difficulties and dementia, presumably well after the individual has stopped working. Frizoni, Rossini, Bianchetti, and Trabucchi (1993) link the practice of farming—relative to "white-collar" work—as a principal lifetime occupation, to a greater likelihood of dementia. Similarly, a variety of studies in a number of countries have shown that the incidence of Alzheimer's disease is lower for people in relatively high status occupations in the United States (Mangione et al., 1993; Stern et al., 1994), and in Japan (Imaizumi, 1993). Similar results regarding memory performance in a sample of nondemented older individuals in France have also been reported (Dartigues et al., 1992). Since high occupational status is very strongly linked to job complexity (Kohn & Schooler, 1983), these findings are consistent with the general hypothesis that complex occupational conditions increase intellectual functioning.

Attitudinal and Motivational Variables

Psychologists and sociologists have examined the relationship between age and work-related attitudes, and have identified a number of variables that are presumably related to job performance. These include job satisfaction, beliefs about work, work involvement, and organizational commitment. In considering this literature, it is important to remember that since most studies are cross-sectional, presumed age effects easily could be due, at least in part, to differences among cohorts.

Job Satisfaction

Studies of the relationship between job satisfaction and age generally report that older workers are more satisfied with their jobs than are younger workers (e.g, Janson & Martin, 1982; Kalleberg & Loscocco, 1983; Rhodes, 1983; Wright & Hamilton, 1978). A number of possible explanations, both structural and psychological, for this relationship have been proposed. Since increased tenure on the job is usually correlated with improvements in job characteristics, one possibility is that older workers are more satisfied than younger workers because they have more desirable jobs (e.g., Wright & Hamilton, 1978; for an alternative view, see Janson & Martin 1982). This relationship may also result from either age or cohort differences in other work-related attitudes and beliefs. For example, older adults may have more "realistic" (i.e., lower) expectations of their jobs than do younger workers (see Kalleberg & Loscocco, 1983). Other possible explanations include life-cycle-related variables, such as family demands on one's time, financial resources, or changes in the relative importance of one's role as worker.

The literature also suggests however, that social change has affected gender differences in the nature of the relationship between age and job satisfaction. Kalleberg and Loscocco (1983) found that males demonstrated the same generally positive age effects in job satisfaction across three time periods (1969, 1973, 1977); the age effects of women surveyed in 1973 and 1977 were more similar to men's than were the age effects of women surveyed in 1969. The authors attributed this sex difference to the effects of social change over the time period investigated. They suggested that women who were employed before 1970 were more likely than women surveyed in later time periods to work outside the home because of financial necessity and would, presumably, have been generally less satisfied with their jobs. In addition, they would be less able to leave the workforce. In either case, the low levels of job satisfaction in women could eliminate any relationship between age and job satisfaction, and yield an illustration of the way in which social change can affect the cohort experiences of men and women.

Worker Involvement and Commitment

In general, older workers are also more likely to demonstrate higher levels of job involvement and organizational commitment than are younger workers (e.g., Mathieu & Zajac, 1990; Rhodes, 1983). Some investigators have suggested that this finding, as well as the age effects on job satisfaction, may be related to the greater strength of the Protestant work ethic in older workers (Aldag & Brief, 1977; Cherrington, Condie, & England, 1979), a result likely to be due, at least in part, to cohort effects. However, the literature regarding this variable is relatively sparse. In addition, other variables, such as job rewards and job autonomy, may contribute to the relationship between age and involvment and/or commitment (Lorence, 1987).

It should be noted that, as was the case for job satisfaction, gender differences in age effects and possible mediating variables are frequently observed. For example, Lorence (1987) found that the relationship between age and work commitment differed between men and women tested over roughly the same time periods as the subjects tested in Kalleberg and Loscocco's (1983) study of job satisfaction. Lorence found that for males, the relationship between age and work involvement was curvilinear, and that the relationship became nonsignificant when job rewards were controlled. In contrast, for women, the relationship between age and involvement was linear and positive, and remained signficant even when job rewards were controlled. Lorence's explanation is similar to Kalleberg and Loscocco's in suggesting that women in the late 1970s were likely to be working "voluntarily," rather than out of financial necessity. Whether such differences between men and women remained after the economic changes of the 1980s remains, to our knowledge, an unanswered question.

Psychological Research on the Older Worker—
Limitations and Conclusions

There are several limitations to the generalizations that can be made from the psychological research dealing with older workers. One is that almost none of the research dealing with actual workers examines reliable samples of what have been called the old old workers—those above 75 years of age. We do not really have a clear picture of how those who continue working at such an advanced age react to the conditions and demands of their work environments. In fact, there is relatively little data on people past their 50s. A second limitation is that in many instances we cannot at present distinguish between possible aging effects and possible cohort effects. This is not merely true for such motivational issues as work ethic, but also for cognitive questions, such as the ability of older people to use computers (for a more thorough attempt to distinguish cohort from aging effects, see Schaie, 1996b.) Perhaps the strongest caveat to generalizing about older individuals in the workforce comes from the most striking generalization that emerges from psychological research on the elderly— the dramatic increase in the heterogeneity among individuals in functioning as they age. For the elderly, the assumption that the mean level of functioning at a given age represents the functioning of a particular worker at that age may be convenient, but it is indefensible.

Bearing these caveats in mind, at present several general conclusions can be drawn about the functioning of older workers. Compared to younger workers, they are more likely to demonstrate high levels of job satisfaction and work involvement. They are also more likely to react more slowly to novel stituations and stimuli but are more motivated to work. Given that most older workers are likely to be highly familiar with their job demands, it is probably not surprising that age is not a very strong determinant of job performance.

GENERAL CONCLUSIONS

This brief discussion of some of the findings of sociology and psychology relevant to older workers illustrates the usefulness of approaches that include many levels of analysis. In considering the relationship between work and the older worker, there exists a complex interplay among levels, ranging from relatively macroconcepts (e.g., social structure) to relatively microconcepts (e.g., individual cognitive abilities). Macro- to microinfluences include how changes in social structure affect the historical experiences of cohorts, including the nature of the jobs they are required to perform. For example, the recent increasing presence of computer technology in the workplace has revealed probable cohort differences in receptiveness to computer training. Another aspect of social change is demonstrated in the period and/or cohort effects of gender differences in the relationship between age and job-related attitudes. In addition, other characteristics of the workplace, such as occupational complexity, have effects on individual functioning across the life span.

Micro- to macroinfluences are also demonstrated. Relatively recent decreases in the age of retirement have had implications for the aging experience of recent cohorts and other aspects of social structure. If, as the evidence suggests, future individuals begin again to continue to work later in life, many of these experiences will change again. In addition, characteristics of the workplace, such as training programs, will probably have to change as well. Together, such changes can be expected to illustrate, once again, a dialectic between aging and social change.

REFERENCES

Aldag, R. J., & Brief, A. P. (1977). Age, work values and employee rections. *Industrial Gerontology, 4,* 192–197.

Arbuckle, T. Y., Gold, D., & Andres, D. (1986). Cognitive functioning of older people in relation to social and personality variables. *Psychology and Aging, 1,* 55–62

Avolio, B. J., & Waldman, D. A. (1990). An examination of age and cognitive test performance across job complexity and occupational types. *Journal of Applied Psychology, 75,* 43–50.

Avolio, B. J., Waldman, D. A., & McDaniel, M. A. (1990). Age and work performance in nonmanagerial jobs: The effects of experience and occupational type. *Academy of Management Journal, 33,* 407–422.

Caplan, L. J., & Schooler, C. (1990). The effects of analogical training models and age on problem-solving in a new domain. *Experimental Aging Research, 16,* 151–154.

Cerella, J. (1985). Information processing rates in the elderly. *Psychological Bulletin, 98,* 67–83.

Charness, N. (1981a). Aging and skilled problem solving. *Journal of Experimental Psychology: General, 110,* 21–38.

Charness, N. (1981b). Search in chess: Age and skill differences. *Journal of Experimental Psychology: Human Perception and Performance, 7,* 467–476.

Charness, N. (1989). Age and expertise: Responding to Talland's challenge. In L. W. Poon, D. C. Rubin, & B. A. Wilson (Eds.), *Everyday cognition in adulthood and late life* (pp. 437–456). New York: Cambridge University Press .

Cherrington, D. J., Condie, S. J., & England, J. L. (1979). Age and work values. *Academy of Management Journal, 22,* 617–623.

Craik, F. I. M. (1983). On the transfer of information from temporary to permanent storage. *Philosophical Transactions of the Royal Society of London, Ser. B, 302,* 341–359.

Craik, F. I. M., & Rabinowitz, J. C. (1984). Age differences in the acquisition and use of verbal information: A tutorial review. In H. Bouma & D. G. Bouwhuis (Eds.), *Attention and performance: X. Control of language processes* (pp. 95–112). Hillsdale, NJ: Erlbaum.

Crawley, B. (1992). The transformation of the American labor force: Elder African Americans and occupational social work. *Social Work, 37,* 41–46.

Czaja, S. J., & Sharit, J. (1993). Age differences in the performance of computer-based work. *Psychology and Aging, 8,* 59–67.

Dartigues, J. F., Gagnon, M., Mazaux, J. M., Barberger-Gateau, P., Commenges, D., Letenneur, L., & Orgogozo, J. M. (1992). Occupation during life and memory performance in nondemented French elderly community residents. *Neurology, 42,* 1697–1701.

DeViney, S., & O'Rand, A. (1988). Gender-cohort succession and retirement among older men and women, 1951 to 1984. *Sociological Quarterly, 29,* 525–540.

Egan, D. E., & Gomez, L. M. (1985). Assaying, isolating, and accommodating individual differences in learning a complex skill. In R. F. Dillon (Ed.), *Individual differences in cognition* (pp. 173–217). New York: Academic Press, 1985.

Elias, P. K., Elias, M. F., Robbins, M. A., & Gage, P. (1981). Acquisition of word-processing skills by younger, middle-age, and older adults. *Psychology and Aging, 2,* 340–348.

Frisoni, G., Rossini, R., Bianchetti, A., & Trabucchi, M. (1993). Principal lifetime occupation and MMSE score in elderly persons. *Journal of Gerontology: Social Sciences, 46,* 310–314.

Hasher, L., & Zacks, R. T. (1988). Working memory, comprehension, and aging: A review and a new view. *Psychology of Learning and Motivation, 22,* 193–225.

Hertzog, C., Schaie, K. W., & Gribbin, K. (1978). Cardiovascular diseases and changes in intellectual functioning from middle to old age. *Journal of Gerontology, 33,* 872–883.

Horn, J. L. (1980). Concepts of intellect in relation to learning and adult development. *Intelligence, 4,* 285–317.

Horn, J. L., & Cattell, R. B. (1967). Age differences in fluid and crystallized intelligence. *Acta Psychologica, 26,* 107–129.

Hultsch, D. F., Hammer, M., & Small, B. J. (1993). Age differences in cognitive performance in later life: Relationships to self-reported health and activity life style. *Journal of Gerontology: Psychological Sciences, 48,* P1–P11.

Imaizumi, Y. (1993). Mortality rate of Alzheimer's disease in Japan: Secular trends, marital status, and geographical variations. *Acta Neurological Scandinavia, 86,* 501–505.

Janson, P., & Martin, J. K. (1982). Job satisfaction and age: A test of two views. *Social Forces, 60,* 1089–1102.

Jessup, D. (1989). Innovative older-worker programs. *Generations, 13,* 23–27.

Kalleberg, A. L., & Loscocco, K. A. (1983). Aging, values, and rewards: Explaining age differences in job satisfaction. *American Sociological Review, 48,* 78–90.

Kliegl, R., Smith, J., & Baltes, P. B. (1986). Testing-the-limits, expertise, and memory in adulthood and old age. In F. Klix & H. Hagendorf (Eds.), *Human memory and cognitive capabilities* (pp. 395–407). Amsterdam: North Holland.

Kohn M. L., & Schooler, C. (1983). *Work and personality: An inquiry into the impact of social stratification.* Norwood, NJ: Ablex.

Levine, M. L. (1988). Age discrimination: The law and its underlying policy. In H. Dennis (Ed.), *Fourteen steps in managing an aging work force* (pp. 97–112). Lexington, MA: Lexington Books

Lipman, P. D., & Caplan, L. J. (1992). Adult age differences in memory for routes: Effects of instruction and spatial diagram. *Psychology and Aging, 7,* 435–442.

Longman, P. (1988). The challenge of an aging society. *Futurist, 22,* 33–37.

Lorence, J. (1987). Age differences in work involvement. *Work and Occupations, 14,* 533–557.

Mangione, C. M., Seddon, J. M., Cook, E. F., Krug, J. H., Sahagian, C. R., Campion, E. W., & Glynn, R. J. (1993). Correlates of cognitive function scores in elderly outpatients. *Journal of the American Geriatric Society, 41,* 491–497.

Mathieu, J. E., & Zajac, D. M. (1990). A review and meta-analysis of the antecedents, correlates, and consequences of organizational commitment. *Psychological Bulletin, 108,* 171–194.

McEvoy, G. M., & Cascio, W. F. (1989). Cumulative evidence of the relationship between employee age and job performance. *Journal of Applied Psychology, 74,* 11–17.

Miller, J., Slomczynski, K. M., & Kohn, M. L. (1985). The continuity of learning-generalization: The effect of job on men's intellective process in the United States and Poland. *American Journal of Sociology, 91,* 593–615.

Mor-Barak, M., & Tynan, M. (1993). Older workers and the workplace: A new challenge for occupational social work. *Social Work, 38,* 45–55.

Preston, S., & Martin, L. (Eds.). (1994). *Demography of aging.* Washington, DC: National Academy Press.

Quinn, J., & Burkhauser, R. (1994). Retirement and labor force behavior of the elderly. In S. Preston & L. Martin (Eds.), *Demography of aging* (pp. 50–93). Washington, DC: National Academy Press.

Rabbitt, P. M. A. (1977). Changes in problem solving ability in old age. In J. E. Birren & K. W. Schaie (Eds.), *Handbook of the psychology of aging* (pp. 606–625). New York: Van Nostrand Reinhold.

Rhodes, S. R. (1983). Age-related differences in work attitudes and behavior: A review and conceptual analysis. *Psychological Bulletin, 93,* 328–367.

Riley, M. W. (1987). On the significance of age in society. *American Sociological Review, 52,* 1–14.

Riley, M. W., Foner, A., & Waring, J. (1988). Sociology of age. In N. J. Smelser (Ed.), *Handbook of sociology* (pp. 243–290). London: Russell Sage.

Riley, M. W., Johnson, M. E., & Foner, A. (1972). *Aging and society: Vol. 3. A sociology of age stratification.* New York: Russell Sage.

Riley, M. W., & Riley, J. W. (1994). Structural lag: Past and future. In M. W. Riley, R. L. Kahn, & A. Foner (Eds.), *Age and structure lag: Socity's failure to provide meaningful opportunities in work, family, and leisure* (pp. 15–36). New York: John Wiley.

Salthouse, T. A. (1982). *Adult cognition.* New York: Springer Publishing Company.

Salthouse, T. A. (1984). Effects of age and skill in typing. *Journal of Experimental Psychology: General, 113,* 345–371.

Salthouse, T. A. (1985). *A theory of cognitive aging.* Amsterdam: North Holland.

Salthouse, T. A. (1990). Cognitive competence and expertise in aging. In J. E. Birren & K. W Schaie (Eds.), *Handbook of the psychology of aging* (3rd ed., pp. 310–319). San Diego, CA: Academic Press.

Salthouse , T. A. (1991). Mediation of adult age differences in cognition by reductions in working memory and speed of processing. *Psychological Science, 2,* 179–183.

Salthouse, T. A., & Maurer, T. J. (1996). Aging, job performance, and career development. In J. E. Birren & K. W. Schaie (Eds.), *Handbook of the psychology of aging* (4th ed., pp. 353–364). New York: Academic Press.

Schaie, K. W. (1990). Late life potential and cohort differences in mental abilities. In M. Perlmutter (Ed.), *Late life potential* (pp. 43–61). Washington, DC: Gerontological Society of America.

Schaie, K. W. (1996a). Intellectual development in adulthood. In J. E. Birren & K. W. Schaie (Eds.), *Handbook of the psychology of aging* (4th ed., pp. 266–286). San Diego, CA: Academic Press.

Schaie, K. W. (1996b). *Intellectual development in adulthood: The Seattle Longitudinal Study.* New York: Cambridge University Press.

Schooler, C. (1990). Psychosocial factors and effective cognitive functioning through the life span. In J. E. Birren & K. W. Schaie (Eds.), *Handbook of the psychology of aging* (3rd ed., pp. 347–358). San Diego, CA: Academic Press.

Schooler, C. (1994). A working conceptualization of social structure: Mertonian roots and psychological and sociocultural relationships. *Social Psychology Quarterly, 57,* 262–273.

Schrank, H., & Waring, J. (1989). Older workers: Ambivalence and interventions. *Annals of the American Academy of Political and Social Science, 503,* 113–126.

Stern, Y., Gurland, B., Tatemichi, T. K., Tang, M. X., Wilder, D., & Mayeux, R. (1994). Influence of education and occupation on the incidence of Alzheimer's disease. *Journal of the American Medical Association, 271,* 1004–1010.

Waldman, D. A., & Avolio, B. J. (1986). A meta-analysis of age differences in job performance. *Journal of Applied Psychology, 71,* 33–38.

Warr, P. (1994). Age and employment. In H. C. Triandis, M. D. Dunnette, & L. M. Hough (Eds.), *Handbook of industrial and organizational psychology* (Vol. 4, pp. 485–550). Palo Alto,CA:Consulting Psychologists Press.

Waugh, N. C., & Barr, R. A. (1980). Memory and mental tempo. In L. W. Poon, J. L. Fozard, L. S. Cermak, D. Arenberg, & L. W. Thompson

(Eds.), *New directions in memory and aging* (pp. 251–260). Hillsdale, NJ: Erlbaum.

Willis S. L., & Schaie, K. W. (1986). Training the elderly on the ability factors of spatial orientation and inductive reasoning. *Psychology and Aging, 1,* 239–247.

Wright, J. D., & Hamilton, R. F. (1978). Work satisfaction and age: Some evidence for the "job change" hypothesis. *Social Forces, 56,* 1140–1158.

Zandri, E., & Charness, N. (1989). Training older and younger adults to use software. *Educational Gerontology, 15,* 615–631.

Commentary: Psychology, Sociology, and Research on Age

Matilda White Riley

It is with great satisfaction that I join the long train of participants in this series of conferences on the Societal Impact on Aging. Once again, Warner Schaie is to be congratulated for designing and sponsoring this series, which began in the 1980s in the Social Science Research Council's Committee on Life-Course Perspectives (Riley, 1989). And Carmi Schooler, Leslie Caplan, and Gary Oates are to be congratulated for their compact, lucid, and informative overview of conceptualizations and findings from the two disciplines of sociology and psychology that are featured in this book. These scholars have demonstrated how a cumulative body of knowledge about age is made possible by examining the connections between theory and research on such a topic as work, and by subjecting such connections to the glare of scientific scrutiny. The Schooler–Caplan–Oates ("SCO") chapter bristles with ideas that merit discussion—too many to comprehend in one short overview.

In my brief discussion, after some preliminary notes, I'll make just two sets of comments: *First,* some general comments that emphasize the conceptual linkage of the "sociology" half of the SCO chapter to the "psychology" half; and *second,* some specific comments about the place of psychology not only in the changing lives of older people but also as a powerful mechanism that emerges, often without notice, in the surrounding social structures.

PRELIMINARY NOTES

The conceptual framework used here, though attributed by SCO to "Matilda Riley," is actually the long-standing product of many scholars. We now call it the "aging and society—A&S—paradigm" (Riley, 1994). This paradigm, still incomplete, is continually emerging. Some aspects requiring recent attention (hence not noted by SCO) include the problem of "structural lag" (resulting from the asynchrony between human lives and social structures) and the tendencies toward an "age-integrated society" (SCO's "age neutrality," chapter 1, p. 4).

The paradigm examines structure in its own right, parallel with lives. SCO deserve rare credit here for avoiding the widespread "life course reductionism" in which structure is treated as merely a "contextual" characteristic of lives.

CONCEPTUAL LINKAGES BETWEEN
SOCIOLOGY AND PSYCHOLOGY

As my first set of comments, I shall merely enlarge a bit on the SCO chapter by emphasizing that the A&S paradigm is multidisciplinary, relevant to the psychology as well as the sociology half of the chapter.

Multidisciplinarity

The paradigm is, to be sure, "sociological" in that its central theme stems from the unique disciplinary focus of sociology: on people and groups and the interplay between them. Beyond this, however, it is designed as a heuristic device for organizing, simplifying, and interpreting the facts and ideas about age and aging from many disciplines.

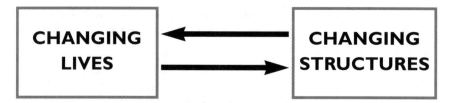

Figure 1.1 Inderdependent dynamisms.

SCO, in transcending their specific focus on work and workers, demonstrate how development of the paradigm has involved communication between sociologists (including Robert Merton, Talcott Parsons, John Clausen, John Meyer, Aage Sørensen, as well as others in this book) and such psychologists as Ronald Abeles, Warner Schaie, Paul Baltes, James Birren, and Robert Kahn.

More generally, however, the broader, multidisciplinary character of the A&S paradigm is evident from a quick review of its central theme. Figure 1.1 simplifies the central components, or "dynamisms": changing lives and changing structures. These dynamisms are connected by two-directional arrows, signifying that the two are interdependent: each influences the other. This simplified scheme represents (as stated by SCO, chapter 1, p. 3) the "continuing dialectical interplay" between the "aging of individuals in successive cohorts and the changing age structures of society." All the "principles" listed by SCO (chapter 1, pp. 2–3) are derived from this central theme.

A moment's thought will indicate how this simplification was designed precisely to capture the linkages among many disciplines. On one side of the paradigm, changing "structures" involve all the social sciences, including economics (as in the work of Thomas Juster), history, and anthropology (when culture is treated as built into structure). Noteworthy is the volume in this series entitled *Age Structuring in Comparative Perspective,* edited by anthropologist David Kertzer in collaboration with Warner Schaie (1989). On the other side of the paradigm, people's "changing lives" involve demography and a "biopsychosocial" integration of disciplines.

Relevance of the A&S Paradigm

When SCO in their chapter turn to the psychological approach to issues of work and the elderly, they emphasize the abilities and attitudes of older as compared to younger workers. Yet, despite the division between psychology and sociology, the very title of the SCO chapter shows the reciprocity between the two, as "Job Affects Older Worker, Older Worker Affects Job." Several of the SCO examples from psychology illustrate the broad connection with the A&S paradigm as a whole, and contribute to its elucidation. As just one of these examples, consider SCO's discussion (p. 10) of the relationship between occupational conditions—which refers to structures and older people's cognitive functioning—which refers to lives. In one direction of the interplay between them, SCO specify such mechanisms as "environmental conditions that foster learning" or the "application of problem-solving skills." Moreover, by showing that early-life work conditions (structures) affect later life performance (lives), they introduce the *dynamic* of "life-span psychology" (as in the work of William Hoyer, Warner Schaie, Sherry Willis, and others.)

In the other direction of the interplay, SCO might have raised the significant additional question: Do those who acquire higher levels of intellectual functioning (lives) exert a reciprocal effect on the character of their jobs (structures)? Perhaps by redesigning existing jobs? creating new jobs for themselves? or simply moving from less to more complex jobs?

Two Caveats

Before leaving this instructive example, I am reminded of two general caveats. First, in their brilliant analysis of the A&S paradigm, SCO allude to the "social-structurally *determined* conditions" to which people "react" (chapter 1, p. 6, italics added). To the contrary, the paradigm assumes that both structures and lives are *not* entirely determined—but are alterable, and that people can act either actively or passively in response to the surrounding environments. At any given moment, to be sure, people's current responses *are* to an extent determined: in part by genetic endowment, and in part by their earlier-life responses made in the "interplay" with successive surrounding structures. Over time, however, even the infant is not only socialized by, but also socializes, the mother. The longer people live, the more their earlier predispositions are modified through their continuing social participation.

The other caveat concerns the distinction made in SCO's "general conclusions" (chapter1, p. 13) between "macrolevel" to refer to structures and "microlevel" to refer to individuals. Although I was at fault in using that distinction in an earlier work, the more useful distinction in the A&S paradigm is between structures and people, both of which can be viewed at various levels. For example, the interplay between workplace and worker can be analyzed at a microlevel by scrutiny of individual workers and their particular environments; or at a macrolevel, as in SCO's long-range historical account of the changing societal nature of occupations and the implications for retirement among workers in the aggregate.

To end this first set of comments, let me repeat: my intention is to reinforce the challenge of the remarkably comprehensive SCO chapter in bringing psychology and sociology together. The authors set out an approach to age that is broad enough for locating and coordinating the diverse ideas and concepts from both sociology and psychology as well as the other relevant disciplines.

PSYCHOLOGY AND THE STRUCTURAL SIDE OF THE A&S PARADIGM

My second set of comments are of another character. Here I pick up one specific question for the future agenda, by reminding us that "psychology" is relevant not only for people's lives, but also for social structures. The question is: Precisely how does psychology fit into the structural side of the A&S paradigm (as in Figure 1.1)?

Confusion in Accepted Concepts of "Structure"

In an earlier conference in the series on the Societal Impact on Aging, it was asked how the successful results of a training program could be sustained after the experimental intervention was ended. The ready answer: "Train the trainers to continue their efforts." But what then? How could this be accomplished? What further efforts would be required? No suggestions were forthcoming. Nor was it immediately recognized that, in training the trainers, we are moving from one side of Figure 1.1 to the other: from the *changing lives* of the focal individuals under study to the *changing structures* to which the trainers belong.

These unanswered questions only illustrate much larger questions. A great deal of research has demonstrated that older people's functioning can be enhanced if appropriate interventions are made in structures (as through introduction of training programs, exercise regimens, greater opportunities for independence). But so far, too little attention has been paid by students of age to the nature of such structural improvements, or to how they might be sustained after the research has ended.

As a consequence, Ronald Abeles and I undertook to identify some of the elements in changing structures as they interact with changing lives—a large assignment that we briefly note here as a further challenge to SCO and their followers. (This work is part of the National Institute on Aging's Program on Age and Structural Change—PASC.)

We began by exploring the familiar elements in structure such as regulations and customs, incentives and rewards, opportunities for practice, community environment, or physical plant and resources. (All these are illustrated in SCO's review of the literature on work.) We called these "institutional elements" in structure. But then we were reminded of another, entirely different, set of structural elements—for which we had no name; it would be confusing to call them "human elements" since they belong on the structural side of Figure 1.1. As we studied the massive literature on social structure and social change, we found a great deal of confusion. Such "human elements" were given relatively little attention, except by a few sociologists such as Robert Merton, James Coleman, Gilbert Brim and Stanton Wheeler, and Carmi Schooler in an earlier article (1994).

Yet this "human" perspective on social structure is of special interest here because psychology is involved. Further pursuit of the structural literature shows that it has been taken for granted that every structure contains an "other"—an "alter" corresponding to the "ego" whose life course is the focus of attention. These "alters" act on behalf of the structures: they make rules and implement them, provide training, allocate resources, and the like. How were we to distinguish the "alters" from the "egos" (the "focal individuals") whose lives are being traced? We decided to accept a new line of thought and to speak of them as "agents." But this recognition of "agents" raised a host of serious questions. How many "agents" are there in particular structures (e.g., the workplace, the nursing home, or the family)? Who are they? How do they participate in the interplay with the changing lives of the egos? And—as we are thinking here about the place of psychology in the structural side of the A&S paradigm, we need to know about their "psychological" processes.

Clarification from the Conference

Happily for our thinking about such questions, the SCO analysis of work provides exemplary clues to processes through which "agents" influence workers' lives and their retirement decisions. Managers make assessments of cognitive skills and send "signals" to older workers about the declining value of their work (chapter 1, p. 4). Coworkers, who are also aging, serve as reference groups. Family members enter into decision making. Outside experts design training materials. Chief executive officers and labor leaders bargain over pension systems. Federal and state legislators alter Social Security arrangements. The list seems endless.

Clearly, then, the dynamism of "changing structures" is far more complex than indicated in the oversimplified Figure 1.1. Researchers studying any given structural change cannot include all this complexity. They can merely keep it in mind as a heuristic guide as they must make selections from it. They can select for scrutiny from a wide variety of "agents." They can select from the manifold ways in which agents influence and are influenced by the lives of the retiring workers. And just as psychology is a necessary tool for tracing the "focal lives" of the workers, it is also a tool for researchers exploring how the "agents," who are themselves aging, engage in their part of the interplay. We pose this topic for future interdisciplinary discussion between psychologists and sociologists.

I conclude with the thought that continuing pursuit of the general formulations in the SCO chapter and its relation to the A&S paradigm bids fair to enlarge theory and deepen understanding. Within this wider compass, insights drawn from specific studies of relationships between work and workers will predictably feed back into the accumulating body of theory and knowledge about age and aging in general and the ties between psychology and sociology in particular.

REFERENCES

Kertzer, D. I., & Schaie, K. W. (1989). *Age structuring in comparative perspective.* Hillsdale, NJ: Erlbaum.

Riley, M. W. (1989). Foreword: Why This Book? In K. W. Schaie & C. Schooler (Eds.), *Social structure and aging: Psychological processes* (pp. xiii–xv). Hillsdale, NJ: Erlbaum.L

Riley, M. W. (1994). Aging and society: past, present, and future [1993 Kent Lecture]. *Gerontologist, 34,* 436–446.

Schooler, C. (1994). A working conceptualization of social structure: Mertonian roots and psychological and sociocultural relationships. *Social Psychology Quarterly, 57,* 262–273

Commentary: The Older Individual in a Rapidly Changing Work Context: Developmental and Cognitive Issues

William J. Hoyer

T he topic of this volume is a response to the fact that the workplace is undergoing rapid and dramatic change. In recent years, some of the most obvious changes in the nature of work activities and in the interpersonal and organizational dynamics of the workplace have been brought about by new technologies. Depending on how new technologies and new organizational configurations are implemented, some workers may experience increased productivity and work satisfaction, while others may experience increased dissatisfaction with the work environment.

Some recent changes in the workplace have resulted in increased workloads for individuals, increased stress associated with quotas and deadlines, and decreased supportive interaction with coworkers and supervisors. In addition to changes in the workplace, the abilities, skills, and attitudes of workers of all ages are changing across time. Societal trends

Preparation of this chapter was supported by NIA Grant No. AG11451.

affecting work behavior include cohort-related differences in pension economics and health care that affect length and quality of work life, as well as educational influences and training that affect the kinds of skills and attitudes that individuals bring to the workplace. Riley (1985, 1987; see also chapter 2, this volume) and others have described cohort differences in entry-level job skills and education, job expectations, and in the composition of the workforce in terms of numbers and proportions of ethnic minorities, women, and older adults. In terms of time-related changes within individuals, age-related declines in late life in memory, information processing speed, sensory functions, movement speed, physical stamina, and changes in other abilities and characteristics may also affect performance in work (e.g., Davies & Sparrow, 1985).

The timeliness of the topic of this volume is also related to the fact that the numbers and proportions of older individuals in the U.S. population are increasing. The "graying of America" requires that we give more attention to both the problems and potentials of an older workforce. This commentary and chapter 1, by Schooler, Caplan, and Oates, are primarily concerned with age-related changes in work performance and attitudes regarding work and leisure, and with relationships between behavioral or psychological changes and changing characteristics of the workplace. We know far too little about the description and explanation of age-ordered changes in work behavior and practical skills, the effects of aging on work motivation, and the larger consequences (both positive and negative) of an aging workforce for society.

An important theme that emerges from the current research literature in the psychology and sociology of work and aging is that the "job affects the older worker, and the older worker affects the job." Indeed, the primary aim of the Schooler, Caplan, and Oates chapter was to explore the interaction between worker and job as it affects older individuals. Schooler, Caplan, and Oates pointed to Matilda Riley's views emphasizing the interplay between the aging individual in successive cohorts and a changing societal structure, as a basis for taking an interactive approach to the understanding of the impact of work on individuals throughout the adult life course.

This chapter begins with a discussion of how older individuals make decisions about their involvement in the role of worker. Since measures of productivity and quality of work performance usually do not show any age-related declines, the individual's investment or commitment to continue to work is an important research focus for understanding worker-workplace interactions. First, I ask *when* and *how* is age a factor in an individual's decision making about work? Second, I briefly and selectively review what is known about the abilities, skills, and other job-relevant characteristics of older workers. Current research suggesting that there are experience-based gains and improvements in some aspects of work performance, as well as age-related losses in some areas, is discussed. Third, following points made by Schooler, Caplan and Oates (chapter 1, this volume) concerning the changing relationships between workers and work contexts, methodological and conceptual issues associated with the investigation of the changing characteristics of older workers in relation to a rapidly changing work context are discussed.

DECISIONS ABOUT WORK AND RETIREMENT

Psychologists and sociologists who study work roles often make strong assumptions about the rationality of human choice behavior. Recently, Ekerdt, DeViney, and Kosloski (1996) examined the timing of the retirement decision and the factors that lead individuals to make a decision to leave work. In response to the question "Why did you retire?" Ekerdt (chapter 3, this volume) noted that individuals often reply with rationales emphasizing personal choice, such as "I felt it was time," or "They made me an offer that was too good to refuse." However, Ekerdt points out that the decision to retire is probably brought about by a change in how the individual interprets and is influenced by subtle prompts that occur in everyday interactions (e.g., shared feelings in conversations among co-workers), influential economic incentives and mandates (e.g., early retirement buyouts and layoffs), and the individual's personal situation in the areas of financial status (i.e., retirement income and benefits relative to expenses), family context (e.g., caregiving roles, change in spouse's situation), and health status (e.g., increased difficulty to continue working or commuting). Consider the possibility that having to sit through an unusually large number of nonproductive meetings, having to deal regularly with massive amounts of unimportant paperwork, or receiving an unpleasant or age-biased derogatory comment from a coworker following a trivial mistake could be enough to trigger an older individual to reevaluate his or her investment in work. An older individual's decision to retire or to continue to work is influenced by an interpretation of an aggregate of minor events as well as by an assessment of one's value and contribution to the workplace. For many older individuals, subjective appraisals and subtle influences may play a larger role than logical processes or objective factors when making decisions about work involvement, which suggests the essential importance of examining work investment issues in terms of a life-span context at the level of the individual (e.g., Featherman, Smith, & Peterson, 1990).

When does age become a factor in evaluating our continued commitment to work? Davies and Sparrow (1985) provided an excerpt from a report made 35 years ago by the director-general of the International Labor Office that bears on this question, as follows:

> Age becomes a significant factor in a worker's life when, simply because of advancing years, he begins to find difficulty either in doing his work or in finding or keeping a job. It is at this stage of his career that he becomes an "older worker" from the standpoint of the world of work. The employment problems which come into being with advancing years differ greatly in kind and in extent from one country to another but they are shared by many nations of the world. Older men and women capable of useful and productive work, needing to work and ready and anxious to do so, tend to meet with increasing difficulties as they get on in years. They may find it hard to adapt to new methods and techniques and to keep up with the fast-changing industrial society. They may find it difficult to maintain the rapid pace and rhythm of many kinds of work. They may have to transfer to other work better suited to their changing capacities. They may encounter discrimination on the job. They may lose their jobs altogether. They may find it hard to get any other job or to obtain retraining. They may be faced with rigid hiring limits. They may find that what they have long dreaded is now happening to them and that for all practical purposes they have been tossed on the "human scrapheap" and that no-one has much use for them or interest in them. (International Labor Office, 1962, p. 14)

The previous statement seems to pertain equally well to the current situation regarding consequences and impact of worker-workplace interactions for older individuals as it did 35 years ago. The amount of cognitive resources and energy that individuals are able to give as well as the effort that individuals are willing to put into the job are affected by a wide variety of societal and individual aging factors. Individual differences and intra-individual changes in cognitive and motivational resources are in part (1) age ordered; and (2) influenced by life history factors as well as prevailing conditions in the workplace and society. Recently, Hanisch (1995) offered a framework for investigating the choices individuals make about job withdrawal and work withdrawal. *Job withdrawal* refers to resigning, retiring, or choosing to be laid off. *Work withdrawal* refers to changes in work behaviors such as tardiness, absenteeism, leaving work early, and general passiveness.

Antecedents that lead to job withdrawal and work withdrawal include pay inequity, health factors, work dissatisfaction, supervisor dissatisfaction, coworker dissatisfaction, and work stress. Factors such as work history, personal values, family situations, coworker pressures, and personal finances influence the likelihood and magnitude of the worker's withdrawal. Hanisch also pointed out that worker-workplace interactions must be understood at the level of the individual. For example, three individuals, Pat, Kim, and Chris might be equally dissatisfied with their jobs, but each can react by engaging in different behaviors. Pat is unable or unwilling to resign or retire, but is frequently absent, and arrives late and leaves early as much as possible. Kim actively pursues plans for an early retirement. Chris chooses to work harder within the corporate context to change the sources of her dissatisfaction. Therefore, researchers need to take into account individual differences in reactions to changes in the workplace (Hanisch, 1995; Hanisch & Hulin, 1990). As suggested in the research by Ekerdt, DeViney, and Kosloski (1996), Hardy and Quadagno (1995), and Maurer and Tarulli (1994), the influence of multiple antecedents on the likelihood and magnitude of the worker's withdrawal is amplified for many older workers in many kinds of work contexts. For example, self-appraisals of work behavior may take on new significance for older individuals, and older workers might be more sensitive to informal remarks or jokes about memory and aging.

AGE AND WORK PERFORMANCE

Some older individuals who choose to retire report that they were less able to keep pace with the continually increasing demands of the workplace. Other workers take the view that they have worked long and hard enough, and that they "deserve" to retire while they are still healthy.

However, many individuals choose to continue to work. These individuals may give reasons why they "have to" work, and they continue to function effectively in their work and other areas of vital involvement (e.g., Baltes & Staudinger, 1993; Brim, 1992; Erikson, Erikson, & Kivnick, 1986). In a variety of work situations, for example, older individuals sometimes hold the most responsible positions, and older individuals sometimes outperform younger workers. Performance of many kinds of real-world job skills, ranging from routine clerical tasks, to artistic and scholarly creativity, to executive or professional decision making, management, and leadership is largely unaffected by aging throughout the working years (e.g., Clancy & Hoyer, 1994; Hunter, 1986; Rhodes, 1983; Salthouse, 1984; Salthouse & Maurer, 1996; Waldman & Avolio, 1986).

The finding from meta-analyses (e.g., McEvoy, & Cascio, 1989; Waldman & Avolio, 1986) that there is no relationship between age and work performance may be accurate at an aggregate level, but it fails to capture a true picture of age-related changes at the level of individual work performance. Some aspects of work performance, especially speed performance, show reliable age-related declines for individuals (Davies & Sparrow, 1985; Welford, 1958; Yokomizo, 1985). It is also well established that older adults experience more difficulty in learning new work tasks, such as using new computer systems, and in benefiting from various kinds of job training programs (e.g., Caplan & Schooler, 1990; Czaja & Sharit, 1993; Kelley & Charness, 1995).

Other aspects of work performance, especially the performance of familiar nonspeeded tasks, appear to be well maintained for individuals across the adult years. Indeed, observations of age-related impairments in job functioning are the exception rather than the rule. When the performance of an older worker is impaired, it is likely to be associated with a change in health rather than with normal aging processes. The apparent lack of age-associated impairments in real work performance is striking and paradoxical, in contrast to findings from laboratory studies indicating that there are age-related declines in basic or fundamental cognitive, perceptual, and motoric abilities (e.g., Salthouse, 1991; Schaie, 1996). How do older adults maintain effective functioning in the work arena, despite laboratory and psychometric evidence indicative of age decline in the basic processes that appear to be requisites?

One explanation has to do with the benefits of experience on how work is performed. Although there are age-related differences in learning new tasks, and in using new technologies (e.g., see Kelley & Charness, 1995), the execution of well-practiced skills is generally unaffected by aging (e.g., Charness & Campbell, 1988; Hoyer & Lincourt, in press; Salthouse & Maurer, 1996). In cognitively demanding tasks in the workplace, the changes as well as consistencies that we observe in individual performance arise from reliance on accumulated knowledge and learned skills. However, work behavior is also affected by age-related changes in the basic processes that control or limit the speed and efficiency of information processing (e.g., Davies & Sparrow, 1985).

Cognition does not show an orderly, across-the-board change with advancing age. Some aspects of cognition show substantial age-related decline, whereas other aspects are or appear to be unaffected by aging, and there are different patterns of change within and across individuals (e.g., see Baltes, 1987; Baltes & Baltes, 1990; Schaie, 1996). Cognitive performance reflects the dynamic interactions of a variety of factors, including characteristics of the information being processed (i.e., its familiarity, salience, and complexity), and age-related and learning-based changes in the speed and efficiency of elementary acquisition and retrieval processes. Further, the individual's tacit knowledge and capacity to access and use previously acquired task-relevant knowledge must be taken into account when assessing performance in real-world domains (Ericsson & Lehmann, 1996; Hoyer, 1985; 1990; Rybash, Hoyer, & Roodin, 1986).

One of the most robust findings in the cognitive aging literature is the gradual albeit global slowing in the speed of mental operations beginning at early middle age and continuing throughout the life span (Birren, 1965; Cerella & Hale, 1994; Myerson, Hale, Hirschman, Hansen, & Christensen, 1989; Salthouse, 1985; Welford, 1958). It is also well known that there are age-related declines in attentional selectivity, working memory, memory retrieval, mental computational abilities, and fluid intellectual abilities (e.g., see Charness & Campbell, 1988; Rybash, Hoyer, & Roodin, 1986; Salthouse, 1991; Schaie, 1996). Age-related changes in the speed and efficiency of basic information processing abilities may be responsible for the deficits observed when older adults perform new and complex tasks in the workplace (Cerella & Hale, 1994; Salthouse, 1985).

Research on age and knowledge utilization suggests that cognitive performance in the workplace and in other kinds of everyday tasks depends on interactions between what the person knows and the computational requirements of the task (Baltes, 1987; Charness & Campbell,

1988; Hoyer, 1985; Hunt, 1993). Results of studies indicating that different patterns of age-related change are obtained for standard laboratory-type assessments of cognitive performance and for everyday cognitive functioning suggest that knowledge utilization plays a key role in enabling individuals to perform effectively even when there is a substantial degree of decline in the speed and computational efficiency of cognitive functioning. In cognitively demanding tasks in the workplace, individuals use their acquired knowledge and familiarity with situations as a way of compensating for normally occurring losses in the speed and efficiency of memory and other cognitive functions (e.g., Bäckman & Dixon, 1992).

Several recent studies have demonstrated the interactive effects of age and domain-specific task variables on cognitive performance (e.g., Clancy & Hoyer, 1994; Salthouse, 1984). Salthouse (1984), for example, examined the typing performance and key-stroke reaction times of skilled typists ranging in age from 20 to 70 years. He found that typing performance was unaffected by age, even though there were reliable age-related declines in the speed of simple key strokes for these individuals. Salthouse investigated the effects of aging on how skilled typists carried out their tasks by varying the extent to which the individuals could preview letters in advance of where they were typing. Skilled older typists used a strategy of looking farther ahead of where they were typing, perhaps as a way of compensating for age-related slowing of the motoric aspects of typing. Similarly, Clancy and Hoyer reported that the efficiency of visual search performance depended on the domain-specificity of the information being processed in medical diagnostics. Age-related deficits in visual search were found between young adults and middle-aged medical technologists for a domain-general visual search task, but no age differences were found for a comparable domain-specific visual search task. Control subjects exhibited age-related deficits in both the skilled visual search task and the general visual search task. In a follow-up study (Hoyer, Ingolfsdottir, & Clancy, 1994), the beneficial effects of domain-specific contextual cues for older skilled subjects were again demonstrated by showing that the visual search performance of older skilled medical technologists was aided by the congruence of targets and display context. Taken together, these findings help us to understand how older adults perform competently in demanding work situations by relying on familiar task cues, despite age-related deficits in the speed and efficiency of basic information processing abilities. Familiarity and prior knowledge of task cues can minimize the negative effects of memory aging on performance when cues serve as mnemonic aids for memory retrieval (see Hoyer & Rybash, 1992).

In addition to reliance on acquired knowledge and the individual's ability to take advantage of information in the task context, individuals learn other effective ways of carrying out their work that minimize or avoid limitations that might otherwise interfere with effective job performance. In a number of research programs, it has been demonstrated that there is considerable plasticity of function in the later years, and considerable potential for compensation for age-related losses by such means as selective optimization and domain-specific knowledge utilization (e.g., see Bäckman & Dixon, 1992; Marsiske, Lang, Baltes, & Baltes, 1995; Rowe & Kahn, 1987; Willis & Dubin, 1990).

The primary implications of models of successful aging as they apply to work behavior are as follows: (a) to describe the positive dimensions of aging, particularly those functions that are maintained or those functions for which declines might be minimized or reversed; (b) to establish assessment markers or measures of aging that reflect the potential for retained or enhanced performance in selected contexts; and (c) to identify persons who perform optimally, and the conditions and background contexts associated with successful functioning. Along these lines, Waterman, Waterman, and Collard (1994) have described the characteristics of career-resilient workers—those individuals who continually succeed in keeping pace with changes in the workplace (see also Cascio, 1995). From a successful aging perspective, there is often an optimal match between the changing demands of the work context and the particular abilities, skills, and other characteristics of individuals at different ages. Workers of all ages can have the potential to make unique and valuable contributions within specific workplace contexts. Some combinations of work contexts and individual abilities may be uniquely successful.

Measurement issues must also be considered in understanding the apparent discrepancy between real-world job performance and measured age-related declines in basic cognitive abilities (Hunter, 1986). Only about 4%–25% of the variance in job performance can be accounted for by standard kinds of cognitive assessments. Several writers (e.g., Avolio, Barrett, & Sterns, 1984; Sternberg, Wagner, Williams, & Horvath, 1995) have suggested that assessments consisting of materials and problems typical of actual performance on the job should be used for predicting and evaluating job performance.

METHODOLOGICAL ISSUES

Although there is general acceptance of a dynamic conceptualization of worker-workplace interactions, there is little empirical work bearing directly on the veracity of this approach. The problem is that the empirical investigation of the interactive effects of person and context is difficult (e.g., Collins, 1996). In a recent review of the literature on work and aging, Salthouse and Maurer (1996) identified several methodological problems that plague the study of the relationship between age-related change and measures of work performance. Salthouse and Maurer pointed out that many of the available studies are weak in terms of statistical power, that the samples used in many of the studies of work and aging represent a limited range of age, and that measures of job performance are frequently biased and insensitive. Further, Salthouse and Maurer pointed out that there are problems in interpreting the available age-comparative data because of failures to consider selective attrition in successive age-cohort samples. It is the case that the more competent workers tend to remain in some job classifications, either by their choice or because employers are more likely to retain and promote these individuals. And it is also the case that the least competent workers tend to remain in other job classifications because these individuals have fewer options to change or improve employment. Further, Salthouse and Maurer suggested that job titles are inaccurate descriptions of individual competency and may not be valid indices for job classification in studies of work and aging. Because older individuals have had more years to advance along particular job tracks, income and job status measures of the proficiency of job performance are confounded with years of work.

There are also substantial challenges to investigating worker-workplace interactive effects in using newly introduced technology. Hunt (1993) noted the tremendous trade-offs that occur between knowledge and effective problem-solving in the rapidly changing workplace. To the extent that experienced workers have already acquired useful problem solving skills, we can expect these skills to be retained and used appropriately in the workplace. However, as the pace of technological advancement accelerates, and depending on the kinds of changes occurring in the workplace, some of the learned skills and particular competencies of experienced workers may become irrelevant and obsolete at a more rapid rate (Willis & Dubin, 1990). As already mentioned, computer training studies have generally produced training benefits for older adults, but older adults usually show more difficulty in acquiring new computer skills compared with younger adults (e.g., Caplan & Schooler, 1990; Czaja & Sharit, 1993; Kelley & Charness, 1995). Further, Kelley and Charness pointed out that these findings do not generalize readily to situations in which older individuals update familiar computer-based skills. Experienced older individuals actually have an advantage when updating their skills because they can build on acquired knowledge. However, anxiety about new technologies may interfere with new learning more for older adults than for younger adults (e.g., see Kelley & Charness, 1995).

Hunt (1993) suggested that the primary benefits of new technology in the workplace are in terms of helping workers to be more productive or to assist the enhancement of the quality of work in ways that complement the various skills of workers. For example, robotic technology and other kinds of automatization can be used to minimize the tedium of repetitive work and in other ways for the purpose of improving the work context. Unfortunately, more often than not, the introduction of new technology and job restructuring are thought of as ways of displacing older workers rather than as a means of helping workers to continue on the job.

SUMMARY AND FUTURE DIRECTIONS

The position advocated in this chapter is that age-related changes in work behavior are best understood in terms of description and explanation of the interactive effects of the aging individual and changing work contexts. The foundations of this approach have been spelled out by other writers (e.g., Baltes, 1987; Riley, 1987). Schooler, Caplan, and Oates (chapter 1, this volume) have discussed specific issues associated with a dynamic conceptualization of worker-workplace interactions.

It should be emphasized that research on the impact of work on older individuals is an area without disciplinary borders. New advances in our understanding of the relationships between work and aging will emerge from the most useful frameworks and the best methods within any of the social sciences (e.g., economics, psychology, sociology). Probably the most important advances in the understanding of effective work contexts will involve integrations of perspectives and methods across traditional disciplinary barriers (Riley, this volume).

The primary criteria for assessing the significance of research on work and aging are in terms of relevance to the worker and the workplace. That is, the primary aims of research on the impact of work on older individuals are to enrich or sustain the value and significance of work life throughout the adult life span, as well as to enhance the productivity and quality of the contributions of workers of all ages. The basic research on age-related changes in work performance is important not only because it dispels false stereotypes about the older worker, but also because it provides a base for employers to utilize the distinctive strengths of older workers. The rapidly changing nature of the workplace raises questions about how to best match people and technology (Hunt, 1993), and about how we can reconstruct the workplace so that individuals of all ages have the opportunity to produce their best work. Consistent with suggestions made by Schooler, Caplan, and Oates, new research on how to tap fully the knowledge, skills, and potential contributions of workers of all ages is likely to be fruitful for both individuals and for increasing productivity in the workplace.

In this chapter, I have tried to emphasize that there are both gains and losses associated with individual aging that affect job performance. Generally, there are only minor declines or no declines in many kinds of work performance. Several issues related to the maintenance of cognitive skills across the adult life span were discussed, including the importance of taking into account the interactive effects of context and individual worker, and increased reliance on learned skills and knowledge as a means of compensation for age-related declines in general abilities. Methodological and measurement issues in the study of the interactive effects of work contexts and aging were also discussed.

Although the available research may give an overly positive portrayal of the older worker because of selective dropout by individuals who are experiencing difficulties in the workplace, probably the general finding that there is no relationship between age and work performance is roughly accurate. However, the aggregate level of analysis obscures the understanding of worker-workplace interactions that operate at the level of the individual worker. In terms of measurement, it was recommended that instruments that tap actual real-world job competencies be used for performance assessment. Thus the main points of this chapter can be summarized as follows:

1. Changes in the worker-workplace relationship occur throughout the working years and are best understood at the level of the individual worker.
2. Successful aging in the domain of work depends on an optimal match between the changing demands of the work context and the particular abilities, skills, and other characteristics of individuals at different ages; workers of all ages can have the potential to make unique and valuable contributions within specific workplace contexts. Some combinations of work contexts and individual abilities may be uniquely synergistic.
3. Older workers can perform effectively in the workplace, in part by relying on domain knowledge and acquired skills, and by using aspects of the work context as support for effective performance.
4. There is evidence to suggest that there are age-related declines in the speed and efficiency of basic information processing abilities, and age differences in the amount of training required when new work responsibilities are introduced.

REFERENCES

Avolio, B. J., Barrett, G. V., & Sterns, H. L. (1984). Alternatives to age for assessing occupational performance capacity. *Experimental Aging Research, 10*, 101–105.

Bäckman, L., & Dixon, R. A. (1992). Psychological compensation: A theoretical framework. *Psychological Bulletin, 112*, 259–283.

Baltes, P. B. (1987). Theoretical propositions of life-span developmental psychology: On the dynamics between growth and decline. *Developmental Psychology, 23*, 611–626.

Baltes, P. B., & Baltes, M. M. (1990). Psychological perspectives on successful aging: The model of selective optimization with compensation. In P. B. Baltes & M. M. Baltes (Eds.), *Successful aging* (pp. 1–34). New York: Cambridge University Press.

Baltes, P. B., & Staudinger, U. M. (1993). The search for the psychology of wisdom. *Current Directions in Psychological Science, 2,* 75–80.

Birren, J.E. (1965). Age changes in speed of behavior: Its central nature and physiological correlates. In A. T. Welford & J. E. Birren (Eds.) *Behavior, aging, and the nervous system* (pp. 191–216). Springfield, IL: Charles C Thomas.

Brim, O. G. (1992). *Ambition: How we manage success and failure throughout our lives.* New York: Basic Books.

Caplan, L., & Schooler, C. (1990). The effects of analogical training models and age on problem-solving in a new domain. *Experimental Aging Research, 16,* 151–154.

Cascio, W. F. (1995). Whither industrial and organizational psychology in a changing world of work? *American Psychologist, 50,* 928–939.

Cerella, J., & Hale, S. (1994). The rise and fall of information processing rates over the life span. *Acta Psychologica, 86,* 109–197.

Charness, N., & Campbell, J. I. D. (1988). Acquiring skill at mental calculation in adulthood: A task decomposition. *Journal of Experimental Psychology: General, 117,* 115–129.

Clancy, S. M., & Hoyer, W. J. (1994). Age and skill in visual search. *Developmental Psychology, 30,* 545–552.

Collins, L. M. (1996). Measurement of change in research on aging: Old and new issues from an individual growth perspective. In J. E. Birren & K. W. Schaie (Eds.), *Handbook of the psychology of aging* (4th ed., pp. 38–56). San Diego, CA: Academic Press.

Czaja, S.J., & Sharit, J. (1993). Age differences in performance of computer–based work. *Psychology and Aging, 8,* 59-67.

Davies, D. R., & Sparrow, P. R. (1985). Age and work behavior. In N. Charness (Ed.), *Aging and human performance* (pp. 293–332). New York: Wiley.

Ekerdt, D., DeViney, S., & Kosloski, K. (1996). Profiling plans for retirement. *Journal of Gerontology: Social Sciences, 51B,* S140–S149.

Ericsson, K. A., & Lehmann, A. C. (1996). Expert and exceptional performance: Evidence of maximal adaptation to task constraints. *Annual Review of Psychology, 47,* 273–305.

Erikson, E., Erikson, J. M., & Kivnick, H. (1986). *Vital involvement in old age: The experience of old age in our time.* London: Norton.

Featherman, D. L., Smith, J., & Peterson, J. G. (1990). Successful aging in a post-retired society. In P. B. Baltes & M. M. Baltes (Eds.), *Successful aging* (pp. 50–93). New York: Cambridge University Press.

Hanisch, K. A. (1995). Behavioral families and multiple causes: Matching the complexity of responses to the complexity of the antecedents. *Current directions in psychological science, 4,* 156–162.

Hanisch, K. A., & Hulin, C. L. (1990). Job attitudes and organizational withdrawal: An examination of retirement and other voluntary withdrawal behaviors *Journal of Vocational Behavior, 37,* 60–78.

Hardy, M. A., & Quadagno, J. (1995). Satisfaction with early retirement: Making choices in the auto industry. *Journal of Gerontology: Social Sciences, 50B,* S217–S228.

Hoyer, W. J. (1985). Aging and the development of expert cognition. In T. M. Schlecter & M. P. Toglia (Eds.), *New directions in cognitive science* (pp. 69–87). Norwood, NJ: Ablex Books.

Hoyer, W. J. (1990). Levels of knowledge utilization in visual information processing. In T. M. Hess (Ed.), *Aging and cognition: Knowledge organization and utilization* (pp. 387–409). Amsterdam: Elsevier.

Hoyer, W. J., Ingolfsdottir, D., & Clancy, S. (1994, August). *Age and expertise in work performance: Supportive effects of contextual factors in visual selective attention.* Paper presented at the annual meeting of the American Psychology Association, Los Angeles.

Hoyer, W. J., & Lincourt, A. E. (in press). Aging and the development of learning. In M. A. Stadler & P. A. Frensch (Eds.), *Implicit learning handbook.* Thousand Oaks, CA: Sage.

Hoyer, W. J., & Rybash, J. M. (1992). Knowledge in visual perception. In R. L. West & J. D. Sinnott (Eds.), *Everyday memory and aging: Current research and methodology* (pp. 79–98). New York: Springer-Verlag.

Hunt, E. (1993). What do we need to know about aging? In J. Cerella, J. Rybash, W. J. Hoyer, & M. Commons (Eds.), *Adult information processing: Limits on Loss* (pp. 587–598). San Diego, CA: Academic Press.

Hunter, J. E. (1986). Cognitive ability, cognitive aptitude, job knowledge, and job performance. *Journal of Vocational Behavior, 29,* 340–362.

International Labor Office. (1962). *Report of the Director General.*

Kelley, C., & Charness, N. (1995). Issues in training older adults to use computers. *Behaviour and Information Technology, 14,* 107–120.

McEvoy, G. M., & Cascio, W. F. (1989). Cumulative evidence of the relationship between employee age and job performance. *Journal of Applied Psychology, 74,* 11–17.

Marsiske, M., Lang, F. R., Baltes, P. B., & Baltes, M. M. (1995). Selective optimization with compensation: Life span perspectives on successful human development. In R. A. Dixon & L. Bäckman (Eds.), *Compensating for psychological deficits and declines: Managing losses and promoting gains* (pp. 35–79). Mahwah, NJ: Erlbaum.

Maurer, T., & Tarulli, B. (1994). Perceived environment, perceived outcome, and person variables in relationship to voluntary development activity by employees. *Journal of Applied Psychology, 79,* 3–14.

Myerson, J., Hale, S., Hirschman, R., Hansen, C., & Christensen, B. (1989). Global increase in response latencies by early middle age. *Journal of the Experimental Analysis of Behavior, 52,* 353–362.

Rhodes, S. R. (1983). Age-related differences in work attitudes and behavior: A review and conceptual analysis. *Psychological Bulletin, 93.* 328–367.

Riley, M. W. (1985). Age strata and social systems. In R. H. Binstock & E. Shanas (Eds.), *Handbook of aging and the social sciences* (Vol. 3, pp. 369–411). New York: Van Nostrand Reinhold.

Riley, M. W. (1987). On the significance of age in sociology. *American Sociological Review, 52,* 1–14.

Rowe, J. W., & Kahn, R. L. (1987). Human aging: Usual and successful. *Science, 237,* 143–149.

Rybash, J. M., Hoyer, W. J., & Roodin, P. A. (1986). *Adult cognition and aging. Developmental changes in processing, knowing and thinking.* New York: Pergamon.

Salthouse, T. A. (1984). Effects of age and skill in typing. *Journal of Experimental Psychology: General, 113,* 345–371.

Salthouse, T. A. (1985). Speed of behavior and its implications for cognition. In J. E. Birren & K. W. Schaie (Eds.), *Handbook of the psychology of aging* (2nd ed., pp. 400–426). New York: Van Nostrand Reinhold.

Salthouse, T. A. (1991). *Theoretical perspectives on cognitive aging.* Hillsdale, NJ: Erlbaum.

Salthouse, T. A., & Maurer, T. J. (1996). Aging, job performance, and career development. In J.E. Birren & K. W. Schaie (Eds.), *Handbook of the psychology of aging* (4th ed., pp. 353–364). San Diego, CA: Academic Press.

Schaie, K. W. (1996). Intellectual development in adulthood. In J. E. Birren & K. W. Schaie (Eds.), *Handbook of the psychology of aging* (4th ed., pp. 266–286). San Diego, CA: Academic Press.

Sternberg, R. J., Wagner, R. K., Williams, W. M., & Horvath, J. A. (1995). Testing common sense. *American Psychologist, 50,* 912–927.

Waldman, D. A., & Avolio, B. J. (1986). A meta–analysis of age differences in job performance. *Journal of Applied Psychology, 71,* 33–38.

Waterman, R. H., Jr., Waterman, J. A., & Collard, B. A. (1994, July-August). Toward a career-resilient workforce. *Harvard Business Review,* pp. 87–95.

Welford, A. T. (1958). *Ageing and human skill.* London: Oxford University Press.

Willis, S. L., & Dubin, S. S. (Eds.). (1990). *Maintaining professional competence.* San Francisco, CA: Jossey-Bass.

Yokomizo, Y. (1985). Measurement of ability of older workers. *Ergonomics, 28,* 843–854.

CHAPTER 2

Gradual Retirement: Japanese Strategies for Older Workers

Chikako Usui

Since the middle of the 1970s, industrially advanced nations have experienced prolonged recessionary trends. During this period, many corporations have introduced structural changes under the general rubric "corporate restructuring" to relieve their cost burdens.[1] As private corporations cut employment, many governments opened up

The research project on which this chapter is based was funded by University of Missouri-St. Louis Research Awards (S-2-00880 and S-2-01070). I would like to thank Carmi Schooler for the initial inspiration for this chapter and K. Warner Schaie, Richard Colignon, and Frances Hoffmann for their valuable comments and suggestions. I would also like to thank the following individuals for their generous donation of time and information: Yoshio Asakura, Mikio Baba, and Kaneo Ito at Gifu Prefectural Government Office, Teruaki Furuse at Japan Airlines, Ken'ichi Ishihara at Gifu University of Economics, Takahiro Ishizaka at Gifu Senior Citizen's Association, Hiroshi Nakamura at the Japan Information File, Takehiro Sakamoto at Japan Federation of Employers' Associations, and Toru Momozaki, Keiko Suehiro, and Ryo Yamanada at the Ministry of Labor.

institutional pathways to address high rates of unemployment by promoting workers' early exit from the labor force. Some European countries followed an "externalization approach," which grants older workers early exit from the labor force with government support. Sweden and Japan adopted an "internalization approach," which provides a transition period between full-time work and complete exit from the labor force through flexible employment options (e.g., part-time work). The United States followed an "early retirement through privatization path," which moves older workers out of the labor force through private pension incentives, without government pension support.

Cross-national studies of retirement conducted since 1986 provide a taxonomy of these pathways for older workers, but they neglect discussions of how and why a particular country institutionalizes a certain approach to the treatment of older workers. This chapter examines the Japanese approach to the "gradual retirement" of older workers to elaborate the how and why of its "internalization" path. A focus on Japanese industrial relations affecting older workers is important for empirical and theoretical reasons. First, most comparative studies of the political economy of retirement have focused on Western countries and assume the convergence of societies to a similar set of structures, practices, and policies. However, the Japanese path of economic development challenges convergence assumptions. Second, much of the discussion about the Japanese postwar economic "miracle" masks the dynamics of the industrial decline and corporate restructuring that occurred since the mid-1970s in Japan. Over the past 20 years, Japanese corporations have continuously restructured themselves to address the fundamental "innovation dilemma." Adverse economic conditions affected the jobs of older workers; yet the Japanese response has been unusual in its emphasis on labor force integration of older workers through active employment policies.

This chapter presents an institutional embeddedness argument for explaining the Japanese approach to gradual retirement. It contends that there is a correspondence between the institutional structures of a society and organizational structures and human resource practices. Organizational systems of worker recruitment, education, training, and remuneration reflect variations in the institutional configurations of societies. Retirement is another organizational feature that follows this societal-specific pattern. This chapter also contends that companies are socially embedded in networks of institutions and do not operate as atomized actors pursuing their particular interests. Further, corporate strategies reflect both the symbolic and material features of the larger institutional configurations, and must be understood in these contexts.

COMPARATIVE RESEARCH AND JAPAN

In general, early retirement in the decade of the 1980s among industrially advanced nations resulted from a conjunction of interests among states, business, and labor unions (Guillemard & Rein, 1993). Governments wanted to reduce youth unemployment by inducing the early retirement of older workers before the age of 60 through various institutional pathways. These institutional pathways offered business greater flexibility in human resource management and opportunities for trimming labor costs. Labor unions supported early retirement as the workers' reward for long service and ending work without embarrassment. Workers saw early retirement as an opportunity to enjoy their nonwork life in good health, particularly in countries where benefits were generous.

Some European governments attempted to absorb older workers by relaxing rules governing unemployment programs, disability pension programs, or preretirement programs—mechanisms of an "externalization" approach. These retirement benefits were given to workers in exchange for their withdrawal from the labor market (Guillemard & van Gunsteren, 1991; Jacobs & Rein, 1993). These arrangements were originally intended to provide a bridge between workers' early exits and the receipt of public retirement pensions. However, older workers became the target for corporate restructuring, thus accelerating the burden on the welfare state.

Alternatively, Japan and Sweden, as exceptions to the European externalization approaches, took an internalization path (de Vroom & Naschold, 1993; Wadensjö, 1991). Internalization models maintain labor force integration through active employment policies for older workers. The Swedish model has been in place for almost 2 decades, providing a flexible alternative to "either work or retirement" for workers between 60 and 65 years of age (Reday-Mulvey, 1995; Wadensjö, 1991). With the availability of part-time jobs, cooperation between the state and private sector, and generous partial pension benefits, the result has been a creation of gradual retirement rather than early retirement. Similarly, Japan maintains relatively high rates of labor force participation with active, proemployment policies for older workers. There is no sign of an early retirement trend in Japan because large- and medium-sized corporations have provided tiered employment. Older workers move from large and medium to medium and small companies between the ages of 50 and 60, while public pensions and other government programs support this transition. This complementary action by the private and public sectors maintains the workers' integration into the labor force, yet moves older workers out of the path of younger cohorts.

The United States has taken a third path (Kohli, Rein, Guillemard, & van Gunsteren, 1991; Sheppard, 1991), neither opening government supported pathways to facilitate the early exit of older workers before age 62 nor engaging in the active integration of older workers into the labor market. Retirement before 62 years of age is a practical option for only a narrow segment of older workers whose employment relationship is terminated by corporate early retirement packages (DeViney & O'Rand, 1988; Hutchens, 1993).[2] Although business firms have facilitated the exit of older workers by offering early retirement incentive packages, the U.S. government has actually moved in the opposite direction. It raised the normal retirement age from 65 to 67 in 1986 to reduce the future costs of the Social Security System. The result has actually been a modest increase in early retirement.

Comparative research on the treatment of older workers provides the context for examining a critical case study. Comparative research on older workers identifies variations in the dependent variable (e.g., retirement), but tends to presume a similar set of independent variables (e.g., unemployment rates, pension apparatus). There is in the literature a strong impulse toward examining a handful of universally relevant, independent variables that are presumed to explain a continuous variation in outcomes. In contrast, this chapter selects Japan for closer examination to identify unique independent variables that explain the Japanese approach to gradual retirement. Rather than seeking a goodness of fit for existing models of independent variables, this chapter attempts to delineate what might otherwise be overlooked independent variables in the Japanese case.

JAPAN AS A CASE STUDY: AN OVERVIEW
OF LABOR MARKETS AND WELFARE INSTITUTIONS

Compared to other industrially advanced countries, a substantial proportion of older persons continue to work in Japan (Tables 2.1 and 2.2).

Among male workers aged 55 to 59, there has been no indication of early retirement, as 91% of men in this age group participate in the labor force. For men between 60 and 64 years of age, there has been a modest decline in the labor force participation rates, from 82.8% in 1965 to 74.2% in 1990. Over 35% of male workers aged 65 and over were in the labor force in 1990. What accounts for this relatively high and stable rate of labor force participation?

Prevailing explanations have typically invoked two factors: (1) poorly developed welfare institutions that provide meager retirement benefits; and (2) a robust economy that provides jobs for older workers.[3] A closer examination of welfare policy changes during the past 3 decades, however, reveals that Japan had diverged from the prevailing Western welfare state models by the mid-1980s. This shift corresponds in time to the adverse economic conditions Japan faced after the two oil-shock recessions. The modern welfare state programs were introduced in Japan in the 1960s and expanded in the "old people's boom years" of the 1970s. However, cost increases in the 1980s resulting from the welfare expansion of the 1970s, combined with a slowing of the economy and the rapidity of population aging, led to drastic revisions in the welfare state course in the mid-1980s. During that period, the government implemented employment programs for workers. It began lobbying business firms to keep older workers on the job by raising the mandatory retirement age. At the same time, the government implemented subsidy programs to foster a smooth transformation of old industries into promising new industries.

The magnitude of changes and economic problems that began in the mid-1970s is often obscured in the literature, which predominantly focuses on the phenomenon of Japanese economic success. The Japanese economy stagnated with the two oil shocks, ending decades of rapid economic growth (Table 2.3). The first oil shock caused a prolonged recession due to Japan's lack of natural resources, including oil. Bankruptcies rose sharply during this period. Because the Japanese economy is export driven, these developments were further aggravated by the continuous appreciation of the yen against the American dollar. The adoption of a flexible exchange rate system in 1971 led to the initial appreciation of the yen, from 360 yen to 270 yen per dollar. Japan's export-led growth ended abruptly in 1980 when the world economy slumped, trade disputes between Japan, the United States, and Europe intensified, and Japanese industries were challenged by the industrializing nations of East Asia.

Table 2.1 International Comparison of the Labor Force Participation Rates, 1965–90

Men, Age 60–64	1965	1970	1975	1980	1985	1990
France	68.8	68.0	56.7	47.6	30.8	23.1
Germany	78.1	71.8	56.2	42.5	32/4	31.5
U.S.	79.2	71.7	64.5	59.8	55.1	53.8
Sweden	83.0	79.5	74.0	69.0	65.1	64.1
Japan	82.8	85.0	79.4	77.8	72.5	74.2

Men, Age 65+	1965	1970	1975	1980	1985	1990
France	28.3	19.5	13.9	7.5	5.3	3.5
Germany	24.0	17.2	10.8	7.0	5.1	4.5
U.S.	26.6	25.7	20.7	18.3	15.2	16.0
Sweden	3.7	28.9	19.9	14.2	11.0	18.8
Japan	56.3	50.0	44.4	41.0	37.0	36.5

Sources: OECD 1993, *Labour Force Statistics.* Ministry of Labor 1988, *Fujin rodo no jitsujo,* App. 110, pp. 96–97.

TABLE 2.2 International Comparison of the Labor Force Participation Rates, 1965–90

Women, Age 60–64	1965	1970	1975	1980	1985	1990
France	31.7	34.3	29.8	27.3	18.9	17.0
Germany	23.3	20.4	15.5	12.0	10.1	12.5
U.S.	34.5	34.8	33.0	32.9	33.2	35.1
Sweden	30.9	38.2	38.3	41.0	46.6	50.5
Japan	39.8	39.1	38.0	38.8	38.5	39.5

Women, Age 65+	1965	1970	1975	1980	1985	1990
France	11.5	8.6	5.9	3.3	1.1	1.5
Germany	7.8	6.1	4.5	3.1	2.3	2.0
U.S.	9.4	9.0	7.8	7.6	6.8	7.4
Sweden	11.6	9.8	6.1	3.7	3.2	4.9
Japan	21.6	17.9	15.3	15.5	15.5	16.2

Sources: OECD, 1993, *Labour Force Statistics.* Ministry of Labor 1988, *Fujin rodo no jitsujo,* App. 110, pp. 96–97.

TABLE 2.3 Annual Rate of Real Growth, 1960–93

Year	Growth rates Japan (%)	Year	Growth rates (%) Japan	Germany	U.S.
1960	7.8	1960–77	7.7	3.3	2.4
1965	9.1				
1970	9.8				
1974 (Oil-shock recession)	-0.2	1970–79	4.6	2.6	3.2
1980	4.2				
1986 (*Endaka* recession[a])	2.9	1986	2.9	2.3	2.9
1990	4.8	1990	4.8	5.7	1.2
1991 (Bubble recession[b])	3.6	1991	3.6	4.5	-0.7
1992 (Bubble recession)	1.2	1992	1.2	1.6	2.6
1993 (Bubble recession)	-0.2	1993	-0.2	-1.9	3.0

Sources: M. Bronfenbrenner and Y. Yasuba, 1987, "Economic Welfare," in K. Yamamura and Y. Yasuba (Eds.), *The political economy of Japan,* Table 1, p. 96. Keizai Koho Center, 1994, Japan 1995, Tables 1–7 and 1–10, pp. 10, 12–13.

Figures for three country comparison derive from Prime Minister's Office, 1983, *Kokusai tokei yoran.,* Table 73, and The World Bank, 1979, *World Development Report,* 1979, Table 2.

[a]Recession caused by rising values of yen.
[b]Recession caused by the burst of bubble economy.

Bubble recession officially started in 1991 and ended in 1993.

However, Japan's continuing trade surplus with Western nations led to the Plaza Accord of 1985, which strengthened the value of the yen, from 273 yen to 168 yen per dollar, causing a second major recession (called the *endaka* recession; Keizai Koho Center, 1994). The number of bankruptcies in 1986 marked the highest level in postwar economic history. [4]

With Japan's international trade surplus still growing, Japan was further pressured to stimulate domestic consumption. This led to the Bank of Japan's drastically loosening of its monetary polices, creating a "bubble economy" with massive asset inflation, share price increases, and booming of speculative markets. When the government finally tightened money supplies in 1989, interest rates rose, asset prices decreased, and the stock market plunged by 60%, causing the bubble to burst. Japan officially entered the bubble recession in 1991. In the meantime, the value of the yen appreciated rapidly, from 145 yen per dollar in 1987 to 101 yen in 1995.

Each major recession forced corporations to engage in restructuring to reduce overcapacity and to address the innovation dilemma (Schumpeter, 1939; 1950). The concept of continuous improvement (*kaizen*) and lean production system are just a few examples of corporate restructuring efforts in meeting external challenges. Although different industries, firm size, and occupational groups were affected in each recession, it was the older workers who were always disproportionately affected (Imai, 1994; Schulz, Borowski, & Crown, 1991; Tanaka, 1977). [5]

Considering the magnitude of macroeconomic changes in the Japanese economy since the mid-1970s, corporate restructuring took place without serious social disruptions. The private and public sectors have forged a complementary strategy for older workers to avoid unemployment. This complementary strategy is distinct from the U.S. model, where business and government efforts work at cross-purposes. The Japanese response is also distinct from European approaches, which created new institutional paths for early retirement. In the following sections, this chapter examines the specific mechanisms that developed or supported the Japanese strategy over time.

The Private Sector: Teinen and Shukko

Teinen and *shukko* provide two mechanisms, internal to Japanese business firms, that contribute to extended participation and gradual retirement of older workers. Many large and medium-sized companies enforce *teinen* (age limit), signifying the end of a worker's primary career. Until recently, the institution of *teinen* left a 5- to 10-year gap before the worker reached age 60, when public pension benefits become available. For example, before 1975 more than 50% of firms with 30 or more employees enforced *teinen* at 55 years of age or earlier. Today, more than 70% of companies with 30 workers or more enforce *teinen* at 60 years of age or later (Ministry of Labor, 1994).

Upon reaching *teinen,* a worker receives company retirement benefits (a lump sum) and shifts from a primary career to a secondary career, sometimes at the same firm but at lower wages with lower status. Many move on to smaller firms through outplacement by their employers. Some workers accept part-time jobs at these firms. Except for those who start up their own businesses or opt for complete retirement, the final exit from work typically occurs 5 years after *teinen,* around 65 years of age.

Firm size has a much more profound impact on Japanese workers' lives than does their occupational status (cf. Ishida, 1993; Kalleberg & Lincoln, 1988; Kerbo, 1995; Kerbo & McKinstry, 1995; Lincoln & Kalleberg, 1985; Naoi & Schooler, 1984). Firm size may modify the effects of *teinen.* Among workers in the same occupational category (e.g., professionals, managers, skilled workers), those employed by large firms are more likely to receive in-house training, long-term job security, seniority-based promotion, higher wages, and fringe benefits than those in small and medium-sized firms. Labor mobility rates are low among large firms but are quite high among small firms. Among small firms, the pay scale is not highly correlated with age or seniority. [6]

The movement of older workers from large and medium firms to medium and small firms results in larger firms maintaining a relatively young age structure, while small firms have a heavy concentration of older workers (Tables 2.4 and 2.5). The implications of this demographic pattern for labor costs and management are significant for companies.

Shukko

Shukko refers to dispatching of workers from one company to another, typically to its subsidiaries or affiliates. *Shukko* is sometimes called "workers on loan." *Shukko* increased among older white-collar workers throughout the 1980s, as companies began to find new ways for the creative use of older workers. [7] Also, large companies began spinning off new satellite firms (*bunsha*) for industrial diversification, creating new posts for workers (Beck & Beck, 1994). The new satellite firms, which are small scale but autonomous, overcome the coordination and contracting problems associated with underdeveloped markets and poorly developed routines of new entrepreneurs (Gerlach, 1992). The experience of older workers makes a valuable contribution to these start-up companies.

Broadly speaking, *shukko* serves four functions (Hirose, 1993): (1) job training and career development of workers in their 30s and early 40s; (2) provision of technical assistance and manpower to smaller subsidiaries or affiliates; (3) employment adjustment device in times of recessions;

TABLE 2.4 Distribution of Older Male Workers by Firm Size, 1973, 1978, and 1988

Year	Male, age	Company size				Government sector	Total(%)[a]
		1–29	30–99	100–999	1,000+		
1973	50–54	27.8	14.6	15.9	25.7	16.0	100
	55–59	33.6	18.6	18.6	15.0	14.2	100
	60–64	42.5	20.0	20.0	8.7	10.0	100
	65+	49.2	19.4	16.4	7.4	7.4	100
1978	50–54	28.0	14.7	16.1	23.2	18.0	100
	55–59	35.0	18.3	16.7	14.2	15.0	100
	60–64	46.0	21.0	17.1	6.6	9.3	100
	65+	53.6	18.9	13.9	5.8	8.7	100
1988	50–54	31.3	15.6	20.5	20.1	12.5	100
	55–59	32.4	17.2	19.2	15.8	14.9	100
	60–64	43.0	19.6	19.6	8.9	8.9	100
	65+	58.1	17.1	14.4	4.0	5.4	100

[a]Due to rounding, figures do not always add up to 100%.

Source: Ministry of Labor, 1989, *White Paper on Labor.* Kimura, Takagi, Oka, & Omori, 1994, p. 250.

and (4) gradual retirement and career development of a post-*teinen* worker. The length of *shukko* varies from 1 to 3 years, but the extension of *shukko* through contract renewal is not uncommon. For all types of *shukko,* much depends on company policies so that individual workers have little choice about dispatching conditions. Except in the last type of *shukko* (gradual retirement), *shukko* does not necessarily lead to a reduction in a worker's salary. Because smaller firms pay a lower salary than do larger firms, larger firms generally pay the difference (about 20% of a worker's original salary). The third and fourth types of *shukko* are effective at keeping a company lean, especially at managerial levels. In addition, *shukko* provides an important liaison between the company and its subsidiary or affiliate in maintaining a network of communications. As the current recession continues, however, it has become more difficult for large firms to find room for *shukko* among their subsidiaries and affiliates.

Workers who are past 50 years of age become prime candidates for *shukko* as a path towards early retirement (described as no. 4 previously).

TABLE 2.5 Distribution of Older Female Workers by Firm Size, 1973, 1975, and 1983

Year	Female, age	Company size				Government sector	Total(%)[a]
		1–29	30–99	100–499	500+		
1973	50–54	43.5	19.2	12.8	12.8	12.8	100
	55–64	48.6	17.1	10.5	11.8	11.8	100
1975	50–54	42.8	19.0	13.1	13.1	11.9	100
	55–64	49.4	17.7	10.1	11.4	11.4	100
1983	50–54	41.8	19.4	13.4	13.4	11.9	100
	55–64	45.1	18.3	13.4	12.2	11.0	100

Source: Ministry of Labor, 1984, *Fujin rodo no jitujo,* App. 16, p. 20.

[a]Due to rounding, figures do not always add up to 100%.

The use of this type of *shukko* has increased, and the age at which it occurs is becoming earlier (Nagano, 1995). A worker may continue to be dispatched until reaching *teinen* (usually age 60). *Shukko* may also lead to a termination of the job contract with the home company, followed by a new job contract with a new employer.

The process of *shukko* follows the tiered pattern of gradual retirement (Table 2.6). *Shukko* is a far more common practice from parent companies to their subsidiaries and smaller affiliates than vice versa. According to a national survey of 2,034 medium- and small-sized firms conducted in 1991, 85.8% of subsidiaries received workers from their parent companies, while 46.1% of parent companies received workers from their affiliates. Over 90% (92.1%) of medium-sized firms sent their workers to their subsidiaries and affiliates, but only 27% (26.7%) of subsidiaries sent their workers to other companies. Forty percent of medium firms sent pre-*teinen* workers, that is, workers who had not reached mandatory retirement age set by their companies. One-third of medium firms (32.1%) sent workers upon reaching *teinen* to their subsidiaries and affiliates. Almost one in four subsidiaries (26.1%) received both pre-*teinen* workers and post-*teinen* workers from their parent firms. Other case studies of *shukko* report that there is a close relationship between the number of new hires and the number of workers sent (see, e.g., Kimura, Takagi, Oka, & Omori, 1993).

TABLE 2.6 Flows of *Shukko* Among Medium Companies and Their Subsidiaries and Affiliates

Direction of *Shukko*	Sending out workers	Sending out workers prior to *teinen*	Sending out workers at *teinen*	Receiving workers from other companies	Receiving pre-*teinen* workers from other companies	Receiving *teinen* workers from other companies
Medium-sized firms	92.1 (%)	40.0 (%)	32.1 (%)	46.1 (%)	13.9 (%)	3.9 (%)
Semi-medium firms	86.8	23.8	24.7	73.2	23.6	17.9
Subsidiaries	26.7	4.5	1.7	85.8	26.1	26.1

Source: From Hirose, 1993, Table 2, Table 3 and Table 4. Surveys were conducted by Hirose from 1991 to 1992. Medium-sized firms are defined as those "*chukaku kigyo*" whose names are listed in the *Tosho jojo kigyo*. A total of 920 medium firms were selected from different industries. In addition, their subsidiaries of 1,114 were included. The total number of firms was 2,034. In the analysis, Hirose reclassified these firms into three categories: medium, semimedium, and subsidiary. Medium firms are those without their own parent companies but with subsidiaries of their own. Semimedium firms refer to those with both parent companies and subsidiaries of their own. Subsidiaries are those without subsidiaries of their own.

Small Firms

Small firms have been the backbone of the Japanese economy, playing vital economic, social and political roles. Small firms, employing one hundred or fewer people, account for over 60% of the private sector employment and produce almost one-half of the private sector GNP (Patrick & Rohlen, 1987). Small enterprises predominate in three sectors—agriculture, retailing, and manufacturing. Reasons for the high number of small firms include the vertical network structure among companies, tax benefits, and workers' desires to become their own bosses. Subcontractors receive technological infusions and other assistance from their parent companies. Parent companies are also able to avoid fixed costs connected with employing more people and they solve problems of space constraints by "spinning off" subcomponent manufacturing to smaller firms (Ballon, 1989; Gerlach, 1992; Patrick & Rohlen, 1987) . Compared to large- and medium-sized firms where a worker's gradual retirement is fostered by the tiered employment system, the institution of retirement among small firms is altogether different. Small firms absorb a large number of people who might otherwise be unemployed, including people forced into early retirement and women returning to work after raising children. Extremely small firms employing 30 or fewer workers account for about 20% of the labor force. The majority of these firms are family owned, and *teinen* is either not enforced or nonexistent. Thus many workers continue to work beyond 60 years of age. This explains the heavy concentration of older workers in small companies as reported in Tables 2.4 and 2.5 .

Public Sector: Government Institutions and Gradual Retirement

Japan introduced a national pension system in 1959 (implemented in 1961) that covered the entire population under three major pension systems: the earnings-related Employee Pension System (EPS), the National Pension System (NPS), and special pensions for public employees (Murakami, 1990). The EPS is the largest pension system of the three, covering slightly over 50% of the labor force. Until the pension reform of 1985, benefits for the EPS were payable at 60 years of age with a minimum of 20 years of contributions. The NPS was based on flat-rate contributions and covered the self-employed population, family workers, agricultural workers, and those who do not work but wish to have their own pensions in old age (e.g., housewives). The NPS covered about 40% of the labor force and provided a small, flat benefits pension at age 65 (with 25 years of contribution). The special pensions for public employees, teachers, and other special occupational groups were known for generous benefits (with 20 years of contribution).

During the 1970s, "old people's boom" years, dramatic increases in pension benefits took place, whose avowed purpose was bringing Japan on a par with other advanced industrialized nations (Campbell, 1992). However, after the oil shock of 1973, the national agenda shifted to the containment of future costs of public pensions and health care benefits. The pension (and health care) reform that took place from 1982 to 1985 signaled "a plateau or deceleration in Japan's march toward the welfare state" (Campbell, 1992).

In 1985, existing public pension systems were consolidated into a simpler, two-tiered system that includes basic (flat) pensions for all the citizens plus employee pensions (Ozawa, 1985). The basic pension is payable at age 65, whereas the employee tier is payable at age 60. Benefits are assessed on the basis of 40 years of flat-rate contributions for the basic pension, with 40 years of income-proportional contributions for the employment-related pensions. This pension reform also raised the original entitlement age for women under the employment-related pension from age 55 to 60 by 2005. [8]

The 1994 pension reform introduced a partial pension between the ages of 60 and 65 and a regular pension (both EPS and NPS) to begin at age 65 (Morito, 1995). The partial pension is designed to strengthen income needs of older workers who are gradually retiring. After age 60, pension benefits are paid according to the level of income of the worker but in a way that encourages continued employment. The new partial pension system will be introduced gradually for men beginning in 2001 and for women beginning in 2006. The tax rate for the employee pension was raised from 14.5% to 17.35% in 1994 (divided equally by employee and employer) and will automatically increase every 5 years by 2.5% until the year 2015. Similarly, contribution rates for flat pensions (NPS) were raised from ¥11,100 ($111) to ¥11,600 ($116) in 1995 and will increase automatically every 5 years by ¥500 ($5), until at least the year 2015

(Nakamura, 1995). In short, the recent policy changes attempt future cost containment through the integration of older workers into the labor force up to the age of 65.

AN INSTITUTIONAL PERSPECTIVE ON
JAPANESE GRADUAL RETIREMENT

In the aggregate, retirement is not a random event caused by frantic business decisions. Japanese firms have engaged in an "organizing logic" that fosters gradual retirement—particularly of regular workers. [9] Economic activities of the firms cannot be separated from the quest for social approval, affiliation, political influence, and reputation of the firm (Granovetter & Swedberg, 1992).

Social institutions influence the nature of competitive business structures and practices developing in different societies. This is seen in the correspondence between the institutional structures of society and organizational structures and human resource management practices (Sorge & Maurice, 1990). Corporations do not act uniformly under pressure for restructuring. Comparative analyses of corporate responses to economic downturns in the United States, Germany, and Japan for the period 1970 to 1985 (Abraham & Houseman; 1989, 1993) show significant differences in their impact on workers.

1. The rapidity and extent of layoffs were slower and less dramatic in scope in Germany and Japan than in the United States. In the United States, corporate adjustment through layoffs took place in close correspondence to falls in production demands. In contrast, Germany and Japan used other measures, such as the reduction of working hours.
2. The distribution of layoffs was more even between white- and blue-collar workers in Germany and Japan than was the case in the United States. In these two countries, the differences in job termination between blue-collar and white-collar workers did not emerge until the recession extended over 1 year. In the United States, at least until the middle of the 1980s, the distribution of layoffs was more concentrated among blue-collar workers, especially less skilled workers.

3. The distribution of layoffs was more concentrated among young
workers in the United States due to less seniority on the job. In
Germany and Japan, older workers were more affected by economic downturns and companies restructuring pressures than were
younger workers.

The context in which Japanese companies operate provides important clues to the pattern of Japanese responses to corporate restructuring
and the treatment of older workers. Four characteristics of Japanese economic, political and cultural institutions account in large measure for corporate adjustment strategies:

1. Japanese management is not driven by shareholder interests in dividends and appreciation;
2. The ownership of company shares is maintained through a network of known firms with durable relationships, not anonymous
securities markets; [10]
3. Gradual retirement policy is implemented by the government
through employment subsidies to firms, funds to targeted industries, and administrative guidance; [11] and
4. The media in Japan constrain company policies because they shape
the reputation of Japanese firms.

Governance Structure of the Japanese Firm

Organizational governance structures of typical U.S., German, and
Japanese firms are different (Aoki, 1987; Gerlach, 1992; Katzenstein,
1987; Useem, 1993). The differences involve such parameters as the
dominant constituency of the firm, the source and level of firm ownership, and the level of independence of the firm's management. The
different combinations of these dimensions of internal organization
result in different organizational policies designed to adjust to economic recession.

Comparing U.S., German, and Japanese modes of corporate governance, various authors have identified "capital" as opposed to "labor"
centered models of governance. The organizational governance structures
in the United States are identified with capital, those in Japan with labor,

and in Germany with a middle path of codetermination. Codetermination refers to the joint participation of owners and workers in their running of the German industry. The system of codetermination provides for employee representation in the workplace and has two components. Workers have a right to form work councils at enterprises with more than four employees. Such councils have codetermination powers in such areas as scheduling, workplace safety, and hiring and firing. Work councils play an important role in negotiating settlements during massive layoffs or plant closings. In large companies, workers also elect representatives to the board of directors (*Aufsichtsrat*) (Abraham & Houseman, 1993; Vogl, 1973).

Codetermination is considered by some authors to be a "third way," a middle course between unlimited capitalism and bureaucratic communism. Streeck (1984) contends that codetermination creates a kind of mutual incorporation of labor and capital, where labor internalizes the interests of capital and capital internalizes the interests of labor. Codetermination has offered employers incentives to change the structure and practice of management to deal with employment flexibility as a means of obtaining economic efficiency (Katzenstein, 1987). Some argue, however, that codetermination has the effect of creating a privileged labor force with relatively secure jobs and strong rights, but that also widens the gap between more and less privileged workers: among the young, old, women, and part-time workers.

American firms are "capital-centered models of corporate ownership" operating within "stock-market-centered capitalism" (Gerlach, 1992). Although a company may have multiple constituencies (i.e., workers, suppliers, creditors, customers, regulators,), it exists primarily for the benefit of stockholders. Useem (1993) suggests that this priority implies that corporate structure and policy are "defined and evaluated according to the criteria of shareholder value" (high dividends and stock price appreciation). The top priority of management is to maximize capital returns.[12]

The experiences of the 1980s exaggerated the governance structure of American firms. These included a prolonged period of profit decline in the 1970s, the emergence of corporate raiders, and the ascent of large aggressive institutional investors (pension funds, investment companies, insurance companies and bank trusts) who increased the control of stockholders over the priorities of American firms (Useem, 1993). The 1980s saw attention focused on shareholder's interests, with frequent and radical "redeployment" and "rightsizings" that left between 500,000 and 600,000 workers unemployed in 1993 alone. The capital-centered model dictates that in times of economic recession, primary effort is devoted to protecting shareholder value. This means dividends must be protected and stock prices maintained continuously. Worker payroll, capital investment, research and development are all reduced before dividends are cut. From the viewpoint of neo-classical economists, "management unilaterally chooses its employment and investment policy in order to maximize share price posterior to individual or collective wage bargaining" (Aoki, 1987).

Japanese firms, by contrast, are characterized by a "strategic" or "labor"-centered model of corporate ownership (Gerlach, 1992) where dividends, profits, and rates of capital return are relatively low. Legally speaking, firms are the property of shareholders, but in practice, firms exist more for the benefit of the employees than for the shareholders. Shareholders stand as investors rather than as controllers of a firm (Abegglen & Stalk, 1985). In time of a recession, Japanese firms cut dividends before cutting payroll. In fact, cutting the dividends is customarily done without the consent of the shareholders in Japan (*Japan Update,* 1992). [13] The major feature of the Japanese model, according to Aoki (1987), is its emphasis on "the mediation postulate, according to which management, possibly in cooperation with the enterprise union, coordinates wage determination and managerial policy making simultaneously in order to achieve an efficient outcome."

The labor-centered governance structure of Japanese firms, in conjunction with other institutional supports, allows Japanese firms to adjust to recession and overcapacity in ways that may seem peculiar to Americans. The Japanese firms' capacity for internal adjustment without worker termination is indicated by the swelling number of redundant workers within firms, known as *in-house unemployment.* Many of the redundant workers are older workers. Various sources estimate that the internalization of redundant workers now involves more than 1 million to 1.5 million regular older workers, or 1.5% to 2.3% of the labor force ("Kigyonai shitsugyosha," 1993). Sumitomo Research Institute estimates that the number of such redundant workers is as high as three million (or 4.8% of the labor force). These figures suggest the severity of overcapacity in Japanese firms. [14]

Industrial Order

In the United States, all aspects of production, price, and authority are incorporated within an institutional framework of independent firms. Price and production are organized by the market and enforced by the Sherman Antitrust Act. In the case of Germany, big business associations or cartels have historically set prices, production, and market allocations. German craft and export-oriented industry, the challenges of diversified export markets, and the legal enforceability of cartel agreements in court have led to a rich variety of interfirm relationships (Chandler, 1990). Japan has a history of price, production, and market controls organized by large holding companies. [15] Furthermore, top corporate executives are prohibited by law from receiving stock options in their companies. This legal regulation partly explains the modest earnings of corporate executives. In 1984, the income gap between the top executive class and the entry-level employee class was 7:1 in Japan compared to 37:1 in the United States (Kerbo, 1995).[16]

Liberalized foreign investment along with the stock market crash of 1964–1965 created widespread fear of unfriendly takeovers by powerful foreign, especially American companies (Johnson, 1982). To insulate the management from outside takeovers, Japanese companies bought each other's shares (primarily among *keiretsu* affiliated firms) [17] so that only about a quarter of the total shares issued by a company were publicly traded. By the 1980s, 66% of all corporate stock in Japan was owned by corporations (Kerbo, 1995). [18]Thus there are significant differences among the United States, Germany, and Japan centering on stock trading and ownership. Stock is privately traded and owned by other corporations within the same *keiretsu* affiliation in Japan. Stock ownership of large German enterprises is highly concentrated (Vogl, 1973). Most of the larger German companies are closely controlled and owned by a small number of large banks, wealthy families, the federal and state governments, trade unions, and foreign investment institutions. In the United States stock is publicly traded yet also controlled by large financial firms (pensions, investment houses, insurance, and bank trusts).

Aoki (1987) suggests that "member-firms (*keiretsu* affiliated) of corporate groups are more risk averse than independent firms and that grouping functions as a mutual insurance scheme." Mutual shareholding, long-term relationships, interlocking directorates, and presidents' club

memberships cement the bonds among firms and provide mutual monitoring mechanisms. [19] One important result of these national differences
in corporate structure is that, compared to American and German firms,
Japanese firms are not subjected to pressures from pension managers,
accountants, and stock analysts for quarterly financial gain.

Government Policy

In general, the U.S. government provides benefits to workers only after
they have lost their jobs; the German government provides prorated support for cuts in working hours that result from job sharing; and the
Japanese government pays corporations to continue to employ their regular workers. German employment protection laws discourage layoffs,
whereas various government programs subsidize the use of alternatives
to layoffs, thereby reducing the cost to employers of providing job security. German law strictly regulates the conditions under which workers
may be dismissed from their jobs. Dismissal for economic reasons is justified only if the individual cannot be transferred within the company and
the company has exhausted all other means of avoiding layoffs, for example, reduction of overtime and short-time week (Abraham & Houseman,
1993). The law requires that age, marital status, number of dependents,
and other hardship factors for the individual and family be considered in
layoffs. Work councils must be consulted before every dismissal.
Dismissed workers may sue in labor court and are likely to be reinstated
or compensated if the company work council opposes the dismissal. If
the dismissal is socially justified, employers must notify the individual
2 weeks to 6 months prior to dismissal, the amount of advance notice
depending mostly on seniority.

   The German government also subsidizes alternatives to layoffs.
Unemployment insurance allows employees whose hours of work have
been reduced to collect prorated unemployment insurance benefits. During
the 1980s, early retirement of workers aged 55 to 59 were facilitated by
changes in unemployment and social security laws. Many companies used
these programs to help finance early retirement by "firing" older workers, who then could collect unemployment benefits for as long as 32
months and begin collecting a state pension at age 60 (Abraham &
Houseman, 1993; Jacobs, Kohli, & Rein, 1991).

In Japan, the government pays distressed companies not to lay off regular workers. Since the first oil shock of 1973, the government has integrated mechanisms for dealing with unemployment and retirement problems as part of general employment policies. In 1974, the government revised the Employment Insurance Law and created the Employment Stabilization Services. It has pursued proemployment policies for workers until the age of 60 and phased retirement between the ages of 60 and 65. Also, it has lobbied business to raise *teinen* from age 55 to age 60 since 1973 and from age 60 to 65 since 1986. [20] In addition, since 1986 business firms are obliged by law to help find postretirement jobs for their workers until they reach 65 years of age. The government enforces this regulation through administrative guidance.[21]

The government has also introduced a number of subsidy programs for the promotion of employment among workers aged 60 to 64 (Ministry of Labor, 1994). These programs include:

1. Subsidies for the promotion of continuous employment or reemployment of workers aged 60 and over;[22]
2. Subsidies to companies for the creation of new enterprises run by older workers (known as "old people's companies);[23]
3. Subsidies for extraholiday and vacations for either full-time or part-time workers aged 45 to 65;[24]
4. Subsidies for companies who hire older workers (aged 55 and over) through public employment services; [25] and
5. Low-interest loan programs for companies that build or remodel buildings to facilitate employment of older workers (or workers with disabilities).[26]

Employee contributions fund these services. The contributions are equal to 1.25% of a worker's salary. The total cost of these subsidy programs was about 127 billion yen (about $1.3 billion) in 1992 and was expected to rise to 230 billion yen ($2.3 billion) by 1995 (Ministry of Labor, 1994).

In addition to the previously discussed subsidy programs targeted for older workers, there are subsidies and tax benefits for small firms. For example, small firms in the agricultural sector are supported by government policies regarding land ownership, taxation, rental, and rice production. The tiny retail outlets of the small enterprise sector are also provided with special financing and tax allowances for family workers in this sector (Ballon, 1989). Patrick and Rohlen (1987) report that the Japanese government provides far more financing to small business than does the American government.

Media and Public Opinion

The media have a powerful effect on the employment policies of Japanese firms. A company's employment records and labor relations are vital to its reputation and ability to attract qualified workers. Once a company breaks with employment routine, it cannot recruit first-class workers for years to come. Extensive reporting on employment records and company performance serve as guides to job applicants. College graduates consider job security and company reputation as the two most important factors in selecting their prospective employers (Economic Planning Agency, 1992). For civil servants, "retirement" may begin as early as age 40, and the assurance of attractive postretirement jobs is critical in recruiting and motivating the most talented and the brightest, who would otherwise seek more lucrative careers in the private industry. The record on each ministry's placement of retiring bureaucrats serves as an important guide to candidates. Private or public, employing organizations are expected to provide job security of regular employees in exchange for their loyalty to companies through good and bad times. In bad times, company managers are expected to cut their own benefits and positions before cutting labor costs of the regular workers.

In Japan, a person's primary social identity is closely tied to the groups to which one belongs. Thus joblessness poses a serious social distress. It has been said that Japanese life consists of movement from "house" (*ie*) to "house" (Nakane, 1970). One's primary identification is said to be one's membership in a particular "house" or set of "houses." Without a house/company identification, others do not know what to make of a person, or how to relate to such a person—neither does the person himself or herself. The person without a house/company identification becomes a *ronin,* literally, a wandering person. In the Japanese language, another form of the word "house" (*uchi*) is the personal pronoun for "I" and "we." House identity, once established, is almost never jeopardized, and the betrayal of one's house is perhaps the worst offense within Japanese society.[27]

Until very recently, no regular employee of a major company would think of moving to another major company. Indeed, "defectors" would be treated with suspicion by any subsequent employer, having proven they could not to be trusted. Consequently, Japan had no trade secret law, at least until 1990. Recently, however, as companies have begun quietly to lay off regular workers, workers have begun pursuing sequential employment, and pay has begun to be linked to performance (Beck & Beck, 1994).

Recent announcements of corporate restructuring received widespread public attention because the restructuring involved large firms. These instances of corporate restructuring symbolized fundamental changes in Japanese labor relations and employment systems. A perusal of Table 2.7 quickly suggests the scope of the issue. [28] The companies are large, but the numbers of employees affected by these employment adjustment strategies are small. However, the events must be understood in the context of contemporary Japan. These changes in employment strategies are seen as drastic by the Japanese, because large companies had not previously taken such measures in postwar Japan. Japanese citizens perceive these events as unthinkable, disgraceful, or even shameful on the part of the companies. The Japanese do not view the termination of the relationship between a company and a long-standing employee in a casual fashion.

The media and the public responded with intense discussions, especially on the "fairness" of dismissing longtime workers by paying extra retirement benefits and without helping them find new jobs (e.g., "Kigyonai shitsugyosha," 1993). The media called into question the procedures some companies used in forcing people out. For example, companies were harshly criticized for their "casual" handling of worker termination. Workers expressed a special kind of anguish for being suddenly forced out. [29] The media also questioned the active use of voluntary retirement in restructuring, by citing cases where workers felt betrayed; morale went down; and most qualified workers took voluntary retirement and left the company ("Kondokoso," 1993).

Surprised by the intense public outcry and harsh media criticisms, many of the companies listed in Table 2.7 *overturned* their decisions to dismiss workers later. Pioneer and TDK, for example, were "taken aback by the publicity surrounding [their] decision[s]" and canceled their plans (Sanger, 1993). The media's reaction and the reversal of forced "voluntary" retirements and worker dismissals by large firms are indicative of

Table 2.7 A List of High-Profile Corporations with Drastic Restructuring Announcement
(Announcement as of Spring 1993)

Company name and characteristics	Major announcement for restructuring
Airlines	
Japan Airlines[1] Operating revenues: ¥1,381,008 mil. Employees: 22,271	Reduction of the workforce from 22,000 to 17,000 by 1997 (2,500 through voluntary retirement and and dispatching; 2,500 through no hiring of new workers).[2]
Japan (Nippon) Air System[3] Operating revenues: ¥266,746 mil. Employees: 5,439.	Reduction in the number of new hiring by 50% for 1994, or 13 positions.
Northwest Airlines, Japan[4]	Hiring of 81 new workers as1-year temporary workers rather than offering them regular positions as originally scheduled.
Automobiles	
Nissan[5] Sales: ¥6,416,931 mil. Employees: 55,597	Permanent closure of one factory (Zama Factory). 2,500 regular workers will not be fired but re assigned/dispatched to other locations.[6] Reduction of company workforce by 5,000 through attrition and no hiring of new workers.

Banking/securities

Cosmo Securities (Shoken)[7]
Operating revenues: ¥41,281 mil.
Employees: 2,395

Reassignment and dispatching of 70 managerial track workers in the central administration office to sales division.

Sakura Bank[8]
Operating revenues: ¥4,049,141 mil.
Employees: 23,095

Reduction of company workforce by 10%, or 3,000 regular workers in 3 years.

Sanyo Securities (Shoken)[9]
Operating revenues: ¥73,461 mil.
Employees: 4,407

Reduction of 10 managerial posts at the central office.
Reassignment and dispatching of 10% of nonsales division regular workers to sales division.

Communications equipment

Oki Electric Industry[10]
Sales: ¥681,283 mil.
Employees: 14,049

Reduction of company's workforce by 2,000, or from 14,000 to 12,000 by March 1995.

Commerce

Itochu[11]
Sales: ¥20,610,475 mil.
Employees: 7,344

Reassignment and dispatching of 300 managers to sales division.
Reduction of managerial personnel to 15% of the company workforce.

continued

Table 2.7 *continued*

Company name and characteristics	Major announcement for restructuring
Computers	
IBM Japan	Reduction of the workforce by 3,000 through voluntary retirement and voluntary dispatching among regular workers aged 50+.[12]
Consumer electronics industry	
Clarion Co. Ltd.[13] Sales ¥184,600 mil. Employees: 9,309	Encouragement of retirement among regular workers aged 40+ with extra pension benefits. (A couple of dozen workers signed up for it.)
Pioneer[14] Sales: ¥613,009 mil. Employees: 2,856	Dismissal of 35 managers aged 50+. (These workers were encouraged to take voluntary retirement first).[15]
Sanyo Electric[16] Sales: ¥1,565,791 mil. Employees: 30,725	Reduction of company workforce by 3,000, or from 30,000 to 27,000, through no hiring.[17]
TDK[18] Sales: ¥534,866 mil. Employees: 8,927	Dismissal of 50 older managers aged 50+ with 90% of salary to be paid until these managers reach the the mandatory retirement age of 60.[19]

Heavy electric machinery

Hitachi[20]
   Sales: ¥1,367,544 mil.
   Employees: 83,821

Reduction of managerial posts by 5–6% at the central administration office. Reduction of company workforce by 3,000 by the end of 1993. Temporary closure of Tokai factory. Two thousand factory workers were given extra holidays.[21]

Iron and steel

Kawasaki Steel[22]
   Sales: ¥1,378,544 mil.
   Employees: 18,599

Reduction of 400 to 500 white-collar workers by 1995.

Nippon Steel[23]
   Sales: ¥3,229,649 mil.
   Employees: 53,049

Reduction of 4,300 positions from the steel division by 1994. Further reduction of 2,500 positions by 1996 or a total of 7,000 by 1996.[24]

NKK (Nippon Koshuha Kogjo)[25]
   Sales: ¥1,931,481 mil.
   Employees: 23,313

Reduction of the company labor force by 15%, or 3,200 workers by 1995.

Sumitomo Metal[26]
   Sales: ¥1,818,089 mil.
   Employees: 20,727.

Reduction of the company labor force by 12%, or 2,600 workers by 1995.

continued

Table 2.7 *continued*

Company name and characteristics	Major announcement for restructuring
Mass media and communications	
NTT (Nippon Telegraph & Telephone)[27] Sales: ¥6,398,374 mil. Employees: 242,743	Reduction of company workforce by 30,000 by 1996 through voluntary retirement of 10,000 each year.[28]
Yomiuri Shinbun, Chubu Honbu[29] Sales: ¥8,514 mil	Reduction of company workforce by 100 through voluntary retirement. One hundred and thirty regular workers signed up for it.
Precision machinery	
Kodak Japan	Reduction of research division's personnel by 70 through voluntary retirement. Cancellation of hiring of 8 new graduates.
Tamuron[30] Sales: ¥12,212 mil. Employees: 576.	Reduction of company workforce by 250 (including regular and temporary workers) through voluntary retirement.
Textiles	
Toyobo[31] Sales: ¥568,879 mil. Employees: 8,010.	Temporary factory closure in 10 factories for 4–8 days per month, affecting 3,000 regular workers. These workers will take extra paid holidays.

Sources: Data are compiled from several sources, including the information given to the authors during company visits in the summer of 1993 in Japan. Other sources include newspaper articles, weekly journal articles (e.g., "Kigyonai shitsugyo," 1993), as cited in the table.

Data on company characteristics derive from *Japan Company Handbook*, 1993. Tokyo: Toyo Keizai, 1993. Statistics for sales and operating revenues are for the March 1992 and September 1992, respectively, expressed in million yen (100 yen equals about 1 US$), unless otherwise noted.

1 Japan's largest airline.

2 The information regarding the exact numbers of voluntary retirement & dispatching, and no new hiring was obtained from "Nikkou, yonende 5,000 nin sakugen" 1994.

3 Japan's third largest airline.

4 Information for company characteristics was not available.

5 Japan's second and the world's fourth largest automaker.

6 That Nissan will not force out 2,500 regular blue-collar workers who used to work at Zama factory was reported in *Shukan Toyou Keizai*, March 13, 1993, p. 14.

7 Cosmo Securities is a medium-sized comprehensive securities closely related to Daiwa Bank and Nippon Life Insurance.

8 The. Nucleus of Mitsui Group. Japan's first commercial bank founded in 1876.

9 One of the major comprehensive securities firms closely related to Nomura Securities.

10 A leading and long-established manufacturer of communications equipment.

11 Japan's one of five biggest trading firms. Belongs to Dai-ichi Kangyo Bank Group.

12 The exact number of positions to be cut was reported in "Shushin koyo no gensou," 1992.

13 The largest maker of audio equipment for cars primarily bound for Nissan.

14 A top manufacturer of audio equipment.

15 Pioneer explained that these managers were selected due to their poor performance record (*Nihon Keizai Shinbun*, January 12, 1993, p. 1). Later, Pioneer overturned its decision to dismiss the 35 managers because of much publicity and criticism.

16 A major producer of consumer electronics.

17 A detailed report was published in *Nikkei Shinbun*, January 12, 1993, p. 1.

73

Table 2.7 *continued*

[18] The world's largest manufacturer of magnetic tapes.

[19] Like Pioneer, TDK withdrew its decision to dismiss its longtime employees. The exact salary information was reported in *Nihon Keizai Shinbun*, January 9, 1993, p. 11.

[20] Japan's largest manufacturer heavy electric machinery.

[21] *Nihon Keizai Shinbun*, January 14, 1993, p. 4.

[22] Japan's third largest producer of crude steel.

[23] The world's largest steel maker.

[24] Reported in *Nihon Keizai Shinbun*, January 4, 1994, p. 1.

[25] One of the world's five largest steel makers.

[26] Japan's third largest producer of crude steel (same rank as Kawasaki Steel).

[27] Japan's largest telecommunications company. Ranks second in the world next to AT&T.

[28] By summer 1993, the company had 4,100 applicants for voluntary retirement and expected to complete the reduction of 30,000 positions much earlier than the targeted date of 1996. With this, NTT announced a drastic *increase* in hiring of new employees (technical positions) for 1995—2.5 to 3 times the number it hired in 1994, or at least 2,000 (*Nihon Keizai Shinbun*, January 3, 1994, p. 27).

[29] One of the major newspaper companies. Figures for sales were for fiscal years 1993 and 1994.

[30] Japan's largest maker of camera lenses.

[31] Time-honored spinning company that has played a locomotive role in Japan's textile industry.

the importance of media pressure and Japanese firms' sensitivity to their public reputation.

CONCLUSIONS

The recent worldwide economic slump provided a generalized stimulus to which governments and corporations in different countries responded with different strategies for older workers. Japanese companies resorted to a combination of restructuring measures that are less socially disruptive. These restructuring measures reflect Japanese companies' distinctive governance structure, affiliations with other companies, and government support. Japanese human resource management is not driven by shareholder interests, and corporate network ties among affiliates and subsidiaries result in labor-centered, long-term management orientations. Corporate actions also are constrained by the media and public opinion, which emphasize the social responsibilities of companies. In addition, the government has shown a propensity to work with business to help declining industries and provide some relief for the employment problems of older workers. This corporate-government relationship lessens pressures on companies to slash personnel payrolls by offering money to companies for retaining workers and sending workers to other firms through *shukko.*

The Japanese approach to older workers reveals a strong commitment to job protection at least until the age of 65, yet combined with a commitment to gradual retirement between 60 and 65 years of age. Tiered employment systems, fostering gradual retirement of older workers, have become over time a vital device for large- and medium-sized firms. This chapter points to the significance of a tiered labor market, based on company size and worker's age, in providing a flexible employment structure capable of adjusting to the problems of older workers.

Prevailing economic views would lead us to believe that the need to remove older workers from the labor force is low in Japan because of a robust economy that provides favorable labor-market conditions. This chapter, however, shows that the Japanese economy has experienced significant industrial decline and adverse conditions since the mid-1970s. The increasing value of the yen in the last 25 years has intensified pressures for corporate restructuring. This study highlights some of the processes and mechanisms through which Japanese firms, in conjunction with other institutional support (the state, industrial groups, governance structure of organizations), undertook a fundamental restructuring of industries and the integration of older workers into the labor force.

The emphasis in this chapter is not a cultural one. Although *shukko, teinen,* and corporate networks reflect and express the cultural values of Japan, it is the configuration of Japanese institutions that creates and sustains these cultural features; and it is that configuration that will determine future cultural changes. In other words, the institutional configuration of Japan is the substructure that holds these cultural features in place.

Several European countries are now shifting toward the concept of gradual retirement (e.g., France, Germany, the Netherlands: Reday-Mulvey, 1995). It is unlikely that the specifics of their approaches will resemble the Japanese pattern, however, because configurations of societal institutions affecting practical and appropriate strategies vary among nations. Yet the importance of tiered employment (by company size and employee age), systems of affiliated firms, corporate governance structures, government policy, and a pervasive sense of a moral economy (Thompson, 1971) sensitize us to factors that may have some applications for other countries.

NOTES

¹ The idea of "restructuring" is to adjust the amount, allocation and costs of facilities, capital and labor to existing demands for products and services to improve organizational performance. "Corporate restructuring" is an abstract, ambiguous and sometimes tautologically defined term. Whatever a corporation does under pressure is considered restructuring. A perusal of the business and organizational literatures suggests various elements of corporate restructuring. Some of these include: increased investment in production technology; elimination of product lines; combining internal units, new stock offerings, early retirements, selling nonessential units; closing plants by eliminating employees; the "externalization of employment" by taking regular employees out and relying more on contract or temporary employees; changing top executives and board members; reallocating employees, changing decision-making location (centralize or decentralize); eliminating positions through attrition, buyouts, retirement incentives, and involuntary layoffs; and changing incentive structures and job descriptions.

2 It is difficult to capture exact numbers of workers who are retiring early with private pensions. John Henrietta estimates that 36% of married men and 21% of single men who exited the labor force before age 62 received private pensions (excluding government pensions) (reported in Sheppard, 1991).

3 To this list, some others add reemployment systems of older workers that are practiced at the firm level (cf. Kimura, Takagi, Oka, & Omori, 1994; McCallum, 1988; Schulz, Borowski & Crown, 1991). This issue is addressed later in this chapter.

4 The number of bankruptcies peaked in 1984 with 20,841. Almost 88% of these cases involved suspension. The bubble recession caused a high number of bankruptcies, but the number is still lower than that of 1984. In 1993, when the recession peaked, the number of bankruptcies reached 14,564 (Imai, 1994).

5 For example, during the first oil-shock recession, blue-collar workers in manufacturing industries were most affected. In the current recession, administrative/managerial and clerical workers are most affected. Further, the problem of excess labor in these occupational categories exists in all sizes of business establishments, large or small, and is not limited to manufacturing industries. It cuts across all types of industries (Usui & Colignon, 1995).

6 This situation reflects the dual structure of the Japanese economy, involving its core and the periphery. The core sector (large firms plus government sector) accounts for about 25% to 30% of the labor force. The core-periphery distinction makes the location of medium-sized firms somewhat ambiguous. Moreover, the core-periphery distinction obscures the vertical linkages that exist between large/medium firms and medium/small firms in Japan. The enforcement of teinen and the use of shukko apply to large and medium-sized firms and thus the discussion of this chapter is not just limited to workers in the core sector.

7 In contrast to white-collar workers, productivity of blue-collar workers has increased consistently over the years, owing to lean production processes.

8 Currently, 96% of older persons receive either the flat pension or employee pension. Public pension receipts amounted to 54.1% of the average household income among the elderly in 1993 or 7.7% of the national income. The current tax rate for employee pension (EPS) is 14.5% (divided equally between employee and employer) and ¥11,100 (about $111) per month for the flat pensions (NPS). In 1994, the average benefits drawn from the EPS among recent retirees was ¥206,300 per month (about $2,000). In the same year, flat pension benefits (NPS) were ¥62,275 per month (about $620).

9 Many contend that "lifetime employment" applies only to regular workers in large organizations in the public and private sectors, or about 20%–25% of the workforce. This position has created confusion, however, about the extent of job security for the rest of Japanese workers. Except for part-time and temporary workers (18% of the work force), regular workers have enjoyed job

security. Japanese courts make it very difficult for employers to fire regular workers unless they exhaust other possible adjustment means, except for cases involving criminal offenses. In this sense, the majority of workers, or about 80% of employed workers, do have job security. One of the difficulties of applying the concept of "lifetime employment" to small and medium-sized firms is the high job turnover rate and bankruptcy rate among these companies. However, the outright dismissal of regular workers is still rare even for these firms; many workers exit from small and medium firms voluntarily rather than involuntarily to seek better jobs or to start their own companies (Abraham & Houseman, 1993; Ballon, 1989; Schregle, 1993).

[10] In addition, stock ownership is often reciprocal, blurring the distinction between owner and owned. Stock ownership loses meaning in Japan because it is only one of many types of relationships taking place simultaneously between any two affiliated firms (e.g., purchases, sales, debts,) (see Gerlach, 1992).

[11] According to Johnson (1982), MITI's administrative guidance was implemented through industry "cooperative discussion groups" during previous recessions. These industrial cartels set production quotas, barriers to entry, market controls, and investment strategies to stave off the consequences of recession.

[12] Even though American companies would emphasize "growth" as their principal goal, a survey of 500 major American and Japanese companies found that executives of American firms placed return on investment as their principal corporate objective. Share price increase and market share were ranked second and third. In contrast, executives of Japanese firms placed market share first, return on investment second, and ratio of new products third. Share price increase came last in Japan (Abegglen & Stalk, 1985).

[13] A common view states that Japanese shareholders receive low profits and meager dividends. Compared with shareholders in the United States. Abegglen and Stalk (1985) report dividends are paid in Japan to "reassure shareholders that the company is healthy." Japanese companies commonly pay dividends equal to about 10% of the par value of the stock, even by borrowing money or selling assets to assure this payment. Moreover, Abegglen and Stalk's analysis of stock price appreciation in the United States and Japan in 16 out of 21 industry leaders shows that Japanese shareholders fared better than their U.S. counterparts.

[14] Anecdotal evidence suggests that *in-house unemployment* involves social and psychological humiliation. Yet, many *in-house unemployed workers* stay with the company for the fear of risking economic security. There is no guarantee of finding a new job at a comparable pay elsewhere.

[15] The historical roots of the Japanese model of corporate ownership date back to the 1950s after SCAP (Supreme Commander of Allied Powers) purged the

power of *zaibatsu* (interlocked corporate groups) by removing family control of major holding companies (Aoki, 1987; Kerbo, 1995). Shares held by the *zaibatsu* families were liquidated, and 40% of the total shares were sold. No one was allowed to acquire more than 1% of any company, and old managers of the *zaibatsu* were replaced by young technocratic managers (Abegglen & Stalk, 1985).

[16] The Antimonopoly Law of 1947 imposed a 5% ceiling on bank holdings in the stock of any single company, but subsequent legislation raised this ceiling to 10%.

[17] Keiretsu (also called kigyo shudan in Japan) generally refers to the network of intercorporate alliances across widely diverse industries. Japanese intercorporate alliances are a complex nexus of reciprocal interests, with cross-shareholding and business-lined equity investment that constrains the decision-making ability of individual firms while simultaneously lending them stability and socially symbolic significance (Gerlach, 1992; Kerbo & McKinstry, 1995). There are two major types of keiretsu structure: the horizontal (or intermarket) keiretsu and the vertical keiretsu. Among the major keiretsu are Mitsubishi, Mitusi, and Sumitomo (former *zaibatsu*) and Daiichi Kangyo, Sanwa, and Fuji (related to bank groups).

[18] Various authors have noted that family stock ownership in Japan is much lower than that in the United States. In the early 1980s, half of all corporate stock was controlled by families and individuals in the United States, whereas it was 27% in Japan (Kerbo, 1995).

[19] Recent studies provide evidence that earnings of employees at member-firms of corporate groups are on the average significantly lower than at independent firms, indicating the trade-off between earnings and job security (Gerlach, 1992).

[20] The Employment Stabilization Act of 1986 mandated teinen at age 60. By 1994, 84% of companies with 30 workers or more had teinen at age 60 or older. As of 1998, companies will be legally obliged to enforce teinen at age 60 or over (Ministry of Labor, 1994).

[21] By 1994, 52% of companies with 30 workers or more had instituted some form of reemployment programs for older workers. Of those with reemployment programs for older workers, one in five countries offered reemployment programs to workers wishing to continue working until they reached 65 years of age (Iwamura, 1995).

[22] This obligation of the government to support companies to employ workers aged 60 and over was clearly stated in the 1986 Employment Stabilization Act.

[23] For example, companies might create new firms by "spinning off" the existing divisions and placing their older workers in these divisions. On the average, one-third of start-up costs are paid.

²⁴ This subsidy program helps workers prepare for increases in leisure time after retirement. If a company offers a worker a minimum of 10 day-holidays with a maximum duration of 3-months, subsidies of up to ¥60,000 per worker per month (about $600) are paid for full-time workers and up to ¥30,000 (about $300) per worker per month for part-time workers.

²⁵ Subsidies equivalent to one-half of a worker's wage (two-thirds, if a company is small or medium) are paid to companies for 1 year.

²⁶ Up to 90% of funds needed can be loaned with interest rates of 4% for small/medium firms and 4.3% for large firms.

²⁷ The Japanese Penal Code, for example, prescribes a penalty of not less than 3 years' imprisonment for murder, but murder of one's lineal ascendant carries a mandatory sentence of life imprisonment or death (article 200). In contrast, Americans are more frightened by random violence caused by unrelated persons, and penalties for these crimes tend to be more severe (Reidel, 1993).

²⁸ The author (Chikako Usui) compiled data from several sources during her visit to various companies in Japan in 1993. The author also added information on company characteristics (Usui & Colignon, 1996).

²⁹ On January 9, 1993, the *New York Times* featured an article with the headline "Shock in a Land of Lifetime Jobs: 35 Managers Dismissed in Japan." The article stated that "the unthinkable has happened in Japan, and it has touched a nerve in the ranks of the nation's middle managers" (Pollack, 1993). It reported the degree of shock and public outrage described in daily newspapers in Japan. On March 3, 1993 the *New York Times* again featured an article with the headline "Layoffs and Factory Closing Shaking the Japanese Psyche" (Sanger, 1993).

REFERENCES

Abegglen, J. C., & Stalk, G. Jr. (1985). *Kaisha: The Japanese corporation.* New York: Basic Books.

Abraham, K., & Houseman, S. (1989). Job security and workforce adjustment: How different are U.S. and Japanese practices? *Journal of Japanese and International Economies, 3,* 500–521.

Abraham, K., & Houseman, S. (1993). *Job Security in America: Lessons from Germany.* Washington, DC: Brookings Institution.

Aoki, M. (1987). The Japanese firm in transition. In K. Yamamura & Y. Yasuba, (Eds.), *The political economy of Japan* (Vol. 1, pp. 263–288). Stanford, CA: Stanford University Press.

Ballon, R. (1989). *The subcontracting system: Challenge to foreign firms.*

Business Series Bulletin No. 127. Tokyo: Sophia University Institute of Comparative Culture.

Beck, J. C., & Beck, M. N. (1994). *The change of a lifetime: Employment patterns amongJapan's managerial elite.* Honolulu: University of Hawaii Press.

Campbell, J. C. (1992). *How policies change: The Japanese government and the aging society.*Princeton, NJ: Princeton University Press.

Chandler, A. D. (1990). *Scale and scope: The dynamics of industrial capitalism.* Cambridge, MA: Belknap Press.

DeViney, S., & O'Rand, A. (1988). Gender cohort succession and retirement among older men and women, 1951–1984. *Sociological Quarterly, 29* (4), 525–540.

de Vroom, B., & Naschold, F. (1993). The dialectics of work and welfare. In F. Naschold & B. de Vroom (Eds.), *Regulating employment and welfare* (pp. 1–15). Berlin: Walter de Gruyter.

Economic Planning Agency. (1992). *Kokumin seikatsu hakusho [White paper on people's lives].* Tokyo: Government Printing Office.

Gerlach, M. L. (1992). *Alliance capitalism: The social organization of Japanese business.*Berkeley, CA: University of California Press.

Granovetter, M., & Swedberg, R. (1992). *The sociology of economic life.* San Francisco: Westview Press.

Guillemard, A. M., & van Gunsteren, H. (1991). Pathways and their prospects: A comparative interpretation of the meaning of early exit. In M. Kohli, M. Rein, A. Guillemard, & H. van Gunsteren (Eds.), *Time for retirement: Comparative studies of early exit from the labor force* (pp. 362–387). New York: Cambridge University Press.

Guillemard, A. M., & Rein, M. (1993). Early retirement: Stability, reversal, or redefinition. In F. Naschold & B. de Vroom (Eds.), *Regulating employment and welfare* (pp. 19-49). Berlin: Walter de Gruyter.

Hirose, T. (1993). Saikin no shukko seido wa do unei sarete iruka. *Rodo Jiho 3109 [How is Shukko being managed and maintained],* 2–89.

Hutchens, R. (1993). The United States: Employer policies for discouraging work by older people. In F. Naschold & B. de Vroom (Eds.), *Regulating employment and welfare* (pp. 395–431). Berlin: Walter de Gruyter.

Imai, K. (1994, May 9). Network bungyo keiei no kosaku ga kyumu [More division-based management is urgently needed]. *Economist* (Japanese ed.), pp. 18–59.

Ishida, H. (1993). *Social mobility in contemporary Japan.* Stanford, CA: Stanford University Press.

Iwamura, M. (1995, March 15). Rodosha no intai katei to ho-taisaku *[Social policies for older workers and their retirement processes].* *Jurist 1063,* 71–81.

Jacobs, K., Kohli, M., & Rein, M. (1991). Testing the industry-mix hypothesis of early exit. In M. Kohli, M. Rein, A. Guillemard, & H. van Gunsteren (Eds.), *Time for retirement: Comparative studies of early exit from the labor force* (pp. 36–66). New York: Cambridge University Press.

Jacobs, K., & Rein M. (1993). Comparative patterns of retirement. *Annual Review of Sociology, 19,* 469–503.

Japan Update. (1992). New York: Japan Business Information Center, p. 4.

Johnson, C. (1982). *MITI and the Japanese miracle.* Stanford, CA: Stanford University Press.

Kalleberg, A. L., & Lincoln, J. R. (1988). The structure of earnings inequality in the United States and Japan. *American Journal of Sociology, 94,* 5121–5153.

Katzenstein, P. (1987). *Policy and politics in West Germany: The growth of a semi-sovereign state.* Philadelphia: Temple University Press.

Keizai Koho Center. (1994). *Japan 1995: An international comparison.* Tokyo: Keizai Koho Center.

Kerbo, H. R. (1995). *Social stratification and inequality* (3rd ed.). New York: McGraw-Hill.

Kerbo, H. R., & McKinstry, J. A. (1995). *Who rules Japan? The inner circles of economic and political power.* Westport, CT: Praeger.

Kigyonai shitsugyosha 300 man nin no ukezara [Redundant labor rising to 3 million: How do companies keep them?]. (1993, November 20). *Shukan Diamond, 20,* 22–31.

Kimura, T., Takagi, I., Oka, M., & Omori, M. (1993). Japan: Shukko, Teinen and Re-Employment. In F. Naschold & B. De Vroom (Eds.), *Regulating employment and welfare: Company and national policies of labour force participation at the end of worklife in industrial countries* (pp. 247–308). Berlin: Walter de Gruyter.

Kohli, M., Rein, M., Guillemard, A. M., & van Gunsteren, H. (1991). *Time for retirement: Comparative studies of early exit from the labor force.* New York: Cambridge University Press.

Kondokoso Nippon wa Karappo ni naru [The de-industrialization of Japan]. (1993, July 24). *Shukan Toyou Keizai,* pp. 10–13.

Lincoln, J. R., & Kalleberg, A. L. (1985). Work organization and work force commitment: A study of plants and employees in the U.S. and Japan. *American Sociological Review, 50,*738–760.

McCallum, J. (1988). Japanese teinen taishoku: How cultural values affect retirement. *Ageing and Society, 8,* 23–41.

Ministry of Labor. (1994). *Koyo no antei no tameni [For employment stability].* Tokyo: Government Printing Office.

Ministry of Labor. (1995, April). Hoken sanjigyo shuyo kyufukin no yosan to shikyu jittuseki [Three types of employment related insurance programs and their fiscal conditions]. [Information given to the author of this chapter (Chikako Usui) during her visit to the ministry in April, 1995].

Morito, H. (1995, May 1–15). Koreisha no intai katei ni kansuru rippo seisaku [Social policies managing retirement processes of older workers]. *Jurist, 1066,* 103–108.

Murakami, K. (1990). *Nenkin no chishiki [A guide to public old pensions].* Tokyo: Nihon keizai shinbunsha.

Nagano, H. (1995, May 1). Kigyonai group-nai jinzai ido [Personnel transfers within a company group]. *Jurist, 1066,* 70–75.

Nakane, C. (1970). *Japanese society.* Berkeley: University of California Press.

Nakamura, S. (1995, March 15). 1994 nen nenkin kaiho no gaiyo [A guide to 1994 public pension reform]. *Jurist, 1063,* 31–37.

Naoi, A., & Schooler, C. (1984). Occupational conditions and psychological functioning in Japan. *American Journal of Sociology, 90* (4), 729–752.

Ozawa, M. (1985). Social security reform in Japan. *Social Service Review, 46,* 12–22.

Patrick, H. T., & Rohlen, T. P. (1987). Small-scale family enterprises. In K. Yamamura &Y. Yasuda (Eds.), *The political economy of Japan* (Vol. 1, pp. 331–384). Stanford: Stanford University Press.

Pollack, A. (1993, January 9). Japan's taste for the luxurious gives way to utility and frugality. *New York Times, p.4.*

Reday-Mulvey, G. (1995). Gradual retirement in OECD countries. *Ageing International, 22* (2), 44–48.

Reidel, M. (1993). *Stranger violence.* New York: Garland.

Sanger, D. (1993, March 3). Layoffs and factory closing shaking the Japanese psyche. *New York Times,* pp. *4.*

Schregle, J. (1993). Dismissal protection in Japan. *International Labour Review, 132* (4), 507–520.

Schulz, J. H., Borowski, A, & Crown, W. H. (1991). *Economics of population aging: The graying of Australia, Japan and the United States.* New York: Auburn House.

Sheppard, H. L. (1991). The United States: The privatization of exit. In M. Kohli, M. Rein, A. Guillemard, & H. van Gunsteren (Eds.), *Time for retirement: Comparative studies of early exit from the labor force* (pp. 252–283). New York: Cambridge University Press.

Schumpeter, J. (1939). *Business cycles* (Vol. 1). New York: McGraw-Hill.

Schumpeter, J. (1950). *Capitalism, socialism, and democracy.* New York: Harper and Row.

Sorge, A., & Maurice, M. (1990). The societal effect on strategies and competitiveness of machine tool manufacturers in France and West Germany. *International Journal of Human Resource Management, 1* (2), 141–172.

Streeck, W. (1984). *Industrial relations in West Germany: A case study of the car industry.* New York: St. Martin's Press.

Tanaka, H. (1977). *Repercussion of the aging society.* Tokyo: Diamond sha.

Thompson, E. P. (1971). The moral economy of the English crown in the eighteenth century. *Past and Present, 50,*76–136.

Useem, M. (1993). *Executive defense: Shareholder power and corporate reorganization.* Cambridge: Harvard University Press.

Usui, C., & Colignon, R. A. (1995). Government elites and Amakudari in Japan: 1963–1992. *Asian Survey, 35,* 682–698.

Usui, C., & Colignon, R. A. (1996). Corporate restructuring: Converging world pattern or societally specific embeddedness? *Sociological Quarterly, 37,* 551–578.

Vogl, F. (1973). *German business after the economic miracle.* London: Macmillan.

Wadensjö, E. (1991). Sweden: Partial exit. In M. Kohli, M. Rein, A. Guillemard, & H. van Gunsteren (Eds.), *Time for retirement: Comparative studies of early exit from the labor force* (pp. 284–323). New York: Cambridge University Press.

Commentary: The Institutional Context of Gradual Retirement in Japan

Carmi Schooler

In her chapter, "Gradual Retirement: Japanese Strategies for Older Workers," Professor Usui provides convincing evidence that the nature and timing of the individual Japanese worker's retirement are affected by the nature of Japan's public and private socioeconomic institutions. These institutions, in turn, reflect several of that country's core cultural values. They can, in a sense, be seen as institutional instantiations of such values. Usui uses comparative data from the United States and Germany to provide persuasive evidence that the Japanese case is an example of a more general matching between the pattern of retirement within a country and the nature of that country's socioeconomic institutions and the cultural values and norms that underlie them.

As Usui notes, her "[c]hapter presents an institutional embeddedness argument in explaining the Japanese approach to gradual retirement. It contends that Japanese firms are socially embedded in networks of institutions and do not operate as atomized actors pursuing their own particular interests. Further, corporate strategies reflect both the symbolic and material features of the [country's] larger institutional configurations" (chapter 2, pp. 46–47). Thus, a company's economic activities cannot be separated from the quest for social approval, affiliation, political influence, and reputation of the firm.

Reflecting the perceived importance to the Japanese of both work and psychological identification with the institutions that employ them, Japanese employers tend to follow a policy of supporting workers through a gradual disengagement from work. As a result, a comparatively large number of Japanese workers continue working until their mid-60s or later. Although the greater proportion of older to younger individuals in Japan than in other countries may also be a factor in the development of such a pattern, the comparatively late retirement of Japanese workers is clearly also a function of the willingness of Japanese companies to undertake the potentially costly burden of supporting such a retirement pattern. Usui attributes the ability of Japanese firms to do so to four particular characteristics of Japanese companies: "(1) Japanese management is not driven by shareholder interests in dividends and appreciation; (2) Most Japanese company stock is not publicly traded but held by other affiliated companies. The ownership of company shares is carried out through a network of known firms with durable relationships, not anonymous securities markets; (3) Gradual retirement policy is implemented by the government through employment subsidies to firms, funds to targeted industries, and administrative guidance; and (4) The media in Japan constrain company policy because they shape the reputation of Japanese firms" (chapter 2, p 60).

According to Professor Usui, it is the embeddedness of Japanese firms in such an institutional network that has led them to feel both the need and the freedom to implement a policy of gradual retirement unconstrained by the possible costs of doing so. Although I agree with her general viewpoint, I believe that her elucidation of the institutional underpinnings of the Japanese gradual retirement system raises some important issues. These include basic questions about the nature and functioning of institutions and more specific questions about the origins, present functioning, and possible future of the particular Japanese institutions that Usui discusses.

SOME GENERAL QUESTIONS ABOUT INSTITUTIONS

Underlying both the general and specific questions about institutions that Usui's chapter raise is the very basic sociological issue of the relationship among the characteristics of a society's institutions and the norms and values of its culture. Perhaps the approach to institutional theory and research that has most directly examined the relationship between different nations' cultural values and their institutions is that in which Meyer (1977) has been a central figure. According to Jepperson (1991), whose views represent this approach, an institution is a social order or pattern from which departures "are counteracted by repetitively activated, socially constructed controls—that is, by some set of rewards and sanctions. . . . Routine reproductive procedures support and sustain the pattern, furthering its reproduction—unless collective action blocks, or environmental shock disrupts, the reproductive process. . . . All institutions are frameworks of programs or rules establishing identities and activity scripts for such identities" (pp. 145–146).

This viewpoint can be restated more formally in terms of Robert Merton's (1957) conceptualization of role, status, and social structure. According to that conceptualization (see also Schooler 1994, 1996), institutions are social structures that tend to be maintained because the pattern of the role relationships among the statuses are so structured that departures from expectations bring about sanctions enforcing conformity to role expectations.

Further light on the psychological mechanisms through which an institution's culture may be transmitted and kept continuous and resistant to change is afforded by a series of experiments by Zucker (1991). The results of the experiments suggest that, even in the absence of sanctions, the transmission of institutional behaviors is not problematic because the actor doing the transmitting simply communicates them as objective facts, and the actor receiving them treats them as an accurate rendition of objective facts. Knowledge of "the history of transmission provides a basis for assuming that the meaning of the act is part of the common-sense world. As continuity increases, the acts are increasingly objectified and made exterior to the particular situation. . . . Acts high on institutionalization will be resistant to attempts to change them through personal influence because they are seen as external facts, imposed on the setting and at the same time defining it" (p. 88).

All in all, institutional theory and research have demonstrated that some social structures (i.e., institutions) are so patterned that they react to threats to their continued existence by selectively punishing role performances that do not meet their norms and rewarding those that do, while at the same time providing psychological mechanisms for aiding their continuance that do not depend on the possibility of sanctions.

This view of institutions also provides us with part of the reason for the apparently greater inertia of social and cultural, as compared to individual, level phenomena. Once some set of cultural norms and concomitant behaviors are institutionalized, they are likely to be maintained. The longer they are maintained, the more likely they are to be seen as legitimate and objectively real.

Cross-national differences in the institutionalization of values such as individualism are demonstrably related to cross-national differences in the manifestation of such values. But at the present, institutional theory and research do not come close to providing a basic explanation of such differences in institutionalization. What remain vague are the socioeconomic conditions under which particular institutions begin, change, and end within a given country. Even less clear are the conditions under which an institution developed in one country is accepted as legitimate in another. For example, if we consider the individualist institutions that Frank, Meyer, and Miyahara (1995) describe in their groundbreaking cross-national empirical study directly linking the prominence of professional psychology to the cultural legitimation and institutionalization of individualism, what is left unanswered by their study from a historical perspective is why individualistic values and institutions were so strongly entrenched in northwestern Europe. In modern times, even taking into account the direct hand that U.S. occupation officials had in writing the Japanese constitution, it would seem simplistically wrong to explain the complex state of individualist norms and institutions in present-day Japan as merely the direct result of spread from "the Anglo-Protestant core countries—the hegemonic source (according to Frank et al., 1995) it seems, of much of the special celebration of the individual in the modern system" (p. 373).

ABOUT JAPANESE INSTITUTIONS

It is a simplification to see the nature of the various forms of institutionalized relationships between the individual and the group in present-day

Japan as completely explainable by the degree to which individualistic Anglo-Saxon norms and institutions have been diffused into Japanese culture. If we reject such simplification, we are left with the questions of how norms and institutions originate, develop, change, or disappear in Japan, or for that matter any country. Because the exact nature of such processes remains among the most basic unanswered questions in sociology, all we can do here is point to the continuing relevance of such fundamental questions. At a less profound level, however, we can raise some questions about the origins and the future of some of the Japanese institutions and cultural norms that Professor Usui sees as critical determinants of the retirement process in Japan.

One set of interrelated institutional characteristics and cultural norms that Professor Usui sees as underlying the gradual retirement process in Japan centers on the norms calling for employees to be loyal to and identify with the organizations for which they work. Those organizations, in turn, take care of and provide security for their workers. Professor Usui sees these norms and institutions as developing directly from the traditional Japanese institution of the *ie* (house, i.e., patrilineal family) that has existed since at least the preindustrial, Tokugawa period.

Many scholars, however, have concluded that the development of the institutions and the norms of company loyalty and lifetime employment are not merely unintended latent consequences of earlier Japanese institutional practices. They would argue, instead, that, although congruent with present-day Japanese cultural norms, these "institutional and organizational arrangements" are not an unplanned by-product of Japanese culture. As Cole (1979) has noted:

> What strikes the observer in reading a historical account of the development of permanent employment is the way it has changed in accordance with economic needs. . . . Although there are some aspects of unconscious persistence of custom in the evolution of permanent employment, for the most part it represents a conscious act of institution building. (p. 24)

Lincoln and Kalleberg (1990) similarly emphasize the importance of strategic choice on the part of Japanese business organizations. They downplay the influence on Japanese company personnel policy of unquestioning adherence to traditional cultural patterns and conclude that "the dedication and commitment of Japanese workers derive from Japan's leading edge status as an adopter and implementer of a new highly successful technology of organization and control" (p. 28). According to this general viewpoint, Japanese business organizations, far from being the passive beneficiaries of economic advantages deriving from traditional Japanese norms and institutions, have actively molded these norms and institutions to meet their economic needs.

The issue of the degree to which Japanese businesses are willing to try to modify existing institutions and norms to meet the requirements for their continued existence is also relevant to the present situation and to the future of gradual retirement in Japan. In chapter 2, Table 2.7, Professor Usui gives a list of 33 Japanese companies that, in response to the most recent economic downturn, have taken steps to reduce their labor costs in ways that are generally seen as seriously violating national norms regarding employers' responsibilities to their permanent workers. She notes that in response to the bad publicity they received, many of the companies have reversed their "offending" decisions. The questions remain, however, of how many companies have not reversed such decisions and of how well companies who violate present national norms regarding retirement eventually do compared to those who do not. Given the present, relatively high labor costs in Japan, which include what may be the substantial costs incurred supporting gradual retirement, it remains an open question whether Japanese businesses will continue to adhere to their old labor practices. Will they, instead, develop new forms and norms of employer/employee relationships—forms that may very well affect the ways in which older Japanese workers both continue to work and to retire. Of course, whatever Japanese firms do will be done within the context of present-day Japanese society. That society's present economic situation, particular demographic characteristics, socioeconomic institutions, and cultural norms will all constrain what actions Japanese companies can take. Nevertheless, although their very nature may limit the speed with which institutions change, the institutional networks in which Japanese companies are embedded are not set in stone, but are themselves open to change.

REFERENCES

Cole, R. E. (1979). *Work, mobility and participation.* Berkeley and Los Angeles: University of California Press.

Frank, D., Meyer, J., & Miyahara, D. (1995). The individualist polity and the prevalence of professionalized psychology. *American Sociological Review, 60,* 360–377.

Jepperson, R. L. (1991). Institutions, institutional effects, and institutionalism. In W. Powell & P. Dimaggio (Eds.), *The new institutionalism in organizational analysis* (pp. 143–163). Chicago: University of Chicago Press.

Lincoln, J. R., & Kalleberg, A. (1990). *Culture, control and commitment: A study of work organization and work attitudes in the U.S. and Japan.* Cambridge: Cambridge University   Press.

Merton, R. (1957). *Social theory and social structure.* New York: Free Press.

Meyer, J. (1977). The effects of education as an institution. *American Journal of Sociology, 83,* 53–77.

Schooler, C. (1994). A working conceptualization of social structure: Mertonian roots and psychological and sociocultural relationships. *Social Psychology Quarterly, 57,* 262–273.

Schooler, C. (1996). Cultural and social structural explanations of cross-national psychological differences. *Annual Review of Sociology, 22,* 323–349.

Zucker, L. G. (1991). The role of institutionalization in cultural persistence. In W. Powell & P. Dimaggio (Eds.), *The new institutionalism in organizational analysis* (pp. 83–107). Chicago: University of Chicago Press.

Commentary: The Institution of Gradual Retirement in Japan

Arne L. Kalleberg

All industrial societies are "graying." This phenomenon results largely from common demographic trends such as declining fertility and increasing life expectancies. For example, about 24% of Americans are projected to be over age 60 by 2,025 (up from 16% in 1980), compared to 31% of persons in Germany (up from 19% in 1980), 30% in Sweden (up from 22%), 25% in the United Kingdom (up from 20%), and 26% in Japan (up from 13%) (Schulz, Borowski, & Crown, 1991). Population aging threatens to strain governmental budgets in all industrial nations, which must care for large aging populations while containing pension costs at the same time. This problem is especially pronounced in Japan, which has experienced an extraordinarily rapid increase in the number of older persons due to a combination of very high longevity rates and decreases in birth rates (Beck & Beck, 1994). Indeed, the elderly's share of the population in Japan will grow faster in the 1990s than in any nation at any time in history (Campbell, 1992).

Chikako Usui's chapter, "Gradual Retirement: Japanese Strategies to

Older Workers" (chapter 2 of this volume) is thus a timely contribution to our understanding of Japan's responses to this major population aging problem. Her chapter also raises a number of important questions about the comparative study of the interrelations among institutions, cultures, and work careers.

THE JAPANESE GRADUAL RETIREMENT STRATEGY

Japan has responded to its "aging society" problem with an "internalization" strategy whereby persons are gradually retired from the labor force. This government-driven employment strategy encourages private-sector companies to employ persons from the time when mandatory retirement takes effect (*teinen*) until age 65, when they are eligible for public pensions. As a result of this system, labor force participation rates among older workers in Japan have continued to remain very high (Usui, Table 2.1 and 2.2). Japan's strategy contrasts with the approaches used by most European countries, which have dealt with their problems of population aging by "externalization" strategies that rely mainly on the provision of government incentives to encourage older workers to withdraw voluntarily from the labor market. The United States has utilized a third strategy, using private pension incentives to facilitate early retirement, with little government support.

The gradual retirement system appears to be a viable solution to Japan's aging worker problem. The system has been fairly successful in helping the public sector in Japan to contain expenditures. Campbell (1992), for example, points out that Japan's pension outlays are substantially lower than those in other countries of comparable worth: Japan devoted only 14.6% of its national income to Social Security in 1986, compared to 40.7% for Sweden, between 25% and 36% each for Germany, France, and Great Britain, and 16.2% for the United States. The gradual retirement system also provides continued opportunities for labor force participation for highly work-oriented older Japanese workers.

INSTITUTIONAL EMBEDDEDNESS

Usui argues that four institutions are responsible for maintaining the gradual retirement system in Japan. These include: (1) a governance structure of firms that features a labor-centered model of corporate ownership where the interests of employees are given higher priority than those of shareholders; (2) patterns of ownership in which many firms are part of holding companies such as the *keiretsu;* (3) government subsidies that have encouraged companies to continue to employ older workers; and (4) media influence that constrained companies from laying off workers.

Usui argues further that these organizational practices and systems are embedded in the institutional structure of Japanese society. The economic actions of firms thus need to be understood in terms of the symbolic and material features of Japanese institutions—such as social networks of organizations and individuals—not as the activities of atomized actors pursuing their individual interests. This view maintains that what is economically rational (e.g., what Hashimoto [1990] calls the "transaction-cost environment") is shaped by cultural-traditional influences and may differ from one society to the next, depending on its institutional structures, cultural values, and legal codes. That economic rationality is socially produced and culturally maintained is a seemingly obvious point, but it is not always recognized by social scientists. Some economists, for example, have attempted to explain Asian economic organization on the basis of neoclassical principles that assume that the individualistic, atomistic characteristics of U.S. markets are rational everywhere (Biggart, 1991). These neoclassical economists are often reluctant to let go of these ideas, despite contrary evidence provided by empirical studies of capitalism in varying cultures. Moreover, some psychologists assume that microlevel phenomena such as motivations and needs are similar from one society to the next, ignoring the diverse ways in which individuals' actions and attitudes are shaped by societal institutions (Kalleberg & Berg, 1987).

Firms, markets, and work in Japan (as well as in other Asian countries such as Korea and Taiwan) illustrate ways of organizing economic activity that are different from Western countries such as the United States and are inconsistent with many of the assumptions of neoclassical economic theory. For example, the "restructuring" and "reengineering" reactions of U.S. corporations to economic crises and technological changes (which have involved severe downsizing and layoffs, among other things) might be considered economically rational in the United States, but these actions would certainly not be seen as economically rational in Japan. (Actually, these actions are not very rational in the United States either;

the evidence overwhelmingly points to the negative consequences of downsizing for both U.S. organizations and their employees—see, e.g., U.S. Department of Labor, 1995.) To the extent that cross-national research on retirement relies on a handful of "universally" relevant independent variables (Usui, chapter 2, p. 48), then, it is useful to be reminded of the need to take into account a society's distinctive features in order to understand its work and industral structures.

An intriguing question is how the gradual retirement system came to be institutionalized in Japan (e.g., Campbell, 1992). Institutional explanations often pay insufficient attention to the processes by which organizational practices and structures become institutionalized (see Tolbert & Zucker, 1996). The gradual retirement system resulted in part from the efforts of government bureaucrats and private-sector actors to reach a consensus that would benefit the common good. This reflects the Japanese preference for indirect government involvement in the economy; the government used incentives and persuasion to encourage private companies to follow public policies. Of course, companies also benefit from this system, since they can rid themselves of higher paid workers (since pay is tied to seniority) and create managerial slots for younger workers. The costs to companies are relatively low, since retirement benefits only amount to a couple of years' salary. However, explanations of how this system was institutionalized should not put too much stress on the harmony and consensus related to its adoption and maintenance. For example, Japanese employers opposed the extension of *teinen* in the 1970s, arguing that compulsory regulation would limit their flexibility (Campbell, 1992).

THE INTERPLAY BETWEEN ORGANIZATIONAL PRACTICES AND CULTURE

Usui contends that Japanese institutions form a substructure that creates and sustains Japanese cultural values. This causal assumption is probably accurate in describing why representations and expressions of Japanese cultural values such as *shukko, teinen*, and corporate networks persist. Nevertheless, the relationship between organizational practices and culture is often more complex than this, and the causal direction may be reversed: cultural values may also shape organizational practices.

Consider the Japanese work ethic, which represents a psychological need to work that supplements—and may often overwhelm—the economic need to work. The Japanese socialization process generates strong pressures on individuals to regard work as a central life interest and to continue working as long as possible. For example, a 1980 survey (cited in Schulz, Borowski, & Crown, 1991) found that only 39% of Japanese men and women over age 59 continued to work because they needed the money. Moreover, the Japanese work more hours than do people in any other country: on average the Japanese worked 2,152 hours annually in 1983 compared to 1,898 in the United States). The Japanese are also well known for behaviors such as their refusal to take their allotted vacation time. The Japanese government even has a program for promoting employment over age 65: the Silver Manpower Center Program of temporary, nonregular work for older persons (Schulz et al., 1991).

This "preference" of Japanese workers for working hard is, of course, embedded in the institutional realities of Japanese life. At the same time, the socialization of Japanese workers into a dependency on work (in addition to the group) reinforces the institutions that underlie the gradual retirement system. This is illustrated by the concerns expressed over recent generational changes in work values and the work ethic: younger Japanese workers are increasingly rejecting the notion that work is the central activity in one's life. This trend is evidenced by a reduction of working hours in Japan (although Japanese employees still work about 10% more hours than the Americans or British). These generational changes in the work ethic concern both Japanese business leaders and government policy makers, who fear that as younger cohorts age and eventually retire, they may be less likely than their elders to be willing to continue to work at low-paying jobs at diminished status and may pressure government bureaucrats to increase pension payouts.

BARRIERS TO GRADUAL RETIREMENT

There are a number of barriers to implementing the Japanese system of internalization in other countries. The Japanese strategy is unlikely to be used in the United States, for example, for many of the reasons Usui notes: the reliance of American companies on short-term stock prices (and managerial compensation tied to them) encourages them to cut costs by reducing the sizes of their labor forces; the relative lack of interorganizational networks such as parent-child linkages in the United States makes it less possible to adopt practices like *shukko*; and the presence of a more individualistic culture in the United States encourages different viewpoints about work. Moreover, the specifics of their institutional environments may hinder the ability of countries such as France, Germany, and the Netherlands—who are now shifting toward gradual retirement—from successfully implementing elements of the Japanese system.

It would be particularly instructive to compare the Japanese experience more explicitly to that of Sweden, the other industrial country that has adopted an extensive gradual retirement strategy and whose social policy is also based on the principle of work. A distinctive feature of the Swedish model of partial retirement is that it enables older persons to combine part-time work with part-time pensions. While opportunities for part-time work are increasing for older Japanese, there is still relatively little provision for early retirement with reduced benefits in Japan. Sweden's partial retirement model is supported by an active employment policy that provides aging workers the opportunity to continue working if they so desire (Wadensjö, 1991).

Even if the institutional barriers were overcome, one might still ask whether it is desirable to adopt a Japanese-style gradual retirement policy in other countries. Is there a "dark side" to this system? Who are the losers? While there are benefits to this system, there are also costs. As in many Japanese institutions, there is a coercive aspect of the gradual retirement system. Older persons are ripe for exploitation by some companies that see them as a source of cheap labor who must work out of economic necessity because private retirement bonuses are too low for them to live on until they are eligible for public pensions (Dore, 1986). Older workers who are past the mandatory retirement age are usually forced to work in lower paid jobs because they have few well-paying options. Japanese workers who are asked to accept a transfer (*shukko*) have little choice but to do this, unlike American workers, who might receive a generous severance package if they decide to leave the company instead of being transferred. This economic necessity is reinforced by the Japanese work ethic, which also coerces individuals by making work a psychological (and social) necessity. The well-documented stress associated with failure to meet societal expectations may add to the other adjustments faced by older Japanese workers.

The retirement experiences of Japanese women suggest another negative aspect of the gradual retirement system. Hashimoto (1990) points out that Japanese women often enter the labor force after their husbands retire, and thus the labor force participation rates of Japanese women over age 65 are twice that of U.S. women (see Usui, Table 2.2). The recession that has hit the Japanese economy has been particularly harmful for women (Lincoln & Nakata, 1997). One reason for this is that women have been traditionally used by Japanese companies as part-time and temporary buffers to protect the permanent employment system. For example, over 70% of the part-time labor force in Japan is made up of women (Work in America Institute, Inc. and The Japanese Institute of Labour, 1995).

PRESSURES FOR CHANGE IN THE JAPANESE GRADUAL RETIREMENT SYSTEM

Changes are occurring in some of the institutions that undergird the system of gradual retirement. Consequently, we might expect this system to change along with other aspects of Japanese organizations' human resources policies. These changes are reflected in the decreases in labor force participation rates of older Japanese men (see Usui, Table 2.1, this volume).

There is growing resistance among many Japanese employers to these retirement-age policies, for example, as Japan faces its deepest recession of the post-World War II period. Japan seeks to respond to increased competitive pressures from Korea, Singapore, Hong Kong and Taiwan, as well as trade pressures from countries such as the United States (Schulz et al., 1991). Lincoln and Nakata (1997) argue that one institution that may be affected by this is the *keiretsu* system of cross-holding among member corporations of a business group. This system has begun to break down partly, making individual companies more sensitive to stock prices and short-term balance sheets. If this is a permanent restructuring rather than a cyclical response to crisis, it may create added pressures for Japanese companies to cut costs by reducing their support for gradual retirement practices. Added pressure on the viability of the *shukko* system results from many parent companies largely abandoning the practice of paternalistically looking after their suppliers and distributors in difficult economic times. One outcome has been the dramatic increase in bankruptcy rates among small firms in recent years.

The economic difficulties faced by Japanese firms have forced them to adopt competitive strategies based on cost reduction, to become more concerned with profit margins, and to moderate their policies about new investment and product variety (Lincoln & Nakata, 1997). These changes have prompted companies to waver in their subordination of short-term profitability to long-term growth and market share. The casualties of this may be the systems of *shushin koyo* (permanent employment) and *nenko joretsu* (seniority grading).

Demographic trends are also putting pressure on the gradual retirement system. The aging Japanese workforce and the increasing proportion of middle-aged employees have made it more difficult for Japanese firms to continue the motivational mechanisms that encourage learning and commitment such as internal labor markets. Many of these systems relied on Japan's unusually young population during the post-World War II period (Campbell, 1992), which made it possible to have fewer higher level positions relative to the number of employees competing for them.

In sum, studies of how macrostructural, demographic, and organizational forces shape work and careers in different national contexts have the potential for increasing considerably our understanding of social institutions and the life chances of the individuals who move through these institutions as they age. Such studies constitute central components of the needed research agenda on aging and retirement as we approach the 21st century.

REFERENCES

Beck, J. C., & Beck, M. N. (1994). *The change of a lifetime: Employment patterns among Japan's managerial elite.* Honolulu: University of Hawaii Press.

Biggart, N. (1991). Explaining Asian economic organization: Toward a Weberian institutional perspective. *Theory and Society, 20,* 199–232.

Campbell, J. C. (1992). *How policies change: The Japanese government and the aging society.* Princeton, NJ: Princeton University Press.

Dore, R. (1986). *Flexible rigidities: Industrial policy and structural adjustment in the Japanese economy, 1970–1980.* Stanford, CA: Stanford University Press.

Hashimoto, M. (1990). *The Japanese labor market in a comparative perspective with the United States.* Kalamazoo, MI: W.E. Upjohn Institute for Employment Research.

Kalleberg, A. L., & Berg, I. (1987). *Work and industry: Structures, markets and processes.* New York: Plenum.

Lincoln, J. R., & Nakata, Y. (1997). The transformation of the Japanese employment system: Nature, depth and origins. *Work and Occupations, 24,* 33–55.

Schulz, J. H., Borowski, A., & Crown, W. H. (1991). *The economics of population aging: The "graying" of Australia, Japan, and the United States.* Westport, CT: Auburn House.

Tolbert, P. S., & Zucker, L. G. (1996). The institutionalization of institutional theory. In S. Clegg, C. Hardy, & W. Nord (Eds.), *Handbook of organization studies* (pp. 175–190). London: Russell Sage.

U. S. Department of Labor. (1995). *Guide to responsible restructuring.* Washington, DC: U.S. Government Printing Office.

Wadensjö, E. (1991). Sweden: Partial exit. In M. Kohli, M. Rein, A.-M. Guillemard, & H. Van Gunsteren (Eds.), *Time for retirement: Comparative studies of early exit from the labor force* (pp. 284–323). New York: Cambridge University Press.

Work in America Institute, Inc. and The Japanese Institute of Labour. (1995). *Employment security: Changing characteristics in U.S. and Japan.* New York: U.S.–Japan Foundation.

CHAPTER 3

Workplace Norms for the Timing of Retirement

David J. Ekerdt

If one views the elements of the life course as beads on a string, then work and retirement are separate, successive matters with a boundary in moments of transition between work and leisure roles. Yet lifetime cannot be so confined. Early experience begets later experience: work structures and roles shape individuals' modes and timing of retirement. And what-is-to-come impinges on the present: in late career, the prospect of retirement is never far from one's mind. Work steers retirement while retirement looms over work.

This chapter is written to support a view of individual retirement behavior as a course of action embedded in the structure of work. As the argument goes, workers anticipate their retirement in advance of the event, entertaining ideas and designs for it along the way. This view runs counter to the model that explains retirement as a time-limited, rational choice between work and leisure. The chapter specifically calls attention to timing norms for retirement as a potential mechanism by which work structures convey people out of their work careers.

A DEVELOPMENTAL VIEW OF
RETIREMENT BEHAVIOR

The literature has long offered the insight that people in late middle age work with retirement in mind. Neugarten (1968) and later Karp (1989) observed—in middle-class workers, at least—that people organize their conception of life's time differently, beginning roughly at age 50. Rather than calculating personal time-since-birth, people come to focus on time-left-to-live. The worker's variant of this projection is time-left-to-work (Ekerdt & DeViney, 1993). Time-left (at work or in the labor force) is indeed calculable by older workers who can foresee the eventuality of retirement: generally in their certain eligibility for Social Security benefits but especially if they participate in rationalized grade, promotion, and employer-pension systems. Time-left is also calculable by others who can encourage the anticipation of retirement with social and organizational cues about its desirability or inevitability. Prompted by the institutionalized rhythm of work careers and perhaps by other life changes, there comes a time when an individual sees work as winding down. As in a game, where early strategy aims to establish competent play, late strategy is governed by the time expiring on the clock.

Gerontology's frequent nod to retirement as a "process" (first enunciated in Carp, 1968) implicitly recognizes the temporal antecedents of later retirement behavior. Yet there really has been only one formal attempt to conceptualize an extended retirement process. Atchley (1976) outlined a framework of several possible "phases" for retirement, beginning with a remote phase of vague anticipation, then a near phase of preparatory rehearsal, and on into phases of postretirement adaptation. Atchley did not offer empirical evidence to support the framework and was purposely indeterminate about the timing and duration of phases. Nevertheless, the idea that an anticipatory process commences long in advance of the exit event became a staple of textbooks in gerontology and life-span development. Research findings have since confirmed that a process of anticipation is under way well in advance of retirement and that a gathering involvement in retirement issues is normative as the event approaches (Evans, Ekerdt, & Bosse, 1985).

Despite the process emphasis and the availability of longitudinal data, the field still lacks models and reports of the time-ordered progression of activities and attitudes that conclude work careers. In one sense, retirement anticipation may seem to be a discouraging topic for research because the end points—events of retirement—are increasingly seen to be variable if not disordered (Henretta, 1992; Ruhm, 1990). Why study people's anticipation of events that may not occur as foreseen? It may seem more sensible to study the outcomes themselves, retrospectively modeling their antecedents.

There has been no dearth of research attention to events of retirement behavior. The single most rugged design in microlevel retirement research designates as the dependent variable workers' events of retirement (variously defined), and then regresses these outcomes on a congeries of financial, health, work, family, and cultural variables. The models of economists and sociologists tend to favor different subsets of these variables because of disciplinary inclinations: economists to disclose preferences for leisure and consumption revealed in retiree's choices, but sociologists to disclose social opportunities and constraints for behavior. These models, it should be said, have been elaborated to consider more than one transition event, such as exit-and-reentry or a series of moves prior to complete retirement. The set of multiple transitions that may precede permanent exit from the labor force are sometimes also labeled a "retirement process" (e.g., Hardy, Hayward, & Liu, 1994).

Models of retirement outcomes do acknowledge the antecedents of later transitions when they incorporate features of the earlier life course (Elder & Pavalko, 1993; O'Rand, Henretta, & Krecker, 1992; Pienta, Burr, & Mutchler, 1994) or emphasize the explanatory power of structural features such as occupation (e.g., Hayward, 1986). Yet the point remains that outcome studies confine their interest in workers' decision making for retirement to the last or late stages of work careers.

I and my colleagues have argued elsewhere that decision making for retirement extends over a considerable period of time—years—prior to the retirement event. Hence the retirement behaviors (which are the focus of so much research) have antecedents in earlier decisions made and remade that will have channeled workers toward particular outcomes (Ekerdt, DeViney, & Kosloski, 1996). The extended stream of decision making for retirement can be observed in the changing plans and intentions toward retirement that workers entertain over time. These intentions are of interest and consequence not just because they may predict behavior, but also because they may prompt interim preparatory behaviors, thereby consolidating a course toward particular retirement outcomes.

This emphasis on extended decision making and interim preparation promotes a view of people as the agents of their retirement behaviors, and not as late-stage deciders or as fated by social structure.

The developmental emphasis is a later life complement to the way that social and behavioral scientists have framed the processes by which adolescents and young adults anticipate and eventually enter career and marital roles. Prior to the 1950s, according to Crites (1989), experts "characterized career decision making as a time-bound, largely static event that occurred at the crossroads of life, usually upon high school graduation, when an adolescent did a self-assessment, analyzed the world of work, and then decided what to do" (p. 142). The subsequent emphasis of the field has been that career development is not a one-time event, but a process that extends approximately from age 10 to 21 (Crites, 1989). Along the way, plans are made and remade. And early plans, when acted upon (e.g., early educational or lifestyle behaviors), can narrow the field of later choices and thereby determine later outcomes (Pimental, 1996).

If people are anticipating retirement for some time prior to the event, and if these behaviors are ultimately more than the enactment of abstract tastes and preferences, what sort of guidance do workers receive about desirable retirement behaviors? Of particular interest here is guidance about the appropriate timing of work exits and retirement.

TIMING NORMS, PAST AND PRESENT

Although timing norms are the focus of this chapter, retirement has other normative content. For example, what activities should occupy one's postemployment leisure? Although the "roleless role" of retirees may indeed be functional and not unwanted (Streib & Schneider, 1971), retirees do recognize a vague, pervasive exhortation to "keep busy" (Ekerdt, 1986). Another issue is the question of where to live. Retirees often feel compelled to make and defend a decision about whether they should relocate to a retirement community (Cuba, 1989).

Norms about the timing of retirement are prescriptions about *when*—at what age or length of service—is the right time to go. Such norms, though, are also bound up with *how* one retires. Retirement at a relatively early age simultaneously means acceptance of reduced, rather than full, benefits. Retirement at a later age tends to preclude postretirement employment. Timing norms may also imply that one should grant or withhold commitment to a work organization. Favoring late work exits could be a compliment to the employer, whereas early exits could signal disfavor. Timing norms, thus, can package expectations about entire modes or styles of exiting.

Norms for the ending of work careers were in circulation long before the Social Security program promulgated its full-benefit age of 65. Pondering the question of an upper age limit on economic efficiency, Todd (1915) described the belief of contemporary social policy that men had an ideal working age of 50 years lying between the ages of 15 and 65. He assembled data on average superannuation ages in various American industries: 55 to 65 for skilled workers, 55 to 60 in the meat industry, 65 to 70 for railroad workers, 50 to 65 for policemen. He also noted the tendency of European pension systems to fix 60 or 65 years as the benefit age.

Focusing on this period, Haber and Gratton (1994) have described how a new, pessimistic, medical model of aging appeared just in time to serve as a rationale for the superannuation of workers in an industrializing economy. There was at hand apparent scientific evidence for an age limit on productive capacity. In 1881 the physician George Miller Beard published results from his historical studies of the relationship between age and creative achievement among "nearly all the greatest names in history." His influential conclusion was that "seventy percent of the work of the world is done before forty-five, and eighty percent before fifty" (Cole, 1992, chap. 8). Beard's work was later a reference point for remarks by the prominent clinician William Osler in his farewell address to the Johns Hopkins University medical faculty in 1905. Osler made jocular reference to the "uselessness of men above sixty," to which may be traced "nearly all of the great mistakes politically and socially, all of the worst poems, most of the bad pictures, a majority of the bad novels, not a few of the bad sermons and speeches." He suggested, fancifully, that after age 60, workers might depart "by chloroform." Shorn of context, these remarks were widely reported, provoking a public uproar that only highlighted Osler's endorsement of age 60 as an ideal retirement age (Berk, 1989; Cole, 1992).

Closer to recent experience, the legislated elimination of modern retirement rules in the 1970s reduced the visibility of timing norms, but there was every reason to believe that age-related pressures to retire were still prevalent (Eglit, 1992). Whether by means coercive or voluntary, retirement has remained necessary for work organizations that need to manage rationally the stock and flow of human resources in a way that conserves worker morale and motivation. The explicit attempt to manage employees' retirement behavior has been clearly revealed by analyses of pension incentives in defined benefit plans (Gustman, Mitchell, & Steinmeier, 1994). As these are structured, workers cannot usually gain any pension advantage in working past the plan's normal retirement age, if not the early retirement age. Indeed, plans tend to penalize financially anything but early retirement (Wise, 1993).

Altogether, then, there is a cultural legacy of public discussion about when retirement should occur, as well as universal recognition of the Social Security benefit ages of 62 and 65, strong suggestions that private pension incentives steer retirement behavior, and narrative evidence that the "right age" for retirement is topical among workers in certain fields (Prentis, 1992). Given all this, it is surprising that discussions of retirement anticipation and decision making have not recognized the potential role of timing norms as a determinant of work-exit behavior. The point is important to a developmental view of retirement because timing norms become the bearer of societal, firm level, or reference group preferences for retirement.

Of three questions addressed in the next analysis, the first is the extent to which workers even recognize a timing norm at work. Surveys of older workers have long featured attitudinal questions about mandatory retirement, about feeling pressure to retire, and about specific mandatory ages on the job. The greater, apparent voluntariness of current retirement practices (Hardy & Quadagno, 1995) requires an updated approach. The data to be examined here come from the national sample of older workers in the 1992 Health and Retirement Study who were asked about the "usual age" for retirement among their coworkers. These responses are taken to represent a local timing norm (after Lawrence, 1988, 1996). The second question is whether reports about the usual age covary with workplace characteristics (i.e., are specific to relations at work) and perhaps arise from the benefit schedules of employers' pensions. The third question is whether norms, in turn, may motivate workers' plans and intentions toward the timing of retirement, as they should.

METHODS

Study Population

Evidence about timing norms comes from the 1992 baseline wave of the Health and Retirement Study (HRS), a nationally representative sample of persons aged 51 to 61 and their spouses regardless of age (Juster & Suzman, 1995). Total sample size for the first wave of this biennial longitudinal survey was 12,652 persons in some 7,000 households. This design affords a sample population that represents the late career and retirement experiences of both men and women. The inclusion of older working women in such a national sample is a particularly welcome feature of the HRS, allowing gender comparisons of experience that may eventually redraw what has hitherto been a "male model" of retirement (Calasanti, 1993; Slevin & Wingrove, 1995).

The study population for the present analysis included all persons in the core sample aged 51 to 61 (born 1931 to 1941); persons from Black and Hispanic oversamples were not included. These 8,077 cases were reduced further to 5,306 by including only current workers who also claimed they had not completely retired. Finally, because timing norms are an inapplicable concept for many of the self-employed, the analysis was limited to wage and salary workers, a study population of 4,331 altogether. The study population was exactly divided between 2,162 men and 2,169 women, was 82.8% White, had a mean age of 55.6 years, and had 84.1% of respondents working 35 or more hours per week.

SURVEY QUESTIONS

The 1992 HRS interview was an omnibus survey of topics, including demographics, physical health and functioning, housing and mobility, family structure, current jobs, work history, disability, retirement plans, cognition and expectations, net worth, income, insurance, and widowhood.

In the interview section on current employment, following a long series on job characteristics, the HRS included a question about local timing norms for retirement. The item asked: "On your main job, what is the usual retirement age for people who work with you or have the same kind of job?" This question is framed to reveal a norm: the customary age for retirement among coworkers. Responses could be given in ages or years of service.

Two other lines of inquiry about retirement timing are involved in this analysis. One involves the age structure of pension incentives that one may obtain at the current job. This was gauged by two questions: one about the full-benefit age ("What is the earliest age at which *you* would be eligible to receive *full* or *unreduced* pension benefits from this job?") and one about the early-benefit age ("What is the *earliest* age at which you could leave this employer and start to receive pension benefits?"). The other line of inquiry concerned plans to leave the current job. These questions about timing immediately followed the question about the local "usual age" for retirement. Respondents were asked: "Are you currently planning to stop working altogether, or work fewer hours at a particular date or age, or to change the kind of work you do when you reach a particular age, have you not given it much thought, or what?" If workers expressed intentions to stop completely, to work fewer hours, or to change jobs, they were asked at what age they planned to do that. For this analysis, this age will be termed the planned "exit age" from the current job, being the same job that was the reference for the usual-age-for-retirement question.

Other survey items were involved in this analysis because they describe circumstances of the job and workplace, as well as demographic and other background factors.

Findings

THE USUAL AGE FOR RETIREMENT

In this population of employed workers aged 51 to 61 in 1992, 73.7% named an age or term of service as usual for retirement at their place of work. Responses given in years of service (by 99 respondents) were recoded to respondents' own ages upon reaching that mark. The distribution of the usual ages is shown in Figure 3.1. Usual ages fall in large concentrations at 62 and 65; cumulatively, 37.5% of these ages fall on or prior to age 62, and 71.0% fall on or prior to age 65. Above this share, almost all of the remaining respondents, 26.3%, cited no usual age for retirement. Thus in the matter of timing norms, current jobs, if they are

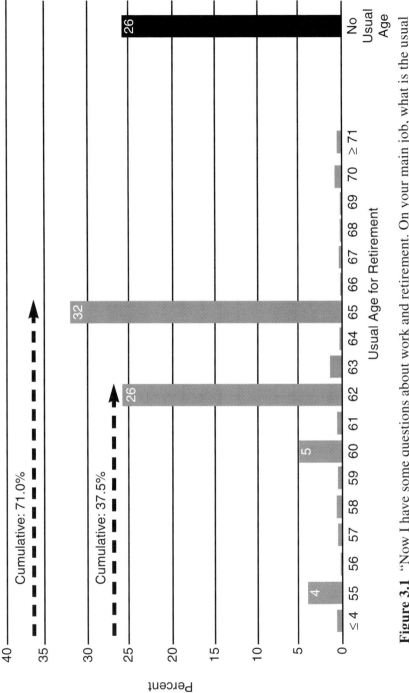

Figure 3.1 "Now I have some questions about work and retirement. On your main job, what is the usual retirement age for people who work with you or have the same kind of job?" (*N*=4,331)

seen as ending at all, are almost all recognized as ending by age 65.

Men and women differed in their recognition of usual ages for retirement, with 80.2% of men but only 67.2% of women recognizing a usual age. However, among those who did recognize a usual age, the *distribution* of usual ages did not differ between men and women. This suggests that male and female workers have varying exposures to timing norms, but the norms that they do see are similar.

The recognition of usual ages also differed across the age range of the study population. After age 55, this cohort of older workers has already begun to become thinned by early retirements, and so its older members were somewhat less likely to recognize a usual age (e.g., 76.2% at ages 51–52 versus 70.9% at ages 60–61).

Table 3.1 shows the prevalence of usual-age reports within categories of other survey items. For this purpose, the distribution of usual ages is shown two ways: whether an age is recognized or not, where higher proportions citing an age would indicate that the timing norm is more prevalent in that circumstance; and cumulated at ages 62 and 65 to convey a sense of the distribution of perceived usual ages for exiting the workplace.

The first issue to consider is whether responses to the usual-age question describe what (in the way of retirement timing) is *typically* done among work peers or what *ought to be* done, whether these are reports about behavioral regularity or behavioral standards. Among the set of HRS questions about job characteristics, workers were asked their extent of agreement with two statements: "In decisions about promotion, my employer gives younger people preference over older people"; and "My coworkers make older workers feel that they ought to retire before age 65" (Table 3.1, Items A and B). Agreement with either question is a claim about local devaluation of older workers. At least 15% of the sample agreed or strongly agreed with the statements, and those so agreeing were more likely to report a usual age, and they were more likely to report that age as falling at or prior to (e.g.) age 62. From this, one cannot leap to the conclusion that workers feel they must retire at the usual age, but it suggests that the awareness of usual ages may be more than just taking note of other workers' transition schedules. Usual ages to some degree seem to be a guide.

Usual ages are conveyed in the workplace, but the next question to answer is whether they arise *out of* the circumstances of work. The question is an important one for theorizing about retirement decision making, especially over an extended period of time. Does one's understanding of retirement norms proceed from social relations in specific organizational and occupational structures, or is it adopted wholesale from the universal entitlement rules of the Social Security program? Of course, local norms can follow the structure of government policy—a glance at Figure 3.1 strongly suggests that the heaping of usual ages at 62 and 65 is no coincidence. Universal eligibility ages notwithstanding, is there evidence that they bend to local context?

The HRS can be mined for several pieces of information about the workplace. All (Items C–F, Table 3.1) suggest that usual ages do vary by work setting. Considering usual-age reports as they vary by the size of the employment location (Item C), the larger the workplace, the greater was workers' awareness of a usual age for retirement, and the greater the likelihood that those ages fell on or before age 62. The pattern for this variable was smooth. Workers in unionized workplaces, too, were far more likely to recognize a usual retirement age (Item D) and to name it as typical by age 62. It was likewise with workers who have employer- or union-sponsored pension plans (Item E); among workers with no pension plan, only half (53.2%) acknowledged a usual age. Finally, usual-age reports differed considerably across occupational categories (selected groupings, Item F), if such broad categories can be viewed as a proxy for type of workplace. In particular, professional-managerial and skilled blue-collar workers reported a greater prevalence of usual ages than did workers in sales, clerical, food preparation, or health services. In the food preparation and health services categories, usual ages were at once less frequent and later (according to the cumulative prevalence by age 62).

Of course, what unifies these observations across workplace size, unionization, pension coverage, and occupational profile is the probability that usual-age reports—timing norms—are more prevalent in the type of large, bureaucratized organizations that typify the core economic sector. These are the work sites that manage larger flows of human resources, characterized by rationalized pay, promotion, and reward systems—places with higher pay, steady employment, and labor unions that are watchdogs for working conditions (Hendricks & McAllister, 1983). The evidence in Table 3.1 is that workers who staff these jobs are more acutely aware of expectations about timing for retirement. The idea is

Table 3.1. Prevalence of a "Usual Age" for Retirement by Other Factors

	No usual age	Some age	Cumulative % by: Age 62	Age 65
Overall (N = 4,331)	26.3	73.7	37.5	71.0
A. In decisions about promotion, my employer gives younger people preference over older people.				
Agree (16.2%)	18.5	81.5	45.3	79.1
Disagree (83.8%)	27.0	73.0	36.4	70.2
B. My coworkers make older workers feel that they ought to retire before age 65.				
Agree (15.0%)	16.0	84.0	51.3	81.8
Disagree (85.0%)	27.6	72.4	35.4	69.6
C. Number of employees at the location where you work:				
Less than 15	37.7	62.3	29.1	60.2
15–24	29.2	71.8	32.9	69.3
25–99	27.7	72.3	35.0	68.8
100–499	18.8	81.2	41.4	78.6
500 or more	15.0	85.0	48.1	82.4

D. Union or employee association?				
Yes (25.9%)	10.7	89.3	57.4	87.0
No (74.1%)	31.7	68.3	30.5	65.5
E. Included in a pension, retirement, or tax-deferred plan with this employer?				
Yes (66.6%)	15.9	84.1	45.4	81.8
No (33.4%)	46.8	53.2	21.7	49.8
F. Selected occupational categories:				
Professional/managerial/technical	19.9	80.1	36.8	76.5
Sales and clerical	31.2	68.8	34.3	66.2
Food preparation services	47.4	52.6	26.3	51.9
Health services	37.6	62.4	29.0	62.4
Skilled trades and operators	18.6	81.3	46.5	80.0

made clearer to them about when it is time to retire, thus maintaining career mobility in these labor markets.

CORRESPONDENCE OF THE PENSION-ELIGIBILITY AGE AND THE USUAL-RETIREMENT AGE

The social construction and communication of retirement timing norms in particular work settings are potentially fruitful topics for life course research. Observational studies and survey techniques can disclose the extent to which timing norms arise from, or are justified by, the physical demands of the job or its skill requirements. In interviews conducted by this author with older workers who are participants in the Boston VA Normative Aging Study (Bosse & Spiro, 1995), policemen and firemen would explain their retirement plans in terms of physical ability: "It's a young man's game." By contrast, managers in large organizations would refer to new supervisors' judgments against their skills, how a "different breed" of workers was wanted now. The construction and communication of timing norms would always need to be considered in light of workers' assumed awareness of the benefit schedules of Social Security and workers' understanding of local pension plan incentives. The evidence is clear that plan incentives steer the timing of retirement behavior (Wise, 1993), and it is reasonable to posit that this occurs because the benefit schedules of the local pension plan become incorporated into the local timing norm.

Findings in Table 3.1 (Item E) suggest as much, where workers with pensions are far more likely to recognize a usual age for retirement. Are usual ages indeed synchronous with the eligibility ages of pensions? The matter can be examined by comparing the two age markers among HRS workers. Of the present study population of 4,331 wage and salary workers aged 51 to 61, 3,190 recognized a usual age for retirement, and of these, 2,407 claimed to be included in one or more pension plans sponsored by their employer or union on their current, main job. For this group, the correspondence between their usual ages for retirement and the ages of eligibility for these pensions is shown in Table 3.2.

Workers whose "most important" pension was of the defined-benefit type (benefits based on a formula involving age, years of service, and salary) were asked about the earliest age at which they would be eligible to receive full, unreduced pension benefits, and the earliest age at which they could receive any benefits. (These questions were asked prior to the usual-age-for-retirement question in the HRS interview sequence.) As shown across the top rows of Table 3.2, some workers did not know or could not answer the questions about eligibility ages.

Among those who could cite a minimum, full-benefit age, 20.2% named a usual age that preceded the full-benefit age. Another 40.6% cited the same age as usual for retirement and as the threshold for full benefits, and nearly the same proportion saw the usual age as following the full-benefit age. Thus the sequence of ages is appropriate for four-fifths of these workers; the usual age is identified as falling on or after the eligibility age.

Yet one-fifth of the workers saw a situation where coworkers usually retire prior to the availability of full pension benefits. This is a puzzlingly high number if pension eligibility is a determinant of local timing norms. The picture, however, becomes clearer when comparing the same pension's early-benefit ages with usual ages (second row of Table 3.2). In this case, only 6.3% of usual ages preceded the pension age. The overwhelming majority of usual ages either fell on or followed the early-benefit pension age.

A very similar pattern obtained among workers whose "most important" plan was a defined contribution plan (money is accumulated in an account). When respondents were aware that their defined contribution plans have a threshold or "youngest" age at which installments or monthly payouts can begin, that age was seen to be preceded by the usual age by only 3.6% of respondents (bottom row of Table 3.2). Thus among workers aware of such details of their defined benefit or defined contribution plans, about 95% said that the usual age falls on or follows the "early" pension-eligibility age. In those roughly 71% of cases where the sequence is pension age first, usual age second, one cannot prove a causal order. Yet the opposite sequence is rare, and so the findings are consistent with an argument that timing norms follow from the age structure of pension incentives.

As a footnote to Table 3.2, the arrays there were also partitioned according to gender (not shown). The correspondence of pension ages and usual ages was very similar for men and women, demonstrating again that given the same exposure, male and female workers acknowledge the same structure of incentives and norms.

Table 3.2 Correspondence of the Usual Age for Retirement and the Pension-Eligibility Age; 2,407 Workers Who Recognize a Usual Age for Retirement and Are Included in a Pension Plan

Type of pension-eligibility age	No pension age given	Precedence of pension age and usual age			N
		Usual age precedes pension age(%)	Usual age matches pension age(%)	Usual age follows pension age (%)	
Defined-benefit type for "most important" plan (N = 1,665)					
Full-benefit age	107	20.2	40.6	39.2	1,558
Earliest benefit age	129	6.3	22.3	71.4	1,536
Defined-contribution type for "most important" plan (N = 742)					
Youngest receipt age	274	3.6	25.4	70.9	468

CORRESPONDENCE OF THE USUAL-RETIREMENT AGE
WITH EXPECTED TIMING OF JOB EXIT

Having followed the question of timing norms upstream, comparing usual retirement ages with pension-eligibility ages, it is also possible to look downstream, to confirm whether timing norms structure workers' own plans to exit their jobs. Immediately following the survey item about a usual age for retirement, HRS respondents were asked the question about current plans to stop working altogether, work fewer hours, change jobs, and so on. Multiple responses could be recorded for each respondent, though few gave more than one response. If responses entailed an intention to make a change from the present job, workers were asked at what age they planned to make the change. For this analysis, workers who foresaw multiple transitions were assigned to the earliest occurring intention.

The question sequence was, thus: When do your coworkers usually retire, and what are you planning to do, and when? The HRS interview elsewhere contains other questions about retirement expectations (self-rated chances of working full time past age 62 or 65, and expected age for retirement in general), but the advantage of the immediate follow-up to the usual-age question is that both explicitly refer to the current, main job.

Of the 3,190 workers who recognized a usual age for retirement, some planned "never" to retire (4.6%), some had not committed to a course of action (39.8%), and some had plans to make a change but did not state an age for the change (2.1%). The remaining 1,707 respondents recognized both a usual age for retirement and followed up with a stated age for an anticipated job change. The latter is called an "exit age" here and encompasses plans to stop work altogether, to change jobs, or to work fewer hours. The last intention, while appearing to connote a change in labor supply in the same position, will likely entail a job exit as well, because opportunities to phase into partial retirement at the same job are not common (Gustman & Steinmeier, 1984).

Table 3.3 reports the correspondence between the usual age for retirement and the expected age of exit from the current job. Overall, 40.5% of respondents planned to exit before the usual age, and another 44.9% at the usual age. Altogether, over 85% of these workers planned to leave at or prior to the local, usual age for retirement. This pattern is in substantial conformity with a timing norm as an upper limit on personal plans for job exits.

Table 3.3 Correspondence of the Usual Age for Retirement and the Expected Age for Exit from the Current Job; 1,707 Workers Who Recognize a Usual Age for Retirement and Have Explicit Plans for a Job Change

	Precedence of exit age and usual age			
Parameters	Exit age precedes usual age	Exit age matches usual age	Exit age follows usual age	N
TOTAL	40.5	44.9	14.6	1,707
Manner of planned exit				
"Stop work altogether"	34.8	50.2	15.0	807
"Work fewer hours"	42.7	44.8	12.5	592
"Change kind of work; Work for myself"	50.7	31.2	18.2	308
Usual Age for Retirement-Level				
Age 59 or younger	9.8	28.9	61.3	173
Age 60 or 61	39.1	32.1	28.8	156
Age 62	30.9	58.1	11.0	635
Age 63 or 64	66.7	17.8	15.5	45
Age 65	52.9	43.8	3.3	651
Age 66 or older	89.4	8.5	2.1	47
Gender				
Male workers	38.5	44.6	16.9	984
Female workers	42.9	45.2	11.9	723

The other rows of Table 3.3 address some variations on this correspondence. The planned manner of job exit affects the proportion planning to exit earlier than the norm. Compared to workers who foresaw a classic, full-stop retirement for themselves, workers who intended to embark on more complex paths into the future—paths such as partial retirement or a change in job—were more likely to exit before the usual age. Yet, whatever the manner of exit, over 80% of respondents did not plan to work beyond the usual age.

The correspondence between usual and exit age is also shown within levels of the usual age. One might observe that the synchrony between timing norms and job-exit intentions is really endogenous to workers' universal awareness of the "super timing" norms of the Social Security program. Usual retirement ages, planned-exit ages, and even pension-eligibility ages all tend to converge, owing to the larger enveloping structure of Social Security arrangements within which American practices play out. The question cannot be settled here, but it is possible to examine whether correspondence is still strong when usual ages are recognized to occur at *other than* 62 and 65. Accordingly, for workers whose usual age fell at 60 to 61, 63 to 64, or 66+, large proportions still planned to exit on or prior to the usual age. The top row of the display, however, illustrates how a number of these 51- to 61-year-old workers were near to, or were already working on past, what were "young" timing norms.

Finally, the gender comparison in Table 3.3 again showed a largely similar pattern for male and female workers. Notwithstanding the concern about women's retiring early due to spousal demands and family obligations (Hatch & Thompson, 1992), female workers here were only slightly more likely than men to foresee an exit prior to the usual age.

CONCLUSIONS

This analysis of information from the 1992 Health and Retirement Study has shown that three-quarters of American workers aged 51 to 61 recognize that, among their coworkers, there is a usual age for retirement. Men are somewhat more likely than women to recognize these regularities. These usual ages vary by workplace circumstances, and they correspond well to the age-scheduled incentives of workers' pension plans. Moreover, usual ages, when acknowledged, appear to be an upper limit on the range of workers' personal plans to exit the job. Usual ages, then, are communicated to workers through their relations at work, and the evidence is that they become a norm for the cessation of the job. These matters were examined in cross-sectional data, but the findings suggest that structure begets a norm and the norm shapes intended behavior.

The ebbing of the defined contribution type of pension plan in the mix of American retirement instruments (Ippolito, 1995; Woods, 1994)— and with it explicit schedules of age incentives and penalties for the timing of retirement—means that timing norms of the future may be more diffuse. Henretta (1992) has detected increased variability in the actual timing of retirement even as the event of retirement has become more of a life course certainty. The legislated rise in Social Security's full-benefit age in the coming decades is likely to spread the timing norms that now nearly universally top out at 65. Still, there will be norms for the timing of retirement. Much as Todd, writing in 1915, could recite usual retirement ages, industry by industry, there is every reason to think that labor markets will continue to have shared ideas about timetables for exit.

This chapter began by insisting that the transition from work to retirement is a course of action rather than a time-limited rational choice between work and leisure, and that retirement is an outcome of social structure. To recapitulate this argument, Sewell's recent (1992) theorizing about social structure is helpful. Setting out to specify the social sciences' "unavoidable epistemic metaphor," Sewell wrote that structure is comprised of cultural "schemas," or generalizable tools of thought, as well as human and nonhuman "resources," including knowledge, that can be used to enhance or maintain power.

Applying these ideas here to the question of retirement, the older individual is already familiar with the "schema" of the life course, being an idealized progression of roles and stages conveying one along from childhood to adolescence and through adulthood. The organizational or occupational version of the life course schema is the career paced by age and time, with retirement looming at its end. Aware of the broad schema—the rules of life—older workers can recognize, use, or interpret an array of "resources" for their retirement behavior. This array is large—it includes their capabilities, family circumstances, wealth and pension prospects, and value in the labor market. Among these resources is knowledge about what is locally regarded as usual retirement behavior or norms, knowledge that is a particular resource for retirement intentions as they are under construction. The schemas and resources do not rigidly determine individual behavior, but rather they endow and enclose individual agency in bringing about retirement. There is engagement with retirement far in advance of the event, which is why we should not be surprised that people are led out of the adult role of work as contentedly as they are.

REFERENCES

Atchley, R. C. (1976). *The sociology of retirement.* Cambridge, MA: Schenkman.

Berk, S. L. (1989). Sir William Osler, ageism, and "The Fixed Period." *Journal of the American Geriatics Society, 37,* 263–266.

Bosse, R., & Spiro, A. (1995). The Normative Aging Study. In G. L. Maddox (Ed.), *The Encyclopedia of Aging* (2nd ed., pp. 688–690). New York: Springer Publishing Company.

Calasanti, T. M. (1993). Bringing in diversity: Toward an inclusive theory of retirement. *Journal of Aging Studies, 7,* 133–150.

Carp, F. M. (1968). Background and statement of purpose. In F. M. Carp (Ed.), *The retirement process.* Public Health Service Publication No. 1778. Washington, DC: U.S. Government Printing Office.

Cole, T. R. (1992). *The journey of life: A cultural history of aging in America.* New York: Cambridge University Press.

Crites, J. O. (1989). Career development in adolescence: Theory, measurement, and longitudinal findings. In D. Stern & D. Eichorn (Eds.), *Adolescence and work: Influences of social structure, labor markets, and culture* (pp. 141–156). Hillsdale, NJ: Erlbaum.

Cuba, L. (1989). Retiring to vacationland. *Generations, 13*(2), 63–67.

Eglit, H. C. (1992). *Age discrimination.* Colorado Springs, CO: Shepherd's/McGraw Hill.

Ekerdt, D. J. (1986). The busy ethic: Moral continuity between work and retirement. *The Gerontologist, 26,* 239–244.

Ekerdt, D. J., & DeViney, S. (1993). Evidence for a preretirement process among older male workers. *Journal of Gerontology: Social Sciences, 48,* S35–S43.

Ekerdt, D. J., DeViney, S., & Kosloski, K. (1996). Profiling plans for retirement. *Journal of Gerontology: Social Sciences, 51B,* S140–S149.

Elder, G. H., & Pavalko, E. K. (1993). Work careers in men's later years: Transitions, trajectories, and historical change. *Journal of Gerontology: Social Sciences, 48,* S180–S191.

Evans, L., Ekerdt, D. J., & Bosse, R. (1985). Proximity to retirement and anticipatory involvement: Findings from the Normative Aging Study. *Journal of Gerontology, 40,* 368–374.

Gustman, A. L., Mitchell, O. S., & Steinmeier, T. L. (1994). The role of pensions in the labor market: A survey of the literature. *Industrial and Labor Relations Review, 47,* 417–438.

Gustman, A. L., & Steinmeier, T. L. (1984). Partial retirement and the analysis of retirement behavior. *Industrial and Labor Relations Review, 37,* 403–415.

Haber, C., & Gratton, B. (1994). *Old age and the search for security: An American social history.* Bloomington, IN: Indiana University Press.

Hardy, M. A., Hayward, M. D., & Liu, M-C. (1994). Work after retirement: The experience of older men in the United States. *Social Science Research, 23,* 82–108.

Hardy, M. A., & Quadagno, J. (1995). Satisfaction with early retirement: Making choices in the auto industry. *Journal of Gerontology: Social Sciences, 50B,* S217–S228.

Hatch, L. R., & Thompson, A. (1992). Family responsibilities and women's retirement. In M. Szinovacz, D. J. Ekerdt & B. H. Vinick (Eds.), *Families and retirement* (pp. 99–113). Newbury Park, CA: Russell Sage.

Hayward, M. D. (1986). The influence of occupational characteristics on men's early retirement. *Social Forces, 64,* 1032–1045.

Hendricks, J., & McAllister, C. E. (1983). An alternative perspective on retirement: A dual economic approach. *Ageing and Society, 3,* 279–299.

Henretta, J. C. (1992). Uniformity and diversity: Life-course institutionalization and late-life work exit. *Sociological Quarterly, 33,* 265–279.

Ippolito, R. A. (1995). Toward explaining the growth of defined contribution plans. *Industrial Relations, 34,* 1–20.

Juster, F. T., & Suzman, R. (1995). The Health and Retirement Study: An overview. *Journal of Human Resources, 30*(Suppl.), 7–56.

Karp, D. A. (1989). The social construction of retirement among professionals 50–60 years old. *The Gerontologist, 29,* 750–760.

Lawrence, B. S. (1988). New wrinkles in the theory of age: Demography, norms, and performance ratings. *Academy of Management Journal, 31,* 309–337.

Lawrence, B. S. (1996). Organizational age norms: Why is it so hard to know one when you see one? *Gerontologist, 36,* 206–220.

Neugarten, B. L. (1968). The awareness of middle age. In B.L. Neugarten (Ed.), *Middle age and aging: A reader in social psychology* (pp. 93–98). Chicago: University of Chicago Press.

O'Rand, A. M., Henretta, J. C., & Krecker, M. L. (1992). Family pathways to retirement. In M. Szinovacz, D. J. Ekerdt, & B. H. Vinick (Eds.), *Families and retirement* (pp. 81–98). Newbury Park, CA: Russell Sage.

Pienta, A. M., Burr, J. A., & Mutchler, J. E. (1994). Women's labor force participation in later life: The effects of early work and family experiences. *Journal of Gerontology: Social Sciences, 49,* S231–S239.

Pimental, E. E. (1996). Effects of adolescent acheivement and family goals on the early adult transition. In J. T. Mortimer & M. D. Finch (Eds.), *Adolescents, work and family: An intergenerational developmental analysis.* Newbury Park, CA: Sage.

Prentis, R. S. (1992). *Passages of retirement: Personal histories of struggle and success.* Westport, CT: Greenwood Press.

Reno, V. P. (1993). The role of pensions in retirement income: Trends and questions. *Social Security Bulletin, 56*(1), 29–43.

Ruhm, C. J. (1990). Career jobs, bridge employment, and retirement. In P. Doeringer (Ed.), *Bridges to retirement: Older workers in a changing labor market* (pp. 92–107). Ithaca, NY: ILR Press.

Sewell, W. H. (1992). A theory of structure: Duality, agency, and transformation. *American Journal of Sociology, 98,* 1–29.

Slevin, K. F., & Wingrove, C. R. (1995). Women in retirement: A review and critique of empirical research since 1976. *Sociological Inquiry, 65,* 1–20.

Streib, G. F., & Schneider, C. J. (1971). *Retirement in American society: Impact and process.* Ithaca, NY: Cornell University Press.

Todd, A. J. (1915). Old age and the industrial scrap heap. *Publications of the American Statistical Association, 14,* 550–566.

Wise, D. A. (1993). Firm pension policy and early retirement. In A. B. Atkinson & M. Rein (Eds.), *Age, work, and Social Security* (pp. 51–88). New York: St. Martin's Press.

Woods, J. R. (1994). Pension coverage among the baby boomers: Initial findings from a 1993 survey. *Social Security Bulletin, 57*(3), 12–25.

Commentary: The Usefulness of Age Norms in Retirement Research

Mark D. Hayward

E kerdt revisits the issue of the role of social norms in life course research in his assessment of "Workplace Norms for the Timing of Retirement" (this volume, chapter 3). His work extends a rich intellectual tradition in aging and life course research. Social norms have played an important role in theorizing about the organization and age differentiation of the life course, and indeed, the much-referenced "life course" perspective rests heavily on this concept. Social norms embody shared expectations about the appropriate time frame bracketing life course transitions such as retirement. Moreover, it is assumed that timing norms are supported by informal sanctions that come into play when transitions occur outside the proper time frame (e.g., Elder 1975, 1978; Neugarten, Moore, & Lowe, 1965).

Partial support of this research was provided by a grant from the National Institute on Aging (R01 AG11758) and NICHD Center grant support to the Population Research Institute (5 P30 HD28263).

Ekerdt, in his analysis, argues that social norms are fundamental elements in understanding both the timing of retirement (e.g., what is the appropriate age to end the work career?) and alternative modes of retirement (e.g., an abrupt end to a career vs. a longer process of job changes). Aware of the life course schemas defined by retirement norms, individuals are presumed to make retirement-related decisions over a long segment of the work career, and these decisions channel workers toward particular retirement outcomes. In many ways, retirement can be viewed from this perspective as a consolidating force in an individual's work career. Individuals are assumed to make career decisions and engage in preparatory behaviors based on the internalization of norms regarding when and how the work career should end. Alternative career decisions are thus made based on conformity with shared expectations about appropriate behavior leading to retirement.

This view of retirement is contrasted in Ekerdt's discussion, albeit somewhat cursorily, with what has become in recent years the dominant conceptual view of retirement in the economic and sociological literatures—that is, retirement decisions are time-limited, rational choices between work and nonwork alternatives. Although social organizational and institutional factors may come into play by affecting an individual's characteristics or by placing constraints on avenues of action, the rational choice perspective portrays the individual as maximizing utility and being a key agent of behavior.

At first glance, this reconsideration of social norms in retirement research is appealing. Certainly, for sociologists, it reintroduces a long-term and closely held sociological concept as a way to better understand the later stages of the life course. Yet, despite a tendency to embrace this attractive concept in sociological theorizing, the utility of social norms is worth a closer look before jettisoning the current utility maximizing models of the human capital, social organizational and institutional determinants of retirement. The central purpose of this chapter is to evaluate the theoretical integrity of the concept of the social norms of retirement. In particular, the discussion focuses on what constitutes a social norm of retirement, what is the utility of social norms in explaining variations in retirement behavior, and what empirical evidence exists in support of this theoretical construct. The issue of operationalizing social norms of retirement in empirical research is also briefly discussed.

THE THEORETICAL INTEGRITY OF THE
SOCIAL NORMS OF RETIREMENT

To evaluate the theoretical usefulness of the general concept of social norms, it is important to note its distinguishing features: (a) a shared evaluation of what ought to be; and (b) the application of sanctions to produce the valued behavior. In terms of retirement, the first feature might be conceptualized in terms of some shared or collective view that individuals *ought* to retire and at certain ages. In Ekerdt's analysis, much as in other analyses of social norms (e.g., Modell, 1980; Neugarten et al., 1965), evidence of this shared view of retirement is based on the Health and Retirement Survey item: "On your main job, what is the usual retirement age for people who work with you or have the same kind of job?" Thus customary age is presumed to reveal the presence of a social norm of retirement, and almost 75% of the sample of men and women ages 51–61 report a usual age for retirement.

Note, however, that although three-quarters of the sample recognize a usual age, 50% expect to retire at the usual age if they plan to "stop work altogether," 45% expect to retire at the usual age if they plan to "work fewer hours," and only 31% expect to retire at the usual age if they plan to "change (the) kind of work" or work for themselves. This comparison illustrates that retirement behavior is more variable than the presumed social norm of retirement, and the variability of behavior surrounding the usual age depends on the manner of retirement. Nonetheless, these findings point to a clustering of retirement behavior surrounding usual ages of retirement.

Is this statistical regularity in behavior sufficient to infer the presence of a social norm of retirement? Remember, a defining criterion of a social norm is what "ought to be." Here, the Health and Retirement Survey (HRS) data provide less convincing evidence of a social norm of retirement. For example, individuals were queried about their agreement with two statements: (1) "in decisions about promotion, my employer gives younger people preference over older people"; and (2) "my coworkers make older workers feel that they ought to retire before age 65." Approximately 85% of the respondents gave responses disagreeing with these statements, indicating that older workers are not devalued in the workplace either by employers or by fellow workers. Although the measurement of what "ought to be" is imperfect, the evidence in support of the presence of a social norm based on this criterion is not overwhelming.

Why then the congruence between the usual age of retirement and individuals' retirement expectations? Usual age denotes regularity in *behavior*. It identifies what workers do or what they will do—it is not necessarily a collective evaluation of what they *ought* to do. In this sense, usual age documents statistical norms of behavior. As noted by Marini (1984, p. 232):

> A norm . . . is not simply a regularity in behavior, represented by a statistical average or typical value. Behavior that is typical may not be normative, and behavior that is unusual is not necessarily nonnormative. Observed regularity in preferred or actual behavior during the [life course] is likely to reflect collectively held values arising from the internalization of predominant behavior patterns, or customs. This regularity may not indicate that a role change ought to *occur* at a particular age, with negative consequences if it does not.

Marini's argument brings us back to the second element of a social norm—the application of informal sanctions when individuals deviate from the expected course of retirement behavior. Two related issues are pertinent. First, what collective of individuals is presumed to be applying the informal sanctions? And, second, what form might those informal sanctions take? The reference group is presumably the collective of persons who share a belief about what ought to occur. Given that retirement is a defining element of the work career, it is plausible to assume that the core reference group is made up of other workers at the job. Other reference groups (e.g., family members and friends) also potentially play a role, yet fellow workers are more likely to be the central group in defining what ought to be with regard to retirement norms. If such is the case, then what are those informal sanctions potentially available to fellow workers to ensure conformity with the retirement norms? Conceivably, these sanctions could take the form of social stigma, discrimination, and other interpersonal means of devaluation.

What evidence is there in the HRS in support of the role of the workplace collective in applying informal sanctions? Let's return to the two items mentioned earlier: (1) whether individuals believed that their employer gives younger people preference over older people, and (2) whether coworkers believed older workers should retire before age 65.

Approximately 85% of the HRS sample disagrees with both of these statements. These findings indicate little support for the application of two
types of informal sanctions to ensure retirement norms. Neither social
stigma nor discrimination appears to be a significant force to ensure retirement conformity in the workplace.

Even granting the possible existence of social norms of retirement,
the role of social norms as an agent of change is ambiguous. Norms, by
virtue of their consensual nature, are typically a conservative social force
preserving the existing social structure. Thus social norms are most appropriate as explanations of social inertia—why social institutions such as
the life course do *not change*. Retirement as a social institution, however,
has undergone substantial changes in recent decades (e.g., Hayward,
Crimmins, & Wray, 1994; Hayward, Grady, & McLaughlin, 1988;
Henretta, 1992). Henretta's work, for example, documents that while
retirement has become a more universal experience of the life course in
the United States since the mid-20th century, it also has become more
variable as the range in timing has increased.

Similarly, Hayward and his colleagues (1988, 1994) found evidence
of substantial changes in the timing and organization of the work-to-retire-
ment transition. During the 1940–70 period, the volume of retirement
increased substantially, and retirement was increasingly seen as a permanent life course status preceding death. Retirement was becoming a
universalistic aspect of the American life course. In the 1970s, this pattern changed. Workers continued to experience contractions in their main
careers; yet these contractions were offset by an expansion of postretirement labor force activity. It became increasingly unclear, therefore,
whether a given retirement marked the end of the work career. Given these
shifts toward increased universality, though greater ambiguity in what
defines retirement as a life course stage, the role of social norms as an
explanatory mechanism is doubtful. Indeed, given the pace of historical
change in retirement behavior in the United States, it is difficult to conceive of retirement norms emerging even as legitimizing agents.

CONCLUSIONS

Ekerdt's proposal to bring social norms back into sociological theorizing about retirement is attractive, given the historical role of social norms

in aging and life course research. Normative conceptions of the life course abound in reference to the transition to adulthood and to the transition to old age. Although social norms of retirement undoubtedly exist in some form, both the theoretical arguments and Ekerdt's own empirical analysis of the HRS suggest that social norms offer little leverage in understanding retirement behavior. Without intending to do so, Ekerdt's normative view of retirement potentially detracts from the institutions of the welfare state, labor market conditions, and the workplace factors that shape the retirement experiences of older workers. The complex interplay of these institutional and social organizational actors has combined to create not only retirement as a universal life course stage, but also a diversity of age schedules and modes of retirement.

It is misleading to construe statistical norms as social norms. Statistical regularities most assuredly denote common pathways to retirement. But such pathways are not necessarily bolstered by social norms. Statistical norms, themselves, may be of significance in understanding retirement behavior. Statistical norms can serve as a useful standard against which individuals' benchmark retirement decisions are based on their own set of circumstances. They enhance the certainty of individuals' decisions by providing information about significant others' behavior in similar circumstances. Statistical norms pertaining to the dominant behavioral patterns of significant others can be internalized through learning or socialization. These norms may be instrumental in shaping individuals' own retirement preferences. Statistical norms, therefore, often stand "side by side" with rationalized, individual decision making.

Ultimately, the test for the usefulness of social norms in retirement research lies in researchers' abilities to measure them. Indeed, it is not clear that retirement social norms have ever been measured successfully. Marini (1984) outlines a range of issues involved in operationalization of social norms in general. Briefly, the measurement issues parallel the theoretical issues raised in this chapter. Measurement of retirement social norms requires both information on the degree of consensus on some valued behavior within a particular population group and information on the strength and form of sanctions invoked when behaviors are at odds with the collective's shared value.

Although it is beyond the scope of this chapter to outline the measurement design to evaluate retirement norms, the development of social normative theories of retirement needs to occur concurrently with the development of measurement strategies to test effectively for social normative effects. Moreover, it is essential to develop measures of social norms that allow researchers to evaluate the effects of norms above and beyond the effects accruing from the micro- and macro-determinants in the utility maximizing models. The open arena of hypothesis testing is the fundamental foundation on which to evaluate the additional leverage that a social normative approach provides in understanding retirement.

REFERENCES

Elder, G. H., Jr. (1975). Age differentiation and the life course. *Annual Review of Sociology, 1,* 165–190. Palo Alto, CA: Annual Reviews.

Elder, Glen H., Jr. (1978). Approaches to social change and the family. *American Journal of Sociology, 84*(Suppl.), 1–38.

Hayward, M. D., Crimmins, E. M., & Wray, L. A. (1994). The relationship between retirement life cycle changes and older men's labor force participation rates. *Journal of Gerontology: Social Sciences, 49,* S219–S230.

Hayward, M. D., Grady, W. R., & McLaughlin, S. D. (1988). Changes in the retirement process among older men in the United States: 1972–1980. *Demography, 25,* 271–386.

Henretta, J. C. (1992). Uniformity and Diversity: Life course institutionalization and late-life work exit. *Sociological Quarterly, 33,* 265–279.

Marini, M. M. (1984). Age and sequencing norms in the transition to adulthood. *Social Forces, 63,* 229–244.

Modell, J. (1980). Normative aspects of American marriage timing since World War II. *Journal of Family History, 5,* 210–234.

Neugarten, B. L., Moore, J. W., & Lowe, J. D. (1965). Age norms, age constraints, and adult socialization. *American Journal of Sociology, 70,* 710–717.

Commentary:
The Decision to Retire or Work

Harvey L. Sterns

T he potential retirees of today may get a very mixed set of messages regarding continued work or retirement from their workplace and society at large. There is much to be said in support of the anticipatory period of the retirement decision as presented by Dr. Eckert in this volume. Clearly, people are trying to make meaningful decisions about their futures. The decision to continue to work, modify work, or retire is influenced by many factors. Time left (at work or in the labor force) is part of a decision process influenced by eligibility for Social Security, employer pension, and norms (Sheppard, 1991). This is an "extended stream of decision making for retirement that can be observed in the changing plans and intention toward retirement that workers entertain over time" (p. 130). The emphasis is on extended decision making and interim preparation with another emphasis on people's agency.

Potential working years range from approximately age 18 to the end of the life span. Industrial gerontology has extended career development concerns from occupational choice and entering the workforce to the study of mid and late careers, including retirement issues (Sterns & Alexander, 1987). Authors such as Havighurst (1982) have taken a life-span approach to the discussion of careers. Havighurst emphasized typical linear career patterns, although he devoted some discussion to people who "have a sequence of different jobs" because of personal factors or external job market changes. Sterns and Alexander reviewed the issues relating to industrial gerontology by emphasizing the decisions of workers throughout the life span. They emphasize that career decisions are not limited to a specific age or stage; decisions are not age-specific. A more recent review by Forteza and Prieto (1994) examines the changes that occur in the life cycle and the implications for the labor cycle. They include an international flavor by considering industrial countries as opposed to just the United States. By adopting a life-span orientation, these reviews consider a range of ages and issues. A life-span perspective emphasizes the continuity of change as individuals move through adulthood and older adulthood.

Psychosocial definitions of older workers (Sterns & Doverspike, 1989) are based on social perceptions, including age typing of occupations, perceptions of the older worker, and the aging of knowledge, skill, and ability sets. The individual's self-perception is also considered. How individuals perceive themselves and their careers at a given age may be congruent or incongruent with societal images. Relatively little research has addressed the quite basic question of how we know when workers will perceive themselves, or be perceived by others, as old. Timing norms are discussed as prescriptions about when and how one retires, influences by level of commitment to the work organization, modes and styles of exiting, and pension incentives. Timing norms become the "bearer of societal, firm level, or reference group preferences for retirement" (p.106) in the Eckert analysis. His analysis of the Health and Refinement Study (HRS) 1992 baseline wave (aged 51–61) reveals support for the concept of a usual age for retirement that may vary in different work settings and occupational categories. Plan incentives clearly influence timing of retirement behavior, and 85% of workers reported that they planned to leave at or prior to the local, usual age for retirement. In addition, over 80% of respondents did not plan to work beyond the usual age.

Lawrence (1987) broadly defines age effects as outcomes within an organization attributed to the age of employees. In her discussion, chronological age and age distributions impact age norms. Age distributions are the actual age distributions in the organization, while the age norms are shared perceptions of the normal ages with an organization or role. Individual age expectations are also important because they reflect the degree to which the individual applies the social norm to himself or herself. Age norms are likely to occur when the range of perceived ages is narrow and agreement on typical ages is high. Organizational tenure is expected to increase recognition of age group distinctions as individuals of roughly the same age and organizational tenure will have shared history and experience. These age norms may provide a context that influences judgments about individuals. This approach supports Eckart's (chapter 3, this volume) analysis.

One can look to parents and peers for models, but each person's circumstances, feelings, and situations may be very different. Recent discussions of the future of retirement (Morris, 1996) tell us that nothing less than a paradigm shift is under way that will affect how people will have to save and invest, how they will fantasize about and plan for the future. Uncertainty regarding what present and future employment will offer is true for individuals who presently have job security, stable working conditions, and choices about their retirement. This can change quickly with corporate buyouts, new public policies, and changing attitudes on the part of workers themselves. The possibility of losing one's job, being faced with an early buyout, or uncertainty regarding future prospects are all part of the current scene. At the same time, there are capable people continuing in fairly traditional careers. Others may lose jobs but are reentering the job search finding that it is a major challenge to find a new position at the same or better salary. Often the person has to settle for a reduced salary and reduced benefits, if any. It appears that about 10% to 20% of older adults want to work beyond traditional retirement age. In any case, it is important to focus on individuals who will continue to work.

Sterns and Sterns (1995) have stated that people may not only wish to work longer, they may have to. They used an early report of the recent survey of 12,600 Americans, which Juster undertook on behalf of the National Institute of Aging, the University of Michigan, and the Alliance for Aging Research (Rich, 1993). This is the same database as that in the Eckert analysis. Reported results indicated that a significant proportion of the next generation of retirees will have few resources on which to retire. The survey results indicated that, in the 1990s, 40% of Americans aged 51 to 60 who were still working would have no pension income other than Social Security were they to retire. Twenty percent of all households had no assets (house, investments, or savings). The survey also indicated that 14% of the respondents had no health insurance and 20% were disabled. All of these individuals, regardless of their health and disability status, will feel the financial pressure to continue working.

The Juster study also reported some positive trends about older people in their 50's. Most were healthy, and many were in good shape economically. The median household income was $37,500, and median net assets, including home and cars, totaled $80,000. But substantial blocks of people in their 50's were not well off, especially among minority groups. While most people were found to be better off financially than their counterparts of decades ago, they may not be ready to face retirement. A logical conclusion from the survey findings is that many older people will continue to work because they will not have the resources to retire (Rich, 1993).

Until recently, many people, now ranging in age from the forties to the mid-60's, had felt that they would have a choice about working after the normal retirement age. This belief was based on the expectation of an expanding economy and a strong economic climate. Many middle-aged and older workers are now surprised by the large numbers of early buyouts, layoffs, and the general trend of downsizing, even by successful companies.

It is apparent that the relationship between employer and employees no longer promises lifelong employment. This places middle-aged and older workers in the position of having to be responsible for their own careers, maximizing the employment opportunities presented to them, and competing with people of all ages in finding new employment.

People will have to fight harder to remain in the workforce longer. The present 50- and 60-year-olds were hired at a time when they could choose among jobs. They were a part of the work-force when there was accelerated growth and numerous promotions. They had to deal with the slower promotions and salary increases of the 1980s, but still expected that they would have control over how long they worked and when they exited the work-force. At the peak of their careers, they now have much less control or no control at all.

Employment benefits, especially retirement benefits, will also change in the future. Individuals may have to pay or copay into pension and health benefit programs both before and after retirement. This will leave fewer discretionary resources in retirement.

As a result, baby boomers may need or desire to supplement their pension or benefits. Dychtwald proposes that the baby boomers are more likely "to do their own thing" and will be comfortable breaking the retirement norm (Dychtwald & Flower, 1989). A new trend toward more cyclic lifestyles (multiple periods of training, work, and leisure) is, and will continue to become, more common. The increasing pressures of changing technology and the need for continuous training to remain competitive in the job market are the forces that will drive multiple-cycle careers (Sterns, 1986).

Older adults have many different reasons for staying longer in the workforce. They want to earn money and have health insurance, and they seek other intrinsic benefits, such as developing new skills, using time productively, and feeling useful and needed. Work allows people to stay in touch with current developments; it provides structure to older people and helps them retain a sense of doing something worthwhile.

People who enjoy work will want to continue to maintain the social interactions and relationships they enjoyed with coworkers, and they will want to continue to participate in meaningful activity. The work one does contributes to identity and a sense of self (Sterns, Matheson, & Schwartz, 1997). An increasing concern for health and youthfulness may also contribute to longer career patterns. Being retired may conflict with a person's youthful image, leading to postponing retirement. We can expect older workers who have expertise to take advantage of additional training in their own or related disciplines and take on new challenges, such as consulting (Kelly, 1971).

Many women, having entered the workforce in midlife, may want to work longer for many of the same reasons as mentioned previouly. They may need to work longer to receive benefits in retirement. A majority of older adults are women, and 60% of women 45 to 60 are employed. Women's participation varies by industry. It is expected that 75% of women will be in the workforce by the year 2000. Women have become a major component of the workforce and will become a larger component in the next decade.

Recently, Barth, McNaught, and Rizzi (1995) and McNaught, Barth, and Henderson (1989) have raised the issue of where the future labor supply should be drawn from now that the workforce expansion may no longer be fueled by the baby boom generation and women shifting into working roles. The 1991 Commonwealth Fund Productive Aging Survey (CFPAS), which interviewed 2,999 older Americans, indicated that 9% (75 and older) to 12% (65 to 74) of nonworking older adults were willing and able to work. Depending on assumptions made about the health of older Americans and acceptable working conditions, the CFPAS results indicated that between 1.9 million and 5.4 million older adults are capable, available, and interested in working.

The CFPAS was conducted in order to understand the interest level and circumstances under which older adults would be willing to work. It examined daily activities, employment, and work attitudes of men and women over the age of 55. Twenty-seven percent of the respondents reported having a job for which they were paid. Those who were employed worked an average of 37.4 hours (median = 39.9).

To determine if respondents were satisfied with the hours worked, they were also asked how many hours they would like to work. The average (29.5 hours) was considerably lower than actual hours worked (median = 34.0 hours); 22% of respondents wanted to work fewer than 15 hours per week, while 29% wanted to work more than 40 hours.

A majority of older adults seemed content to have retired and wanted to remain retired. For the 72% of the sample who were not employed, 73% of that group had not worked since 1985. The unemployed group were asked if they would prefer to be working: 31% responded "yes" and 4% responded "not sure."

The 31% who indicated they would work were asked, "If a suitable job were available in your area, would you be able to work or would it not be possible for your to work?" Forty-six percent said "yes, it would be possible." Fifty-one percent responded, "No, it would not be possible," and 3% responded "not sure." The large percentage of "not possibles" may be due to health or caretaker responsibilities, or other competing activities. Of those willing and able to work, two thirds were willing to work part time, and one third wanted more than 35 hours of work.

The CFPAS data implied that those older adults who are working would like to continue to work, but work fewer hours per week. Most older adults who were not working said they would like to remain retired. However, approximately 14% of those nonworking older adults said they would like to return to work. Based on this percentage, of the 32 million older adults who are currently not in the workforce, some 4.5 million are potential full- or part-time older adult employees.

Over the past 2 decades, employees' attitudes toward working have become increasingly more important to organizations in their efforts to predict worker behavior (Warr, 1994). General attitudes about work contribute to a desire to continue to work and to maintain the skills required to excel. The work environment also influences employees' attitudes about their job performance and whether they want to continue to work.

The desire to continue working in an organization has been researched under the topic of organizational commitment. Meyer and Allen (1984) distinguish between two dimensions of organizational commitment that affect work attitudes in different ways. The first, *continuance commitment* is the employee's perceived cost of leaving or a perceived lack of alternatives to make up for investments in the benefits of the current job. Individuals remain at work because they are not willing to risk loss of salary, health benefits, or pension investment. This aspect of organizational commitment is especially relevant to older adults. As workers increase their tenure with an organization, they may feel increasing continuance commitment because they have established a home and friendships in the area, have become specialized in a skill that they feel cannot be transferred, or believe that they could not get the same salary or benefits if they moved to a new organization.

Affective commitment, the second dimension of organizational commitment, refers to the employee's affective, or emotional, orientation to the organization. Affective commitment is concerned with the individuals' interest in the work and loyalty to the organization and its goals. This emotional tie to the organization motivates them to remain, not because they cannot afford to leave, but because they feel a sense of contribution and growth by staying with the organization. Other things being equal, an organization that encourages maintenance at one's job, provides challenging work, and offers opportunities to inject new ideas will not only be more likely to stay ahead of competitors, but will also reduce turnover and retain more productive employees.

An organization can measure the success of its efforts to improve the work environment by examining organization-based self-esteem (Pierce, Gardner, Cummings, & Dunham, 1989). Organization-based self-esteem is measured by the degree to which organization members believe they are valuable, worthwhile, and effectual employees (Pierce et al., 1989). Matherson (1991) studied the influence of organization-based self-esteem on job satisfaction and commitment. She divided the employees in a northeastern investment company into three groups (aged 20 to 35, aged

36 to 50, and aged 51 and older) and collected attitudinal information using a questionnaire and objective measures of absenteeism and turnover. She found that organization satisfaction, continuance commitment, and global self-esteem (a measure of a person's overall perceived self-worth) increased with age. However, after controlling for job and organizational tenure, two variables that have been found to be related to age, she found that only global self-esteem was significantly associated with age. Employees over age 50 had significantly higher global self-esteem than did younger age groups. Those who perceived that they were valuable as organizational members were more satisfied with their jobs and the organization, were committed to the organization in terms of both loyalty and their career investment (e.g., position, salary, seniority, and pension), and were less likely to leave.

Evidence is mounting that the intrinsic rewards of work—satisfaction, relationships with coworkers, and a sense of participating in meaningful activity—become more important as an individual ages. The abolishment of the mandatory retirement age allows working older adults to continue to participate in these benefits until they feel that they have the financial resources and personal network outside the workplace to retire (Brady, Fortinsky, Norland, & Eichar, 1989). Contemporary research has established that financial incentives influence retirement behavior, although the relative importance of economic factors compared to affective and social factors is not known (Ruhm, 1990). There is considerable disagreement about the effect of economic factors (Quinn & Burkhauser, 1990).

In surveys of employed adults, job satisfaction shows consistently that work-related attitudes are more positive with increasing age (Rhodes, 1983). Older adults may have a different perspective on work than younger adults. For older workers, survival needs are less likely to be urgent as they will probably have reached a maximum income for their jobs. Desire for more control over the job is still strong. However, older workers have seen less evidence that hard work leads to promotions, salary increases, or other rewards. Goals may not change with age, but expectations of achieving these outcomes can diminish.

Phillips, Barrett, and Rush (1978) found that older groups preferred more responsibility, interesting work, and attention demands, whereas younger workers preferred autonomy and social opportunities. Some studies have shown that motivation measures predict performance more for older adults than for younger adults. Younger workers may lack the knowledge to make accurate judgments about likelihoods of efforts paying off. Older workers report that job satisfaction is more closely related to intrinsic factors or internal rewards of work.

Organizational views toward older workers recognize that the effects of age and tenure are necessarily related (Sterns & Doverspike, 1989). Individuals age in both jobs and in organizations. An older worker has often spent a substantial amount of time in a job and substantially more in an organization. A definition of older worker based on the aging of individuals in organizational roles is more commonly discussed under the topics of seniority and tenure. The effects of aging may often be confounded by the effects of tenure and vice versa. Organizations, too, may age (Schrank & Waring, 1981). An organization may be perceived as old because of the average age of its members. As the average age of its members increases, new demands are placed on the organizational subsystems such as human resources.

The life-span approach to older workers (Sterns & Doverspike, 1989) advances the possibility for behavioral change at any point in the life cycle. Substantial individual differences in aging are recognized as vital in examining adult career patterns.

Three sets of factors are seen as affecting behavioral change during the life cycle.

1. The first set includes normative, age-graded biological and/or environmental determinants. These bear a strong relationship to chronological age.
2. The second set of factors includes normative, history-graded influences that affect most members of a cohort in similar ways.
3. The third set of events is nonnormative. This includes unique career and life changes, as well as individual health and stress-inducing events. The unique status of the individual is the result of the joint impact of these factors.

According to this approach, there are more individual differences as people grow older (Baltes, Reese, & Lipsitt, 1980).

These differences create difficulty in developing theories that adequately address the broad range of differences. Late careers are often more difficult to study than early careers because there is less consistency in the developmental tasks. For example, in early career, individuals must choose a career. In late career, a person may continue a career, start a new career, modify a career, or retire.

Bronte (1993) interviewed individuals who had long careers into their 80s and 90s. The participants are proof that it is possible to continue being creative and productive past age 65. They present a positive view of what can be accomplished late in one's career or even early in a career started late in life. While it is not a rigorously designed study, it provides portraits of individuals who break the stereotypes of older adult careers.

Although Bronte found a great deal of variety in careers, she identified three basic career patterns.

1. The "homesteaders" are individuals who stay in the same job or profession for their entire careers. Many of these individuals are in artistic or scientific fields. They are still deeply engaged in their careers and feel that they have more potential for growth.
2. The "transformers" change jobs once. Early transformers change careers shortly after starting an occupation. This process seems to be part of the trial-and-error process. In contrast, late transformers tended to be well established financially and personally, giving them the freedom to pursue another interest later in life.
3. The "explorers" changed careers from as few as 3 to as many as 10 times. The reasons for the shifts were varied as were the career paths.

Bronte's study illustrates the variability in career pattern and ages of career peaks and contributions.

Early models of career development were linear, which assumed individuals moved through predictable career stages and then retirement. For older adults, maintaining skills for a period of time and then declining was the predicted pattern. This notion that career stages are linked to age will lead practitioners to incorrectly develop career development opportunities that are congruent with the age and stage of various cohorts. These models ignore individual differences and the contributions that older workers make. People may be aware of norms and expectations regarding their expected retirement. At the same time, workers may have the options of part-time or full-time work in the same career, in a new career, or a new job in the later part of their lives.

REFERENCES

Baltes, P. B., Reese, H. W., & Lipsitt, L. P. (1980). Lifespan developmental psychology. *Annual Review of Psychology,* 31, 65–110.

Barth, M. C., McNaught, W., & Rizzi, P. (1995). Older Americans as workers. In S. Bass (Ed.), *Older and active* (pp. 35–70). New Haven: Yale University Press.

Brady, E. M., Fortinsky, R. H., Norland, S., & Eichar, D. (1989). *Predictors of success among older workers in new jobs.* Final Report. University of Southern Maine: Human Services Development Institute.

Bronte, L. (1993). *The longevity factor.* New York: HarperCollins.

Dychtwald, K., & Flower, J. (1989). *Age wage: The challenges and opportunities of an aging America.* Los Angeles: Jeremy P. Tarcher.

Forteza, J. A., & Prieto, J. M. (1994). Aging and work behavior. In M. Dunnette, L. Hough, & H. Triandis (Eds.), *Handbook of industrial and organizational psychology* (Vol. 4, pp. 447–483). Palo Alto, CA: Consulting Psychologists Press.

Havighurst, R. J. (1982). The world of work. In B. B. Wolman (Ed.), *Handbook of developmental psychology* (pp. 771–787). Englewood Cliffs, NJ: Prentice-Hall.

Lawrence, B. S. (1987). An organizational theory of age effects. *Research in the Sociology of Organizations, 5,* 37–71.

Kelly, H. H. (1971). *Attribution and social interaction.* Morristown, N J: General Learning Press.

Matherson, N. S. (1991). *The influence of organizational-based self-esteem on satisfaction and commitment: An analysis of age differences.* Unpublished doctoral dissertation, University of Akron, Akron, OH.

McNaught, W., Barth, C. B. & Henderson, P. H. (1989). The human resource potential of older Americans. *Human Resource Management, 28, 47–64.*

Meyer, J. P., & Allen, N. J. (1984). Testing the "side-bet theory" or organizational commitment: Some methodological considerations. *Journal of Applied Psychology, 69,* 372–378.

Morris, B. (1996,). The future of retirement: It's not what you think. *Fortune,* pp. 86–94.

Pierce, J. L., Gardner, D. G., Cummings, L. L., & Dunham, R. B. (1989). Organization-based self-esteem: Construct definition measurement and validation. *Academy of Management Journal, 32,* 622–648.

Phillips, J. S., Barrett, G. V., & Rush, M. C. (1978). Job structure and age satisfaction. *Aging and Work, 1,* 109–119.

Quinn, J. F., & Burkhauser, R. V. (1990). Work and retirement. In R. H. Binstock & L. K. George (Eds.), *Aging and social sciences* (pp. 308–327). San Diego, CA: Academic Press.

Rhodes, S. R. (1983). Age-related differences in work attitudes and behavior: A review and conceptual analysis. *Psychological Bulletin, 93,* 328–367.

Rich, S. (1993, June 13). A grim outlook for retirement. *Akron Beacon Journal,* p. A12.

Ruhm, C. J. (1990). Determinants of the timing of retirement. In P. B. Doeringer, (Ed.), *Bridges to retirement* (pp. 23–32). Ithaca, NY: Cornell University Press.

Schrank, H. T., & Waring, J. M. (1981). Aging and work organizations. In B. B. Hess & K. Bonds (Eds.), *Leading edges: Recent research on psychosocial aging* (pp. 99–118). Washington, DC: U.S. Department of Health and Human Services, National Institute on Aging.

Sheppard, H. (1991). The United States: The privatization of exit. In M. Kohli, M. Rein, A. M. Guillemard, & H. Van Gunsteren (Eds.), *Time for retirement* (pp. 252–283). Cambridge University Press.

Sterns, H. L. (1986). Training and re-training adult and older adult workers. In J. E. Birren, P. K. Robinson, & J. E. Livingston (Eds.), *Age, health, and employment* (pp. 99–113). Englewood Cliffs, NJ: Prentice-Hall.

Sterns, H. L., & Alexander, R. A. (1987). Industrial gerontology: The aging individual and work. In K. W. Schaie (Ed.), *Annual review of gerontology and geriatrics* (pp. 243–264). New York: Springer Publishing Company.

Sterns, H. L., & Doverspike, D. (1989). Aging and the training and learning process in organizations. In I. Goldstein & R. Katzel (Eds.) *Training and development in work organizations.* San Francisco, CA: Jossey-Bass.

Sterns, H. L., Matheson, N. K., & Schwartz, L. S. (1997). Work and retirement. In K. Ferraro (Ed.), *Gerontology: Perspectives and issues* (2nd ed., pp. 171–192). New York: Springer Publishing Company.

Sterns, H. L., & Sterns, A. R. (1995). Age, health and employment capability of older Americans. In S. Bass, M. Barth, & B. McNaught, (Eds.), *Older and active* (pp. 10–34). New Haven, CT: Yale University Press.

Warr, P (1994). Age and employment. In M. Dunnette, L. Hough, & H. Triandis (Eds.), *Handbook of industrial and organizational psychology* (Vol. 4, pp. 485–550). Palo Alto, CA: Consulting Psychologists Press.

CHAPTER 4

Organizational Structure of the Workplace and the Older Worker

James L. Farr, Paul E. Tesluk, and Stephanie R. Klein

A number of important demographic, economic, and workplace trends have made understanding issues related to the older worker in the organizational context an increasingly critical area for both human resource practice and research. First, organizations are facing a combination of demographic trends that have resulted in a situation in which older workers are accounting for an increasingly larger proportion of the workforce. In fact, workers 55 and older are the fastest growing segment of the workforce. By the year 2010, the median age of the workforce will rise to 40 (Capowski, 1994). This is due to the aging of the baby-boomer generation (those born between the end of World War II and 1964) and a decrease in the number of young adults (ages 20–34) entering the labor market as a result of the relatively small numbers of births between 1964 and the 1980s (often known as the "baby-bust" generation) (Greller & Nee, 1989; Guzzo, Nelson, & Noonan, 1992; Park, 1994).

As a result of the workforce becoming increasingly older and with fewer younger workers, a number of pension funds have become over-burdened, and now the Social Security system has become threatened. With their financial security following retirement more tenuous, it is likely that many employees will want to work beyond traditional retirement ages (Park, 1994). Trends in the workplace present numerous challenges to older workers, however. As organizational downsizing and restructur-ing activities continue, many organizations are using early-retirement strategies and even layoffs to reduce layers of management and to stream-line middle-management levels (Jarratt & Coates, 1995). These work-force reductions often are targeted at the types of jobs frequently occupied by older workers (Capowski, 1994). In the 1990s, displacement and unem-ployment rates have grown faster for older workers than for other age groups (Herz, 1995).

Another important workplace trend that has direct implications for older workers is the changing nature of work. For example, workers can no longer anticipate a career with a single company; rather, multiple careers and frequent job transitions are becoming the norm (Price & Vinokur, 1995). In addition, the pattern of jobs is changing from indus-trial manufacturing to service jobs. This means that younger and older workers will be less likely to perform manual labor, but, instead, will have to rely on cognitive and interpersonal skills (Warr, 1994a). Moreover, the shift to knowledge-based work that is required of new information and computer technologies (Zuboff, 1988) will require older workers to possess a new set of knowledge and skills.

These interrelated demographic, economic, and workplace trends have numerous implications for organizations and employees. Organizations need to be concerned with performance-related issues that may be affected by having a workforce that is composed of a larger per-centage of older workers. How and to what extent is age related to job performance, work-related attitudes, work motivation, participation in skills updating and training activities, and employees' physical and psy-chological health and well-being? These are critical questions that have direct implications for organizational functioning and effectiveness. They raise the issue of how organizations can structure themselves to facilitate the work and well-being of older workers.

Another important area of concern deals with the topic of age dis-crimination. With the 1986 amendment to the Age Discrimination in

Employment Act (ADEA), which prohibited employers from using mandatory-retirement policies, the decision to retire is largely in the hands of employees themselves (Avolio, Waldman, & McDaniel, 1990). Although corporate restructuring and downsizing and accompanying buyouts and layoffs have meant that many older workers are tending to retire earlier from their long-tenure, career jobs, many are choosing to return to work either as full- or part-time employees in new jobs. Thus the labor force participation rates of early retirees (those under age 65) has increased in recent years (Herz, 1995; Kramer, 1995). If these trends continue, employers will encounter an increasingly older workforce. Therefore, employers need to be concerned with the possibility of age discrimination in areas such as hiring, promotions, training opportunities, and terminations by taking steps to minimize its occurrence and defend against possible age-discrimination suits that may be filed under the ADEA. The dramatic increase in the number of age-discrimination cases that have been filed in recent years and the fact that approximately three fourths of all older workers believe that they have been discriminated against in some way in their employment are testimonials to this concern (Bird & Fisher, 1986; Sparrow & Davies, 1988). Moreover, the number of age-discrimination cases being filed actually appears to be increasing in the 1990s as early retirement incentive plans and downsizing activities continue (Capowski, 1994).

In order to meet these issues and challenges, organizations need to develop structures, practices, policies, and procedures that create a work environment that maximizes the strengths of older workers in terms of their performance, work attitudes and motivation, and physical and psychological well-being. The fact that most organizations are ill prepared to meet the impending challenges associated with older workers is a point that has been raised recently by practitioners (Buonocore, 1992; Capowski, 1994). Until now, little research has been conducted relating organizational features to the older worker that can be used to guide the development and implementation of effective human resource management practices for the aging workforce (Warr, 1994a).

An examination of the range of organizational factors that may affect older workers in various ways requires some type of a theoretical orientation or guiding framework. Systems theory (Katz & Kahn, 1978) is especially useful for understanding how organizational structures, practices, policies, and procedures fit together across levels of the organization to operate in an interrelated fashion. A systems perspective is particularly useful, therefore, for making recommendations to organizations on how to develop structures and practices that combine and mutually reinforce each other to support the work of older employees. Research into organizational structures and practices and of the older worker that adopts a systems perspective can benefit theory as well. Very little of the existing research on aging has been conducted in organizational settings; most research has taken place in laboratory environments and has considered a rather limited range of variables (Warr, 1994a). Thus there is a need for research that examines how organizationally relevant variables (e.g., structures and practices) operate as environmental factors to influence older employees' performance, behaviors, and attitudes. Much of the research relating to age and work has also been cross-sectional rather than longitudinal in design (Forteza & Prieto, 1994). A systems orientation places a greater orientation on the long-term influences of environmental factors, continuous patterns of behavior, and physiological changes on worker behaviors and attitudes, however. This type of approach is also needed in understanding the relationship between organizational structures and older employees (Warr, 1994b).

Other important theoretical questions that arise concern the extent to which basic relationships between variables such as age and performance on a given task are modifiable by organizational conditions. Finally, do older workers' personal attributes interact with features of the environment in a way that shapes their work behaviors, attitudes, and motivations? What individual characteristics are particularly important and with what types of organizational conditions do they interact?

These important practical and theoretical questions require a comprehensive course of research that is now in an early stage. The intent of this chapter is to offer an integration and review of the literature that has considered the relationship between organizational structures and practices and the older worker. Following this integration, we offer suggestions to guide future research and practice that are organized around the general question of how organizations can structure themselves to support older employees.

Our integration is organized around a systems theory-based model that attempts to integrate the range of findings into a more coherent perspective. The model resembles an onion and is presented in Figure 4.1. The different layers represent the levels in the larger work environment that indirectly and directly affect the older worker. At the outermost layers of the model, macrofactors such as organizational design, structure, and strategy serve to specify the range of possible technologies, work practices, policies, procedures, and human resource activities in an organization. For instance, many organizations are currently undergoing a shift from hierarchical, rigid structures designed to maximize productive efficiency to more flexible designs, flatter structures, and strategies designed to promote innovation in an increasingly competitive and fast-paced technological and business environment. These changes in basic organizational structures and designs require changes in work organization, organizational policies, and human resource practices. Job descriptions now include a wider range of tasks, work is more often team based, and policies and practices are designed to encourage active participation and continuous learning on the part of employees (Lawler, 1992). Changes in organizational and human resource policies, practices, and procedures may be experienced by older workers through their immediate work environment, for instance, by changing work-group norms and climate, the nature of supervision, and the specific types of tasks required in their jobs. These types of changes also may have more direct effects on older workers, for example, in the form of early retirement incentives that are offered as part of the organization's downsizing efforts. Together, these multiple layers of the "onion" function as the set of organizational "structures" that influence the older worker.[1] It is important to note that these structural influences operate at multiple layers in the organization and are interrelated. Finally, at the heart of the model is the older worker, who is certainly affected by the organizational environment, but whose personal attributes (e.g., experience, existing knowledge and skills, personality) interact with these organizational factors to influence performance, behaviors, and attitudes.

Before working through the layers of this model and reviewing the literature on organizational structures and practices and the older worker, we need to address the work-related implications of aging. In other words, what are the relationships between age and work outcomes such as performance, work attitudes and motivation, withdrawal behaviors, and skills updating and training? An initial, brief examination of these questions is useful because it suggests multiple areas where organizational structures and practices may be instrumental in influencing the effectiveness of older workers within a variety of criteria that are important to organizations and to workers themselves.

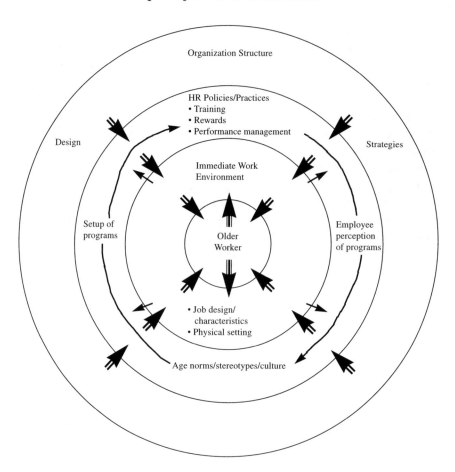

Figure 4.1 Model of organizational structure influences on older worker.

WORK-RELATED IMPLICATIONS OF AGING

The impact of aging in the work context spans a number of different outcomes including performance; work attitudes and motivation; accidents; withdrawal behaviors such as retirement, absenteeism, and turnover; and decisions to engage in skills updating and training. Our intent is not to provide a detailed review of the impact of aging on work performance, behaviors, and attitudes. Excellent reviews of this sort already exist (e.g., see Warr, 1994a). Instead, we describe the general nature of these relationships as they have been identified in the research literature and note that in each of these areas, organizational structures and practices can have important effects on moderating the relationships between age and work-related outcomes. We focus our attention on work-performance outcomes, but also suggest how organizational structures are important to work attitudes, withdrawal decisions, and training and skills updating.

Age and Work Performance

The relationship between age and job performance has been considered in a number of studies and meta-analyses. For instance, Avolio et al. (1990) found an age-performance correlation of .07 across five different occupational types; in a sample of firefighters, investigated by Jacobs, Hofmann, and Kriska (1990), the correlation was .17; and Cleveland and Shore (1992) identified a correlation of -.08 in a sample of employees that included a variety of job descriptions. Meta-analyses of the age–work-performance relationship have found an average correlation that is close to zero, while the range of correlations across studies has varied widely (McEvoy & Cascio, 1989; Waldman & Avolio, 1986). For instance, in McEvoy and Cascio's meta-analysis, the correlations ranged from -.44 to .66. Reviews of studies on age and job performance have made similar conclusions saying that, in sum, the results are "ambiguous" (Stagner, 1985) or "mixed" (Rhodes, 1983). This is surprising as cognitive abilities, which are highly correlated with job performance, have been found to decline with age (Park, 1994). In short, the best general conclusion that can be made regarding the relationship between age and performance is that there is no consistent relationship across settings.

Instead, it appears that the age–job performance relationship appears to be moderated by a number of other variables (Forteza & Prieto, 1994; Park, 1994; Waldman & Avolio, 1993; Warr, 1993, 1994a, 1994b). In their meta-analysis, Waldman and Avolio (1986) found that the type of work performed appeared to moderate the relationship between age and performance. A stronger negative relationship was found between age and work performance for those in nonprofessional jobs as compared to those in professional jobs. Avolio et al. (1990), in their study of workers from five different occupational groupings, also found evidence that performance tended to flatten or decline more quickly for employees in low-level clerical jobs as compared to higher level craft and service types of occupations. A similar finding was reported by Sparrow and Davies (1988), who reported that peak job performance in terms of quality occurred at a significantly higher average age for jobs that required greater task complexity.

One critical factor that may help explain this pattern is the level of complexity in different types of jobs (Avolio et al., 1990; Waldman & Avolio, 1993). More complex jobs provide employees with challenge and stimulation and can enhance skill development and maintain motivation over time, which leads to positive work performance (Schooler, 1987). In contrast, employees in jobs with low levels of complexity that involve simple and highly routine task functions may eventually feel unchallenged and bored and thus their performance may deteriorate over time. Less complex work also offers fewer opportunities for cognitive stimulation over the course of a career, which is important in maintaining the individual cognitive abilities over time that are necessary for continued effective work performance (Avolio & Waldman, 1987). Thus workers in more challenging jobs that require the continuous use and practice of critical cognitive abilities are able to perform effectively into old age.

There may be limits on the extent to which the complexity inherent in a job can help maintain effective performance as one ages, however. Warr (1994b) has reported that in jobs where there are high levels of cognitive demands in areas such as information processing and decision making, older workers are rated as less knowledgeable and autonomous than younger workers. It may be that there is a range of optimal levels of task complexity and cognitive demands that can provide workers the stimulation, motivation, and skill development that lead to continued effective performance but do not require extremely high levels of processing and working memory demands in terms of decision-making speed, concentration, and problem solving that may be taxed by the slight declines in older workers' basic cognitive abilities. Factors in the immediate work environment that can help ease processing demands (e.g., reduced time pressures, written presentation of materials and information) can help minimize these declines (Warr, 1994a).

Features of the work environment can vary in other ways to influence the age-work performance relationship. Warr (1994b) has suggested that the pace of change can be important. If a job undergoes continuous changes in terms of job demands and work procedures, an older worker has to unlearn the old, well-established routines and work methods and learn new ones, whereas a younger worker just coming into the job does not have to unlearn these outdated routines and is more likely to have been recently trained in the new knowledge and skills. Possibly compounding this problem is that older workers have been reported to have greater difficulty in unlearning old patterns of behavior and replacing them with new ones, especially if the new routines are inconsistent with the older ones (Sterns & Doverspike, 1989). Problems associated with maintaining professional competence for older workers are especially likely to be the case in certain technologically intensive occupations. For example, since about 1975, the half-life of an engineering degree (the amount of time necessary for half of an engineer's knowledge and skills to become obsolete) has decreased from 5 years to as little as $2^{1}/_{2}$ years in some fields of engineering (Kaufman, 1995). Older engineers may be at a particular disadvantage if they intend to stay in the technical side of operations.

The pace of change of the work environment may set off a negative spiral (Lindsley, Brass, & Thomas, 1995) for older workers between their self-efficacy regarding the development of new knowledge and skills, keeping up-to-date with new work practices, developing new knowledge and skills, and their subsequent performance (Warr, 1994b). The process may begin any number of ways. For instance, supervisors and managers may act on commonly held negative stereotypes that depict older workers as less flexible, adaptive, and interested in learning new skills (Buonocore, 1992; McEvoy & Cascio, 1989; Stagner, 1985). These stereotypes can spur a self-fulfilling prophecy as supervisors and managers fail to provide the environmental conditions necessary for maintaining professional competence, such as opportunities for retraining, social support for developing new knowledge and skills, and resources and conditions that facilitate participation in updating activities (Kozlowski & Farr, 1988; Kozlowski & Hults, 1987).

As a result of these conditions, older workers are likely to experience low levels of self-efficacy regarding their potential to succeed in retraining, decreased motivation to learn new knowledge and skills, and will be less likely to perceive the benefits of updating activities. Poor self-efficacy, low motivation, and lack of perceived benefits result in a failure to engage in the training that will lead to knowledge and skill development (Farr & Middlebrooks, 1990; Noe & Wilk, 1993). The downward spiral continues as older workers who do not keep pace with the rapid changes in work environments are likely to be viewed as less competent and motivated by their supervisors and managers and therefore may be provided fewer opportunities for challenging work and skills updating, which can result in even further obsolescence and declines in subsequent performance. Suggestions offered for breaking these types of negative, individual efficacy-performance spirals (e.g., Lindsley et al., 1995) point to the important role of restructuring the work environment so that more appropriate feedback, encouragement, positive expectations, and opportunities for becoming involved in retraining and skills updating activities are provided to older workers. In summary, managers need to be highly cognizant of the need for middle-aged employees' skills to be updated continuously to avoid skills obsolescence. As Park (1994) summarized, "it seems clear that older workers who do not gradually and continuously upgrade work skills may have difficulty acquiring new skills if the to-be-acquired skills are extremely complex, resource-demanding, and not related to earlier areas of expertise" (p. 200).

The critical point in this review of the literature on the age–job performance relationship is that several features of the job and organizational context play important roles as moderators. Models of work performance (e.g., Waldman & Spangler, 1989) have highlighted the importance of contextual factors for influencing individuals' performance directly, for instance, through the physical environment or the availability of resources for effective task completion, or indirectly in the form of policies and practices that affect workers' knowledge and skills and motivation. Organizational structures and practices, in the form of methods of arranging work, human resource policies, and training and reward systems, to name just a few, are important in the age–performance relationship. It is also important to note the role of the social structure in the form of attitudes, norms, and stereotypes directed toward older workers. The social structure is also part of the work environment and can be influenced by management's actions, organizational employment policies, and work practices, as well as serve as a source of influence on these more tangible structures. As Avolio et al. (1990) concluded, "the implication for future research is that there is a need to come to a better understanding of the specific types of work experiences and employment practices that may affect the relationship between age and work performance" (p. 418). In sum, a close examination of the research on age and work performance indicates that contextual factors in the organizational environment may accrue over time and influence individuals over the course of their careers (Howard & Bray, 1988).

Age and Work Attitudes and Values

Age appears to be related to work attitudes, such as job satisfaction (e.g., Lee & Wilbur, 1985; Rhodes, 1983) and work values, the underlying beliefs driving attitudes and behavior (Engle, Miguel, Steelman, & McDaniel, 1994). For example, Lee and Wilbur (1985) discovered that total job satisfaction increases as employees age, even with the effects of salary, education, job tenure, and a motivation score removed. White and Spector (1987) suggested that the increase in job satisfaction is due to perceptions of job congruence and locus of control (which are themselves related to age), proposing, "older workers get more of what they want out of work" (p. 261). Rhodes (1983) presented a model in which present environment, past environment, chronological age effects, and sources of systematic error, such as selective sampling and selective dropout, contribute to age-related differences in work attitudes and behaviors. In a review of over 185 research studies, Rhodes, too, stated that there is a positive correlation between aging and work attitudes. Research on the relationship between age and work attitudes and work values indicates that older workers can continue to maintain a positive relationship with and regard toward their jobs as they age. As Rhodes (1983) summarized, "[O]lder workers have been found to have work attitudes and to demonstrate work behaviors that are generally consistent with effective organizational functioning" (p. 356). However, she noted that the worker's environment will affect his or her attitudes and behaviors, which provides further evidence that as the nature of the labor pool changes and grows older, organizations need to devote increasing attention toward cultivating work environments that may enhance the work attitudes of their older employees.

Age and Withdrawal Behaviors

The nature of an employee's relationship with his or her organization in part can be illustrated by a variety of withdrawal behaviors, such as decisions to retire, absence and punctuality, and turnover. For example, Beehr (1986) suggested that as the workforce ages, and as mandatory retirement has been eliminated in most occupations, an understanding of retirement decision processes, as well as the effects of retirement, will be valuable. Reviews of the retirement literature (e.g., Beehr, 1986; Feldman, 1994) have noted that in addition to personal factors (e.g., health and economic well-being) and macroeconomic factors (e.g., eligibility for Social Security), organizational factors (early retirement counseling programs, treatment of older workers) can influence retirement decisions and reactions to retirement. These decisions have profound effects on retirees in terms of their adjustments to retirement and on organizations in terms of staffing and the composition of their workforces.

Absence and punctuality are additional outcomes of the effect of aging in the work context. Absenteeism among older workers is higher for reasons of illness but lower for voluntary reasons than among younger workers. Specifically, older workers are less likely to take time off without organizational approval (Hackett, 1990; Martocchio, 1989). In addition, punctuality is higher for older workers (Forteza & Prieto, 1994). These qualities have been noted by organizations, such as Days Inn and Travelers Insurance, who have calculated bottom-line savings by retaining older workers in various forms of postretirement employment (e.g., part-time or temporary workers). However, Warr (1994a) has argued that while age-related social roles or health factors may influence absence rates, it is important to remember that organizational norms and policies can have a noticeable effect on absences (cf., Nicholson & Johns, 1985).

Skills Obsolescence

As organizational goals and technology change, and organizational structures are redesigned, workers' skills become obsolete and new skills are needed (Fossum, Arvey, Paradise, & Robbins, 1986). Older workers, by virtue of having learned their skills in earlier years, are likely to have skills that are more obsolete than younger workers; Fossom et al. (1986) noted that obsolescence tends to increase after workers reach their mid-30's. However, organizational policies and reward practices frequently do not encourage employees to engage in skills updating activities (Farr & Middlebrooks, 1990; Fossum et al., 1986), especially older workers who ask for training (Forteza & Prieto, 1994). When older workers are provided with training, inappropriate methods are often used, which perpetuates the myth that older workers cannot be trained as successfully as younger workers (Warr, 1993; Sterns & Doverspike, 1989). Specific training issues will be discussed later in this chapter, but it is important to note that organizations will need to address issues of skills obsolescence if they want to remain competitive. Thus various organizational structures, including training design and availability and rewards for skills updating, are important considerations for their influences on older workers' maintaining and developing new knowledge and skills.

Conclusions on Age and Work Outcomes: The Importance of Organizational Structures

Organizational factors may play a critical role in determining many of the relationships between age and various work-related outcomes. Our position is that organizational factors—ranging from the organization's strategy, structural characteristics, and design, to its human resource practices, such as training policies and reward systems, to the nature of the immediate work environment in terms of supervisory practices and the way in which work is performed—can have a strong and pervasive effect on relationships between aging and work outcomes. Understanding the influences that different features of the organizational context have on older workers is particularly important given the dramatic changes that organizations are currently facing. These changes range from new organizational designs and arrangements to new work methods and technologies. As organizations attempt to keep pace with these changes, they will need to assess the demographic makeup of their workforces and consider the roles of older workers.

Our approach to understanding how the organizational context relates to the functioning of the older worker draws on a systems-level perspective. A long history of research and practice in the area of organizational design has demonstrated the importance of developing and configuring aspects of the organization—its structures, policies, practices, and operations—so that they mutually reinforce and support each other (Galbraith, 1977; Galbraith & Lawler, 1993; Nadler & Tushman, 1988). For instance, while policies and procedures may be established to encourage hiring and retaining older workers, these policies and procedures need to be supported by performance management and incentive systems that encourage older workers to engage in continuous learning and self-development. Moreover, these factors reside at multiple levels and are interconnected, as illustrated earlier in Figure 4.1. We follow this perspective as we now turn to describing how the structures, practices, policies, and procedures that operate at different functional levels within the organization are interrelated and influence the older worker.

INFLUENCES OF ORGANIZATIONAL STRUCTURES, SYSTEMS, POLICIES, AND PRACTICES ON THE OLDER WORKER

The subsequent discussion reviews the literature on the effect of organizational structures, systems, policies, and practices on the older worker. Following our model in Figure 4.1, this section is organized by beginning with macroorganizational factors and proceeding to microfactors in the work environment. Throughout this section, we consider how factors in the organizational context may influence the older worker and how these factors are related to factors at lower levels that may have other relationships with older workers.

Organizational Strategy, Structure, and Design

Organizations are now in a state of flux. In the face of increasing global competition over the past 2 decades, organizations have been striving to improve on cost, quality, and responsiveness to customers (Galbraith & Lawler, 1993). To meet these challenges, organizations are being forced to change their strategies, designs, and management practices. Strategic initiatives of cost-effectiveness, total quality, customer service, and time-based competition require concurrent changes in design and structure. To increase their speed and flexibility in developing responsiveness to customer demands and getting new products to market, organizations are moving to flatter, more streamlined, decentralized structures organized around products, services, or customers, rather than functions (Lawler, 1992). These types of changes in the structure and design of organizations

have important implications for older workers. Some of these relationships are more direct than others.

Influences Associated with Restructuring and Downsizing

The first immediate implication is that as organizations restructure and
downsize, they are removing the middle levels of the hierarchy (Brockner
& Lee, 1995). In large part, because these positions tend to be filled by
employees with greater seniority, these cuts have been particularly hard
felt by older employees. Reflecting the dramatic downsizing trend of the
early 1990s, displacement rates were significantly higher for older workers for the first half of this decade than during the first half of the 1980s
(Gardner, 1995). In many cases, organizations have attempted to avoid
layoffs by offering early retirement packages to older employees. Herz
(1995) has reported that a survey of major corporations indicated that the
percentage of companies offering some form of early retirement plan
increased from 17% in 1984 to 43% in 1991. The results also demonstrated that some workers have opted to accept these plans because they
are attractive, while others have done so to avoid impending job loss. In
this particular survey, nearly two-thirds of the employers indicated that
the plans were to avoid mandatory layoffs. What this has meant is that
either through involuntary displacement or by exercising early retirement
options, workers have been retiring from their long-tenure or career jobs
at an earlier age.

Although downsizing has been one major initiative associated with
organizational restructuring in recent years, so, too, have been outsourcing activities and making more extensive use of "contingent"—otherwise
known as part-time, temporary, or consultant—employment practices.
For organizations interested in reducing labor costs and increasing flexibility and responsiveness to cyclical changes in the economy, making
use of temporary workers makes sense. Wage levels for temporary workers tend to be lower than for full-time employees; fringe benefits, which
have undergone a tremendous increase in cost over the decade (particularly medical coverage), are infrequently provided; training, orientation,
and development costs are lower because these workers already have work
experience, and training is often provided by temporary employment
agencies; and extensive layoffs of permanent employees during business
downturns are less likely to be necessary if temporary workers are used.

As a result, the use of part-time workers has increased from 1957 when temporary workers constituted 12% of the workforce to today, where they make up 24% of the workforce (Feldman, 1994).

A large number of these temporary workers are older employees who either were laid off or took advantage of early retirement incentives during periods of downsizing and are looking for some form of "bridge employment" between the end of their long-tenured career positions and permanent retirement (Feldman, 1995). Many of these older workers are looking to take temporary or part-time employment simply to make ends meet. Even some of those who took attractive early retirement packages are finding it necessary to return to work either because the lump-sum payments they received did not go as far as they thought, their pension annuities have eroded due to inflation or have been reduced as a result of changes in pension plan arrangements made by employers, their health insurance costs have increased because once they retired their benefits were reduced, or some combination of these factors (Herz, 1995). Basic economic necessity is coupled with the fact that many older workers do not want to leave the workforce when they retire, so they seek some form of bridge employment, whether it be in part-time work, temporary positions, or consultant roles. The availability of these types of jobs, as a result of the organizational restructuring and emphasis on outsourcing more work, creates "pull" factors that induce older workers to leave their long-tenured jobs and seek alternative forms of employment (Feldman, 1994). As a result, more and more older workers are taking positions in some form of bridge employment, such as in part-time jobs. As of 1990, 25% of the workforce aged 55 and older were part-time employees (defined as working fewer than 35 hours per week) compared to only 19% in 1970 (Kramer, 1995).

Thus changes in the basic structures of organizations as they have undergone downsizing have had and will continue to have more dramatic effects on the nature of employment of older workers. The combination of displacement and early retirement of older, permanent, long-tenured workers, with the increasing use of contingent employment sources, signifies a fundamental change for the work of many older individuals. Specifically, as Feldman (1995) has observed:

> although 33 percent of the workforce leave their long-term jobs by age fifty-five and 50 percent leave by age sixty, less than one in nine workers in this country has fully retired by age sixty. Instead, most of these

workers take "bridge jobs" between the time they end their full-time jobs
and the time they begin full-time retirement. (p. 136)

This trend in the nature of employment for older workers suggests
that we need to pay more attention to the nature of contingent work and
older employees. Feldman's research on various forms of contingent
employment practices (e.g., Feldman, 1990, 1994, 1995; Feldman &
Doerpinghaus, 1992a, 1992b) has demonstrated that, particularly for part-
time and temporary work, there are often problems associated with worker
productivity and commitment. Is this because contingent workers:

1. tend to have lower skills than permanent workers and they tend to
   self-select themselves into temporary or part-time work?
2. lack the training and skills updating needed?
3. do not work for long enough periods at a time to acquire or maintain their knowledge and skill sets and proficiency levels?
4. are not provided the types of financial incentives necessary to provide high levels of motivation and consistent performance? or
5. are not provided the types of work activities that they are used to
   performing or that are motivating?

Most likely, it is a combination of these factors that explains performance and other work-related implications of the shift toward contingent
employment relationships. Although at this point there is too little research
on how contingent employment practices affect employees' attitudes and
performance in general, let alone for older employees, to make conclu-
sive statements (Feldman, 1995), this demonstrates our point that it is
important to trace how changes in macroorganizational strategies and
structures can affect older employees both directly and indirectly.

We have already described the direct effects on employees through, for
example, layoffs or early retirement options that have an immediate impact
on the employment status of older workers. The more indirect effects are
the results of changes in the nature of work and human resource policies
and practices that accompany new contingent forms of employment. For
instance, approximately half of those retirees who take bridge jobs change
occupation and industry (Feldman, 1995). These older workers are thus
responsible for learning what is likely to be a new set of skills. Because
managers often assign temporary or part-time workers different types of
tasks (e.g., those that require less organization-specific knowledge) than

full-time employees (Pearce, 1993), older employees who make the transition to some form of contingent employment may be working on very different sets of tasks, even if they continue to work in the same occupation.

The massive restructuring and downsizing efforts that are so common in today's large organizations can touch older workers in other ways than by changing their employment status. Those workers who remain following an organizational downsizing frequently find that the requirements of their jobs have changed both qualitatively and quantitatively (Kaufman, 1995). Due to qualitative changes in the nature of their jobs, for older employees to be able to perform at their standard levels, training is necessary for tasks with which they are less familiar. Issues associated with retraining older employees thus take on critical importance in an era of corporate restructuring. As we will discuss in more detail in the section on human resource policies and practices, if older employees are given appropriate training practices, they can acquire new knowledge and skills and perform effectively in their new tasks (Sterns & Doverspike, 1989; Warr, 1994a). Older employees may find themselves not only performing different types of work, but also more work. On the one hand, there is evidence that those who are older may be able to deal with stressors more effectively than those who are younger because they can draw from past experiences to know what types of responses are most effective (Aldwin, 1991). However, for older workers who report feeling older than their actual chronological age and tend to experience greater job strain (Barnes-Farrell & Piotrowski, 1989), increases in their workloads may be particularly detrimental to their psychological well-being. We see that, once again, changes in organizational restructuring are likely to have effects that reverberate through the organization to influence older workers.

Influences Associated with the Adoption of New Technologies and Work Practices

Changes in organizational strategies and structures are changing the nature of work for older employees in other ways as well. With the growing use of new information technologies and computerized systems, the nature of work is changing from physical work to knowledge work (Zuboff, 1988). Certain organizational strategies and structures speed the rate of change and the introduction of these new methods of work. For instance, the adoption of new manufacturing techniques and processes, such as advanced manufacturing technologies, total quality management, and just-in-time inventory controls, which together fall under the rubric "integrated manufacturing," is dramatically changing the nature of traditional work methods in a number of manufacturing industries (e.g., autos, steel) (Snell & Dean, 1994). Control-room-type manufacturing situations are appearing with increasing frequency in capital-intensive technologies such as petroleum, chemicals, paper, glass, and food processing. In these types of work environments, effective organizational functioning is becoming more dependent on the knowledge and skills of employees, particularly in the areas of planning, decision making, and problem solving, than on the physical execution of work (Lawler, 1992; Zuboff, 1988). These types of changes put a premium on the development of new and expanded skill sets. For instance, changes in manufacturing have produced new skills sets, including computer and statistical skills, and also have expanded the job domain to often include direct contact with customers, and thus require the use of interpersonal skills (Greller & Stroh, 1995).

Many employees in general and older workers in particular may see these changes as threatening their sense of control over the way they perform their work. This is particularly true if employees do not have the knowledge, skills, and level of familiarity with these new methods of work, and training is not readily encouraged or available. Providing stress coping workshops that focus on the needs of older workers, specifically, by increasing their understanding of the types of changes occurring and providing them the means to gain necessary new knowledge and skills is particularly useful during these transitions (London, 1990). Although these efforts will be discussed in more detail in a later section, organizations need to develop practices that encourage and facilitate self-directed learning and career development that promote continuous learning and change. As Greller and Stroh (1995) have noted, it is imperative that older workers are made aware that they will need to learn and reshape their skills to remain employable.

For organizations in traditional manufacturing industries (e.g., steel, autos), issues related to transitioning to new methods of production in order to gain competitive advantage and the older worker are especially critical. In these traditionally unionized environments, seniority provisions that specify "last hired, first fired" mean that the massive layoffs of blue-collar employees that were particularly pronounced during the 1980s served to increase the average age of these workforces. More than 10 years later, now in the 1990s, few new employees are being hired, even as companies in these industries regain their profitability. Instead, through a combination of the use of advanced manufacturing technologies, just-in-time inventory practices, and new, more flexible team-based work methods, organizations have been able to meet increasing demands without substantial increases in their workforces. In short, they are managing to do more with less—with a workforce that is significantly older.

Savoie (1990) has described Ford's experience with an older workforce in attempting to rebound from the crisis that hit the auto industry in the early 1980s. Like many other firms in the "mature" industries, as a result of the massive blue-collar layoffs of primarily less-senior employees (who tended to be younger), Ford experienced a high age compression of its workforce. In the period from 1978 to 1987, as the hourly workforce was cut nearly in half from 200,000 to 100,000, the average age of the blue-collar workforce at Ford increased by 7.3 years, from 37.2 years to 44.5 years. According to Savoie, in the face of severe competition, Ford "had to alter everything, from how products looked and worked to the fundamental ways in which the company addressed its customers, employees, unions, dealers, and the rest of the world" (p. 277). In doing so, Ford introduced new forms of teamwork to redesign entire product lines, focused employee involvement practices on improving quality and efficiency, and developed new cooperative labor management relations with the UAW. Of critical concern to Ford was whether its older workforce would have the flexibility, resourcefulness, and motivation necessary to make these changes.

The experience of older workers provided valuable knowledge, particularly with regard to problem-solving efforts focused on improving product quality. According to Savoie, the older workers tended to be just as creative and involved in decision making as their younger counterparts. Participation by older workers in extensive training and education efforts in areas ranging from basic education to computer programming was the same as for younger workers. Also, the older workers were absent less often, tended to demonstrate greater commitment to the organization, showed more patience with the transitions, and were more likely to recognize the severity of the situation facing the company.

There were, however, some potential negative features associated with having an older workforce. First, the older workforce led to significant internal cost increases associated with average wage rates becoming skewed at the upper end of compensation ranges, greater retirement plan obligations, and higher health care plan rates. Second, there was the potential that the older workers might resist the new work methods, prefer the traditional adversarial approach to bargaining, and adhere to the old style of top-down management. Based on Ford's success, Savoie emphasized that this second set of problems was largely avoided with the effective design of organizational training and skills updating activities, reward systems, communication and information sharing, and job security contract provisions. The message conveyed in Ford's experience clearly points to the importance of developing specific human resource practices that complement the types of changes initiated by the movement toward new organizational strategies and structures designed to face an increasingly competitive environment.

Influences Associated with Basic Strategic Approaches to Human Resources

An organization's basic strategic orientation, in response to the demands of its business environment, is linked with the set of approaches it takes in managing its human resources (Miles & Snow, 1984). As such, organizations with different strategies may have employment practices and human resource systems that treat older workers in distinctly different ways. For instance, organizations with the strategic orientation of a "defender" have limited and stable product lines, are focused on efficiency and quality, and tend to have highly centralized structures. Because these organizations place a premium on stability and slow, incremental improvements in production processes, individuals' organization-specific knowledge and skills are highly valued. To achieve a workforce with a deep understanding of the organization's operations and product knowledge, defender organizations adopt an approach that enables them to "build" or "make" their human resources. These organizations typically have internal promotion practices, well-developed career ladders, and extensive training and skills-building programs, and strive for low turnover rates.

In contrast, "prospector" organizations operate in changing markets, emphasize responsiveness to customer preferences, and have decentralized structures. Since these organizations emphasize flexibility, change, and an entrepreneurial orientation, they take a "buy" or "acquire" perspective in their human resource functions and focus on recruiting new employees with a new set of skills. The different strategic approaches can influence older workers indirectly by determining whether emphasis is placed on providing internal promotion, career development, skills updating, and retraining opportunities for its employees or on focusing efforts on acquiring new employees who have the particular knowledge and skill sets that are desired. If organizations take the first approach, they need to consider how appropriate their career- and skill-development practices are for older workers. It may be the case that organizations that aggressively take the latter approach are the more frequent, or at least more deliberate, violators of age discrimination laws and may tend to have "ageist" cultures (Rosen & Jerdee, 1985). Moreover, if the impending shortage of younger, highly skilled workers comes true as predicted, then organizations that have emphasized recruiting newly trained younger employees will need to reconsider the viability of that approach and focus more efforts on retraining and skills development for the existing older workers.

Organizational and Human Resource
Policies and Practices

As organizations restructure, downsize, and pursue the use of new technologies and advanced work methods, organizational and human resource policies and practices need to be given careful attention for how they relate to older workers. These policies and practices can be considered the more immediate structural aspects of the organization that influence the older individual at work. In this sense, as we peel back another layer of structural influences, we see that these policies and practices function as the "critical levers" for organizations in effectively managing older workers. But before we examine these policies and practices, we shall consider the role of the social structure that is intricately bound with the policies and practices.

Organizational Age-Related Social Structures: Cultural Norms and Values and Stereotypes of the Older Worker

An organization's culture, especially in terms of norms and stereotypes, will have a profound effect on its policies and practices. Currently, age-

are now beginning to be classified as older workers. These workers appear to be less concerned with hierarchical advancement in the organization; they are more oriented toward utilizing their potential, developing new skill sets, and being constantly challenged in their assignments and responsibilities (Hall & Richter, 1990). For instance, Miner and Smith (1982) found that motivation to advance in management and assume leadership roles began declining for college students in the 1960s and leveled out by the early 1970s. Howard and Wilson (1982) and Howard and Bray (1988) have compared motivational profiles of AT&T managers hired in the 1950s to those hired in the 1970s. Compared to those hired in the 1950s, managers hired in the 1970s (who are baby boomers) had less of a desire for advancement in the organization and movement into leadership roles. Instead, realizing that opportunities for advancement were limited and that they might not be able to get ahead in their work, baby-boom managers have focused instead on self-fulfillment and personal growth.

Career paths are becoming more self-directed and differentiated as companies can no longer promise steady upward mobility in the organization, but instead require employees to be adaptable and capable of learning new knowledge and skills as well as managing the demands of working in novel situations. The notion of protean careers (Hall, 1976; Hall & Mirvis, 1995)—where the career is the responsibility of and shaped by the individual, not the organization—fits well with the work values of the baby boom generation, who are now approaching midlife. Hall and Mirvis see the career of the future as involving a series of periodic cycles of skill learning, mastery, and reskilling that are required to make lateral moves to new positions, jobs, and assignments. These types of career trajectories define growth not as upward mobility, but as the continuous development and use of new skills and abilities that allow individuals to take on new assignments and positions as needs arise. Workers need to adjust their expectations about career success and focus on the intrinsic rewards that come from challenging assignments and developing new skill sets.

This shift emphasizes that employees—old and young alike—develop the "learning-how" or "learning-how-to-learn" skills that allow them to adapt to new situations. Thus new career development practices for workers should be focused on facilitating the process of continuous self-directed learning. This process can be supported by the organization in multiple ways. The organizational values as articulated and acted on by management should replace the "promotion culture" with a "learning and psychological success" culture. This type of a culture can be developed through the implementation of policies on promotion from within, cross-training and cross-functional moves, using assignments for developmental purposes, and making managers accountable for subordinate development. To make employees more self-aware and self-directed in their development of new skills and control over their own careers, self-assessment methods must be made readily available. For instance, DuPont's Individual Career Management Program assists in the assessment of employees' own values, skills, and interests and in the development of action plans for acquiring new knowledge and skills and applying them in their careers (Hall & Richter, 1990).

Job placement practices can be an effective means to manage older workers. Older employees may be placed in assignments and positions that play to their strengths. Warr (1994a) has summarized a number of studies that have found that older employees' work behaviors and performance tend to be characterized by greater consistency, quality, and conscientiousness than that of younger workers. Older workers also tend to demonstrate higher levels of commitment and loyalty to the organization, are absent less often, and are less likely to leave. Many of these behaviors, such as exerting extra effort to assist others with work and personal problems, supporting the organization, volunteering suppositions for improvements, and orienting new employees can be classified as aspects of contextual performance—the job performance behaviors that support the larger organizational, social, and psychological environment rather than the technical core of the organization (i.e., task performance) (Borman & Motowidlo, 1993). Qualities such as strong commitment to the organization and conscientiousness have also been noted as important in contextual performance. Older workers appear to be particularly well suited for organizations, assignments, and roles where contextual performance composes a large part of the performance domain. For instance, in service-oriented organizations, where customer satisfaction, quality, and consistency in service delivery are considered especially important, older workers' contextual performance assets of attention to quality and conscientiousness make them particularly well suited for employment. Older workers may be very effective in assignments involving quality control and providing ideas for quality improvements (London, 1990). In this way, human resource staffing and placement can play a critical role in maximizing the fit between the older worker and the organization.

From a long-term perspective, career practices can play a critical role in determining the types of experiences individuals accrue over the course of their employment. Although highly correlated with age, the quantitative and qualitative aspects of experience demonstrate a much more consistent relationship with work performance than does chronological age because experience is considered to contribute directly to the development of knowledge and skill that contribute to effective performance (Tesluk & Jacobs, 1995; Waldman & Avolio, 1993). Career management practices, by providing employees exposure to the types of situations, events, and challenges that develop critical knowledge and skills or the "lessons of experience" (McCall, Lombardo, & Morrison, 1988), can help ensure continued motivation to learn, positive work attitudes, and effective job performance (Morrison & Hock, 1986; Waldman & Avolio, 1993). These types of assignments that involve transfers across units or departments have been especially recommended for older workers as a means to build skills and maintain interests by offering a new setting with new challenges (London, 1990). Changes in the form of lateral exploratory and enrichment moves, reassignments, and relocations can also provide greater self-esteem, sense of identity, and control (Brockner & Lee, 1995).

The benefits of structuring careers to ensure the development of critical knowledge and skills over the long term can be particularly beneficial as employees become older by providing them valuable experiences that can facilitate more effective work performance. Warr's (e.g., 1994a, 1994b) taxonomy of work tasks, task performance as a function of age, and the role of experience suggest that there are certain types of tasks where experience can either offset a negative age-performance relationship or enhance a positive age gradient. For tasks that require skilled manual labor, the effects of age-related declines in information processing or physical capabilities on performance may be counteracted by accumulated experience. The benefits of experience may come from learning specific behaviors that help compensate for age-related limitations. For instance, by

1. avoiding situations and activities where the effects of their age-related deficits may be more pronounced (e.g., activities that involve a great deal of physical exertion);

2. applying different work methods (e.g., scanning the text ahead for upcoming characters while typing; Salthouse, 1984); or
3. using aids to compensate for possible sensory and memory losses (e.g., eyeglasses or written notes), older workers can maintain effective performance.

An example of this first instance comes from Landy and Vasey's (1991) study of the task frequency ratings provided by police officers. Older, more experienced officers gave higher frequency ratings to the less physically demanding tasks, such as noncriminal investigations and court-related activities, while younger, less experienced officers provided higher ratings for the more physically demanding tasks, such as conducting raids and traffic duties. This may be explained by Landy and Vasey's observation that police officers have some discretion in determining the specific tasks they engage in while on duty. Officers working in teams often divide tasks on the basis of seniority, where the older officers select the less physically demanding activities and the younger officers defer by taking responsibility for the tasks that involve greater physical effort and exertion. To the extent that these types of employee-initiated restructuring of roles and responsibilities help to maintain effective performance, organizations may want to consider ways to provide older workers greater opportunities for allocating their tasks.

Development of the types of career management systems that can provide older workers opportunities for challenging responsibilities that provide motivation for learning and self-development is influenced by the social structure in terms of the norms and stereotypes of older workers held by members of the organization. As Warr and Pennington (1994) demonstrated, managers tend to reserve particular job classifications for older workers based on the job's ability requirements. Through this type of an "age-grading" process, older employees are placed into jobs that are slower paced, require less expenditure of energy, and require fewer cognitive resources. Such assignments are based on a negative stereotypical view of the older worker as being resistant to change, physically and cognitively slower, and less capable of learning new skills. It is likely that in organizations, divisions, and units where managers operate with these types of negative stereotypes, occupational segregation based on age will be more prevalent. Here we see how the social structure and human resource practices can interact in a way that has direct implications for older workers.

Whether it be through the placement of older employees into less demanding jobs and assignments by management as an age-grading process, older employees' own efforts to restructure the set of tasks that define their jobs, or through accumulated experiences that make the job more familiar, Park (1994) has suggested that one reason for the lack of a significant age-job performance relationship is that older employees typically work in situations that require limited demands on their cognitive resources. She refers to this as the maintenance hypothesis. That is, because older workers typically have responsibilities that involve a large proportion of maintenance situations—tasks that are familiar and make limited cognitive and physical demands—their job performance is not adversely affected by natural declines in cognitive resources that accompany aging. Although this hypothesis is supported in part by a few studies that have found declines in older workers' performance in situations that involve new learning or dealing with novel situations, the types of work settings and situations and how they have developed (e.g., through older employees' redefinition of their core job tasks or through managerial assignments) that apply to the maintenance hypothesis need to be specified in detail.

Reward and Feedback Systems and the Older Worker

Because stereotypes abound regarding older workers, such as their lower performance, lower motivation, or higher absences than their younger counterparts (e.g., Forteza & Prieto, 1994), reward and feedback systems can be a source of discriminatory treatment. Sterns and Alexander (1988) suggested that measures be taken to ensure the fairness of performance appraisal systems, emphasizing that evaluations should be reasonable, relevant, and reliable. If the managers conducting performance appraisals are thoroughly trained, an awareness of possible bias, then evaluations can be conducted properly. Given an accurate appraisal of an older worker's capabilities, decisions can be made regarding pay and promotions. In addition, more accurate decisions can be made regarding assigning workers to training programs, so they can adapt to changes in technology and the work environment. Rewards and feedback are especially important to older workers, given the stereotypes that frequently lead to underestimation of their skills and abilities.

Training Systems and the Older Worker

Training issues affect older workers in several ways. As noted earlier, changing technology can lead to skills obsolescence, or job changes may occur due to movement to a new organization or even a new industry (Goldstein, 1993). Research, however, has indicated that older workers may be less adaptable, and therefore less successful in training, than their younger counterparts (Warr, 1993; Kubeck, Delp, Haslett, & McDaniel, 1996); older workers are frequently ignored when employees are assigned to training programs (Sterns & Doverspike, 1989). But this issue of lack of adaptability may be due in large part to misconceptions and stereotypes regarding older workers. Employers sometimes feel that it is not worthwhile to train older workers who will not be in the organization for as long as younger workers—although, in reality, as noted earlier, older workers have lower turnover rates (Forteza & Prieto, 1994). In addition, older workers themselves may be reluctant to be trained, due to nervousness in feeling that they are less able to learn than when they were younger (Warr, 1993). Moreover, when older workers are provided with training, inappropriate methods are often used, which perpetuates the myth (to managers and to older workers themselves) that older employees cannot be trained as successfully as their younger counterparts.

Older workers are indeed responsive to training efforts, however. Warr (1994a) discussed learning strategies that can be used to train older workers more successfully, such as structuring a program so that trainees experience success early in the program, thus promoting self-confidence in their ability to learn. Warr also suggested that extra steps be taken to ensure transfer of training, which older workers may have more trouble with than younger workers. In addition, Park (1994) concluded that if older workers do not engage in continuous learning and skills updating, they may have trouble mastering complex new skills, especially those unrelated to current areas of expertise. However, she suggested that these difficulties will likely be overcome if the older workers are allowed to learn new skills in an appropriate training situation. Warr's (1994a) and Park's (1994) conclusions are consistent with Sterns and Doverspike's (1988, 1989) suggestions for structuring training programs that are appropriate for older workers.

In 1988, Sterns and Doverspike emphasized the importance of a needs analysis, not just for the organization and the job, but also to determine the specific training needs of the people who will be trained. They also identified five dimensions that need to be considered when designing a training program: motivation, structure, familiarity, organization, and time. Sterns and Doverspike suggested that while employees of all ages need motivation to participate in skills updating, older workers may need additional encouragement to overcome the stereotypes and nervousness described previously. They agreed with Warr's (1994a) suggestions for structure, advising a format where trainees receive frequent positive feed-back; they also addressed Park's (1994) concerns by proposing that tasks be arranged in increasing complexity. With this structure, trainees would have the confidence acquired from each newly mastered task supporting them as they advanced to the next one. Familiarity (building training on past skills and abilities whenever possible), organization (providing knowledge organizing skills for older workers, who frequently organize information differently than younger workers), and time (sufficient for older workers, who may take longer) also addressed concerns important in the training of older workers. In 1989, Sterns and Doverspike added two categories for consideration in designing training programs for older workers, active participation and learning strategies. Specifically, they noted that older workers, who frequently feel intimidated or alienated by a lecture format in training, can benefit when encouraged to participate actively. In addition, training older workers in learning strategies will increase their ability to not only complete the training tasks, but to retain the information and transfer it to their jobs.

Other researchers have addressed the development of training programs for older workers. Hill and Elias (1990) suggested that self-efficacy regarding ability to learn affected employee success in training programs. In their research, they determined that career history, such as previous, relevant, formal training and advancement potential, had an effect on self-efficacy. However, seniority was negatively correlated with self-efficacy in learning, and that effect was only partially moderated by prior training relevance and potential for advancement. Hill and Elias's research, then, suggests the importance of addressing self-efficacy in older workers. Although prior training and advancement potential were found to be insufficient to compensate for seniority, the suggestions of Warr (1994a) and Sterns and Doverspike (1988, 1989) to build early success and positive feedback into the training program may also work to increase self-efficacy beliefs concerning the ability to learn.

Immediate Work Context

An additional factor to consider as organizations restructure, downsize, or alter their technologies is the effect of these changes on the immediate work environment of their employees. Warr (1994a) proposed four categories of job activity, which consisted of knowledge-based judgments with no time pressure; relatively undemanding activities; skilled manual work; and continuous, paced data processing. The latter two categories are most relevant in the present discussion. As noted earlier, the pattern of jobs is changing from industrial manufacturing to service-type jobs. Therefore, older workers must expect a shift in the nature of the jobs they are expected to perform—from physical work to work that is more dependent on cognitive skills. Meier (1988) noted that an important source of employment for older workers is durable goods manufacturing. As manufacturing organizations implement computer aided design (CAD) and computer aided manufacturing (CAM) technologies, many older workers must expect considerable shifts in the nature of their jobs. Meier explained that some occupations may experience "deskilling," or a reduction in the skills required to perform a job; other occupations will demand expanded skills.

However, this move away from physical labor may benefit older workers. Warr (1994a) noted that older workers often experience some decline in physical capabilities. Berkowitz (1988) explained that, in general, older workers are in poorer health than younger workers. On the other hand, Forteza and Prieto (1994) cautioned against moving older workers away from jobs involving moderate physical effort merely because of their age, warning that staying in the same position for extended periods in a sedentary job may be uncomfortable or even harmful. As Berkowitz (1988) concluded, "the key is intelligent placement which makes the most of the . . . capacity of . . . older workers" (p. 112). A final point, suggested by Waldman and Avolio (1993), is that physical characteristics of an employee's work area, such as an ergonomic design, can decrease physical strain and perhaps help compensate for the declines in physical capabilities that can occur with aging. The creative use of computer technology may be particularly beneficial for older workers by functioning as a cognitive support (e.g., as a way to monitor productivity, have easy and quick access to information) and as a means to overcome physical impairments (e.g., by allowing employees to work at home) that occur with greater frequency in older adults (Park, 1994).

The extent to which a shift away from physical labor is beneficial for older workers will in turn depend on the organization's structure and its human resource practices. For example, the training issues discussed previously will be relevant here (e.g., on the use of computer hardware and software) in terms of whether retraining is accepted by workers, valued by the organization, and successfully completed. Likewise, if the organizational culture supports growth, learning, and change, job redesign and organizational restructuring can be received positively by employees. Because older workers are frequently ignored or discriminated against in learning and training situations due to stereotyped attitudes, older workers will be especially vulnerable to an unsupportive culture.

The Role of the Older Worker and Interactions with Organizational Structures

Our discussion has largely considered how various features of the organizational structural context influence older workers. But older workers are not passively influenced by the organizational environment. For instance, the nature of the tasks reported by police officers in Landy and Vasey's (1991) study suggests that older workers in certain occupations may have the ability to restructure their immediate work environment to help facilitate performance as they age. However, for older employees to be able to exert more control over their immediate work situations, certain opportunities need to exist, such as providing employees a certain amount of discretion in structuring their job duties. Providing opportunities for older workers to exert control over the structural characteristics that influence their own attitudes and behaviors at work may be a particularly effective strategy for organizations. As organizations continue to undergo restructuring and downsizing, the responsibility for career management is increasingly falling on employees themselves. Formal career ladders that involved a series of upward promotions through the organization and involved a long-term relationship with the organization are no longer tenable (Brockner & Lee, 1995). Instead, the assessment and planning involved in the career development process are now beginning to rest with employees. In the area of career management, in particular, the outward arrows in Figure 4.1 from the older worker to the larger organizational context will need to be strengthened. Researchers in career development are beginning to make recommendations for how organizations can do this (e.g., Hall & Mirvis, 1995; Hall & Richter, 1990). For instance, providing self-assessment methods and activities for older workers to think about and plan their own career objectives can provide them the information necessary to take a number of steps, including making a career change, seeking training and skills development, or retirement to either some form of bridge employment or a more permanent form (London, 1990).

If greater attention is to be directed toward enabling older workers to influence more control over their own work environment, we need to develop a better understanding of the role of older workers' individual characteristics and how they interact with aspects of organizational structure. For instance, individual difference variables, such as self-efficacy, goal orientation, autonomy, locus of control, and need for achievement, and others have been suggested as important characteristics that may moderate the effectiveness of organizational interventions designed to encourage employees to engage in skills-updating activities (Farr & Middlebrooks, 1990; Fossum et al., 1986). As a second example, cognitive ability has been suggested as an individual difference characteristic that may combine with features of the work environment to affect outcomes for the older worker. More specifically, general cognitive ability may influence their recognition of the need to acquire knowledge and skills unrelated to previously acquired competencies through participation in developmental activities (Willis & Tosti-Vasey, 1990). Individuals' financial status and standard of living are important factors that will influence how an older worker reacts to an early retirement offer in terms of retiring permanently, accepting the offer, and then pursuing either other full-time work or some form of bridge employment, or rejects the offer entirely (Feldman, 1994).

CONCLUSIONS: IMPLICATIONS FOR PRACTICE AND RESEARCH

In many ways, the content of this chapter has been both descriptive, in terms of describing the types of influences that organizational structures have on older workers' behaviors attitudes and behaviors, and prescriptive, by noting demographic, economic, and workplace trends that point to the important role of older workers in organizational operations. Human resource practitioners need to be concerned with both pieces of information. As Greller and Nee (1990) concluded:

> Changing demographics will turn companies into case studies of successful and unsuccessful adaptation. How each employer forecasts, plans, and takes action to accommodate the change is what will determine the difference. Although the older workers are not the only resource, they represent one of the most available alternatives. There is no way any employer can avoid the aging of its workforce. (p. 191)

Clearly, a critical issue facing organizations is how to structure themselves in order to successfully make these transitions and meet these challenges.

In this period of change, it is important that human resource planning systems be connected with business strategy. The organization needs to first determine issues related to the company's strategic objectives and demographic trends in the relevant labor market. Understanding the organization's strategic strengths and weaknesses and basic business strategies provides direction for developing structures, processes, and interrelationships that foster competitiveness. It also provides context, meaning, and direction to understanding what is to be required of the organization's human resources (Cascio, 1987). Information on conditions of the relevant labor market can be linked to structures and strategies that involve the employment and management of older workers (Warr, 1994a). Information on the age composition of the labor market can even be used to modify business strategy to take advantage of demographic shifts (Greller & Nee, 1990). An organization facing an increasingly competitive environment may decide to pursue a high-service or high-quality-oriented strategy, rather than continue to try to survive being a low-cost, high-volume producer, in part because the local labor market can provide a means to recruit midcareer and older workers, who tend to be particularly focused on quality and providing a high level of service.

Basic strategic planning, human resource forecasting, and analysis of the appropriate labor market conditions can provide direction for a coordinated set of organizational structures that maximize the capabilities and qualities of older workers. As we have stressed in this chapter, a systems orientation where structures are coordinated and complementary is necessary. For example, a service-oriented strategy needs to have a flexible structure to allow employees to be responsive to customer needs, a recruitment and selection system that can attract high-quality older workers who enjoy and have experience working with customers, a training and reward system that encourages the development and maintenance of customer-service-related skills and high-quality service, and a preretirement planning system that encourages quality employees to continue their association with the organization as part-time employees. This means not only coordinating basic human resource structures at the organizational level, but also understanding how organizational level structures influence work structures at more immediate levels, such as nature of the older employee's task or the physical work environment.

Because we spend such a large part of our lives working in organizations, striving for the development of an understanding of how organizational structures influence older individuals can provide valuable insights into the long-term influence of environmental factors as people age. Understanding how organizational structures influence the older worker can provide us with valuable knowledge about the role of context and environment in the aging process and its outcomes in general and in other nonwork situations. So much of what we know to date about the aging process and the effects of aging on outcomes such as attitudes, behaviors, and performance has been context-deficient, that it is time to focus our energies on what occurs in natural environments, such as work organizations.

NOTES

[1] Many of the effects of these structures on older workers are "unintended consequences" (Marshall, this volume), rather than planned consequences.

REFERENCES

Aldwin, C. M. (1991). Does age affect the stress and coping process? Implications of age differences in perceived control. *Journal of Gerontology, 4,* 174–180.

Avolio, B. J., & Waldman, D. A. (1987). Personnel aptitude test scores as a function of age, education and job type. *Experimental Aging Research, 13,* 109–113.

Avolio, B. J., Waldman, D. A., & McDaniel, M. A. (1990). Age and work performance in nonmanagerial jobs: The effects of experience and occupational type. *Academy of Management Journal, 32,* 407–422.

Barnes-Farrell, J. L., & Piotrowski, M. J. (1989). Workers' perceptions of discrepancies between chronological age and personal age: You're only as old as you feel. *Psychology and Aging, 4,* 376–377.

Beehr, T. A. (1986). The process of retirement: A review and recommendations for future investigation. *Personnel Psychology, 39,* 31–55.

Berkowitz, M. (1988). Functioning ability and job performance as workers age. In M. E. Borus, H. S. Parnes, S. H. Sandell, & B. Seidman (Eds.), *The older worker* (pp. 87–114). Madison, WI: Industrial Relations Research Association.

Bird, C. P., & Fisher, T. D. (1986). Thirty years later: Attitudes toward the employment of older workers. *Journal of Applied Psychology, 71,* 515–517.

Borman, W. C., & Motowidlo, S. J. (1993). Expanding the criterion domain to include elements of contextual performance. In W. C. Borman & Associates (Eds.), *Personnel selection in organizations* (pp. 71–98). San Francisco: Jossey-Bass.

Buonocore, A. J. (1992). Older and wiser: Senior employees offer untapped capabilities. *Management Review, 81(7),* 49–52.

Brockner, J., & Lee, R. J. (1995). Career development in downsizing organizations: A self-affirmation analysis. In M. London (Ed.), *Employees, careers, and job creation* (pp. 49–70). San Francisco: Jossey-Bass.

Capowski, G. (1994). Ageism: The new diversity issue. *Management Review, 83*(10), 10–15.

Carnazza, J. P., Korman, A. K., Ference, T. P., & Stoner, J. A. F. (1981). Plateaued and non-plateaued managers: Factors in job performance. *Journal of Management, 7,* 7–25.

Cascio, W. F. (1987). *Applied psychology in personnel management* (3rd ed.). Englewood Cliffs, NJ: Prentice-Hall.

Chao, G. T. (1990). Exploration of the conceptualization and measurement of career plateau: A comparative analysis. *Journal of Management, 16,* 181–193.

Cleveland, J. N., & Landy, F. J. (1983). The effects of person and job stereotypes on two personnel decisions. *Journal of Applied Psychology, 68,* 609–619.

Cleveland, J. N., & Landy, F. J. (1987). Age perceptions of jobs:

Convergence of two questionnaires. *Psychological Reports, 60,* 1075–1081.

Cleveland, J. N., & Shore, L. M. (1992). Self-and supervisory perspectives on age and work attitudes and performance. *Journal of Applied Psychology, 77,* 469–484.

Dennis, H. (1988). Management training. In H. Dennis (Ed.), *Fourteen steps in managing an aging work force* (pp. 141–154). Lexington, MA: Lexington Books.

Engle, E. M., Miguel, R. F., Steelman, L. A., & McDaniel, M. A. (1994). *An examination of the relationship between age and work values.* Paper presented at the Ninth Annual Conference of the Society of Industrial and Organizational Psychology, Nashville, TN.

Farr, J. L., & Middlebrooks, C. L. (1990). Enhancing motivation to participate in professional development. In S. L. Willis & S. S. Dubin (Eds.), *Maintaining professional competence: Approaches to career enhancement, vitality, and success throughout a work life.* San Francisco: Jossey-Bass.

Feldman, D. C. (1990). Reconceptualizing the nature and consequences of part-time work. *Academy of Management Review, 15,* 103–112.

Feldman, D. C. (1994). The decision to retire early: A review and conceptualization. *Academy of Management Review, 19,* 285–311.

Feldman, D. C. (1995). Managing part-time and temporary employment relationships: Individual needs and organizational demands. In M. London (Ed.), *Employees, careers, and job creation* (pp. 121–141). San Francisco: Jossey-Bass.

Feldman, D. C., & Doerpinghaus, H. I. (1992a). Missing persons no longer: Managing part-time workers in the '90s. *Organizational Dynamics, 21,* 59–72.

Feldman, D. C., & Doerpinghaus, H. I. (1992b). Patterns of part-time employment. *Journal of Vocational Behavior, 41,* 282–294.

Forteza, J. A., & Prieto, J. M. (1994). Aging and work behavior. In H. C. Triandis, M. D. Dunnette, & L.M. Hough (Eds.), *Handbook of industrial and organizational psychology,* (Vol. 4, pp. 447–483). Palo Alto: Consulting Psychologists Press.

Fossum, J. A., Arvey, R. D., Paradise, C. A., & Robbins, N. E. (1986). Modeling the skills obsolescence process: A psychological/economic integration. *Academy of Management Review, 11,* 362–374.

Galbraith, J. R. (1977). *Organizational design.* New York: Free Press

Galbraith, J. R., & Lawler, E. E., III (1993). Introduction: Challenges to the established order. In J. R. Galbraith, E. E. Lawler, III, & Associates (Eds.), *Organizing for the future* (pp. 1–12). San Francisco: Jossey-Bass.

Gardner, J. M. (1995). Worker displacement: A decade of change. *Monthly Labor Review,118*(4), 45–56.

Goldstein, I. L. (1993). *Training in organizations: Needs assessment, development, and evaluation* (3rd ed.). Pacific Grove, CA: Brooks/Cole Publishing.

Greller, M. M., & Nee, D. M. (1989). *From baby boom to baby bust: How business can meet the demographic challenge.* Reading, PA: Addison-Wesley.

Greller, M. M., & Nee, D. M. (1990). Human resource planning for the inevitable—the aging workforce. In M. London, E.S. Bassman, & J. P. Fernandez (Eds.), *Human resource forecasting and strategy development* (pp. 181–193). New York: Quorum Books.

Greller, M. M., & Stroh, L. K. (1995). Careers in midlife and beyond: A fallow field in need of sustenance. *Journal of Vocational Behavior, 47,* 232–289.

Guzzo, R. A., Nelson, G. L., & Noonan, K. A. (1992). Commitment and employer involvement in employees' nonwork lives. In S. Zedeck (Ed.), *Work, families, and organizationss* (pp. 236–271). San Francisco: Jossey-Bass.

Hackett, R. D. (1990). Age, tenure, and employee absenteeism. *Human Relations, 43,* 601–619.

Hall, D. T. (1976). *Careers in organizations.* Glennview, IL: Scott Foresman.

Hall, D. T., & Mirvis, P. H. (1995). Careers as lifelong learning. In A. Howard (Ed.), *The changing nature of work* (pp. 323–361). San Francisco: Jossey-Bass.

Hall, D. T., & Richter, J. (1990). Career gridlock: Baby boomers hit the wall. *Academy of Management Executive, 4,* 7–22.

Hill, L. A., & Elias, J. (1990). Retraining midcareer managers: Career history and self-efficacy beliefs. *Human Resource Management, 29,* 197–217.

Herz, D. E. (1995). Work after early retirement: An increasing trend among men. *Monthly Labor Review, 118*(4), 13–20.

Howard, A., & Bray, D. W. (1988). *Managerial lives in transition:*

Advancing age and changing times. New York: Guilford Press.

Howard, A., & Wilson, J. A. (1982, Summer). Leadership in a declining work ethic. *California Management Review, 24,* 33–44.

Humple, C. S., & Lyons, M. (1983). *Management and the older workforce.* New York: American Management Associations.

Jacobs, R., Hofmann, D. A., & Kriska, S. D. (1990). Performance and seniority. *Human Performance, 3,* 107–121.

Jarratt, J., & Coates, J. F. (1995). Employee development and job creation: Trends, problems, opportunities. In M. London (Ed.), *Employees, careers, and job creation* (pp. 1–25). San Francisco: Jossey-Bass.

Katz, D., & Kahn, R. L. (1978). *The social psychology of organizations.* New York: Wiley.

Kaufman, H. G. (1995). Salvaging displaced employees: Job obsolescence, retraining, and redeployment. In M. London (Ed.), *Employees, careers, and job creation* (pp. 105–210). San Francisco: Jossey-Bass.

Kozlowski, S. W. J., & Farr, J. L. (1988). An integrative model of updating and performance. *Human Performance, 1,* 5–29.

Kozlowski, S. W. J., & Hults, B. M. (1987). An exploration of climates for technical updating and performance. *Personnel Psychology, 40,* 539–564.

Kramer, N. (1995). Employee benefits for older workers. *Monthly Labor Review, 118*(4), 21–27.

Kubeck, J. E., Delp, N. D., Haslett, T. K., & McDaniel, M. A. (1996). Does job-related training performance decline with age? *Psychology and Aging, 11,* 92–107.

Landy, F. J., & Vasey, J. (1991). Job analysis: The composition of SME samples. *Personnel Psychology, 44,* 27–50.

Lawler, E. E., III. (1992). *The ultimate advantage.* San Francisco: Jossey-Bass.

Lee, R., & Wilbur, E. R. (1985). Age, education, job tenure, salary, job characteristics, and job satisfaction: A multivariate analysis. *Human Relations, 38,* 781–791.

Lindsley, D. H., Brass, D. J., & Thomas, J. B. (1995). Efficacy-performance spirals: A multilevel perspective. *Academy of Management Review, 20,* 645–678.

London, M. (1990). Enhancing career motivation in late career. *Journal of Organizational Change Management, 3,* 58–71.

Martocchio, J. J. (1989). Age-related differences in employee absenteeism:

A meta-analysis. *Psychology and Aging, 4,* 409–414.

McCall, M. W., Lombardo, M. M., & Morrison, A. M. (1988). *The lessons of experience: How successful executives develop on the job.* New York: Lexington Books.

McEvoy, G. M., & Cascio, W. F. (1989). Cumulative evidence of the relationship between employee age and job performance. *Journal of Applied Psychology, 74,* 11–17.

Meier, E. L. (1988). Managing an older work force. In M. E. Borus, H. S. Parnes, S. H. Sandell, & B. Seidman (Eds.), *The older worker* (pp. 167–189). Madison, WI: Industrial Relations Research Association.

Miles, R. E., & Snow, C. C. (1984, Summer). Designing strategic human resource systems. *Organizational Dynamics, 36–52.*

Miner, J., & Smith, N. (1982). Decline and stabilization of managerial motivation over a 20-year period. *Journal of Applied Psychology, 67,* 297–305.

Morrison, R. F., & Hock, R. R. (1986). Career building: Learning from cumulative work experience. In D. T. Hall, & Associates (Eds.), *Career development in organizations* (pp. 236–273). San Francisco: Jossey-Bass.

Nadler, D. A., & Tushman, M. (1988). *Strategic organizational design.* Glenview, IL: Scott, Foresman.

Nicholson, N., & Johns, G. (1985). The absence of culture and the psychological contract—who's in control of absence? *Academy of Management Review, 10,* 397–407.

Noe, R. A., & Wilk, S. L. (1993). Investigation of the factors that influence employees' participation in development activities. *Journal of Applied Psychology, 78,* 291–302.

Park, D. C. (1994). Aging, cognition, and work. *Human Performance, 7,* 181–205.

Pearce, J. L. (1993). Toward an organizational behavior of contract laborers: Their psychological involvement and effects on employee coworkers. *Academy of Management Journal, 36,* 1082–1096.

Price, R. H., & Vinokur, A. D. (1995). Supporting career transitions in a time of organizational downsizing. In M. London (Ed.), *Employees, careers, and job creation.* San Francisco: Jossey-Bass.

Rhodes, S. R. (1983). Age-related differences in work attitudes and behavior: A review and conceptual analysis. *Psychological Bulletin, 93*(2), 328–367.

Rosen, B., & Jerdee, T. H. (1985). *Older employees: New roles for valued resources.* Homewood, IL: Dow Jones-Irwin.

Salthouse, T. A. (1984). Effects of age and skill in typing. *Journal of Experimental Psychology: General, 113,* 345–371.

Savoie, E. J. (1990). The aging of organizations: Strategic issues. In I. Bluestone, R. J. V. Montgomery, & J. D. Owen (Eds.), *The aging of the American work force: Problems, programs, policies* (pp. 275–289). Detroit, MI: Wayne State University Press.

Schein, E. H. (1990). Organizational culture. *American Psychologist, 45*(2), 109–119.

Schooler, C. (1987). Psychological effects of complex environments during the lifespan: A review and theory. In C. Schooler & K. W. Schaie (Eds.), *Cognitive functioning and social structure over the life course* (pp. 24–49). Norwood, NJ: Ablex.

Snell, S. A., & Dean, J. W., Jr. (1994). Strategic compensation for integrated manufacturing: The moderating effects of jobs and organizational inertia. *Academy of Management Journal, 37,* 1109–1140.

Sparrow, P. R., & Davies, D. R. (1988). Effects of age, tenure, training, and job complexity on technical performance. *Psychology and Aging, 3,* 307–314.

Stagner, R. (1985). Aging in industry. In J. E. Birren & K. W. Schaie (Eds.), *Handbook of the psychology of aging* (2nd ed., pp. 789–817). New York: Van Nostrand Reinhold.

Sterns, H. L., & Alexander, R. A. (1988). Performance appraisal and the older worker. In H. Dennis (Ed.), *Fourteen steps in managing an aging work force* (pp. 85–93). Lexington, MA: Lexington Books.

Sterns, H. L., & Doverspike, D. (1988). Training and developing the older worker: Implications for human resource management. In H. Dennis (Ed.), *Fourteen steps in managing an aging work force* (pp. 97–110). Lexington, MA: Lexington Books.

Sterns, H. L., & Doverspike, D. D. (1989). Aging and the training and learning process. In I. L. Goldstein (Ed.), *Training and development in organizations* (pp. 299–332). San Francisco: Jossey-Bass.

Tesluk, P. E., & Jacobs, R. R. (1995). *Experience, tenure, and seniority: A review and directions for future research.* Unpublished manuscript.

Waldman, D. A., & Avolio, B. J. (1986). A meta-analysis of age differences in job performance. *Journal of Applied Psychology, 71,* 33–38.

Waldman, D. A., & Avolio, B. J. (1993). Aging and work performance in perspective: Contextual and developmental considerations. *Research in Personnel and Human Resources Management, 11,* 133–162.

Waldman, D. A., & Spangler, W. D. (1989). Putting together the pieces: A closer look at the determinants of job performance. *Human Performance, 2,* 29–59.

Warr, P. (1993). In what circumstances does job performance vary with age? *European Work and Organizational Psychologist, 3*(3), 237–249.

Warr, P. (1994a). Age and employment. In H. C. Triandis, M. D. Dunnette, & L. M. Hough (Eds.), *Handbook of industrial and organizational psychology* (2nd ed., Vol. 4, pp. 485–550). Palo Alto: Consulting Psychologists Press.

Warr, P. (1994b). *Age, psychology, and work.* Paper presented at the 23rd International Congress of Applied Psychology, Madrid, Spain.

Warr, P., & Pennington, J. (1994). Occupational age-grading: Jobs for older and younger nonmanagerial employees. *Journal of Vocational Behavior, 45,* 328–346.

White, A. T., & Spector, P. E. (1987). An investigation of age-related factors in the age-job-satisfaction relationship. *Psychology and Aging, 2*(3), 261–265.

Willis, S. L., & Tosti-Vasey, J. L. (1990). How adult development, intelligence, and motivation affect competence. In S. L. Willis & S. S. Dubin (Eds.), *Maintaining professional competence* (pp. 64–84). San Francisco: Jossey-Bass.

Zuboff, S. (1988). *In the age of the smart machine.* New York: Basic Books.

Commentary: Organization, Self-Directed Learning, and Chronological Age

Gerald A. Straka

S ystem theory describes and explains the complex interrelations among organizational structures, human resource politics and practices, immediate work environments, and workers. As a consequence, there is a range of immediate work environments individuals are interacting with, and those work environments change over time. Another set of issues arise with respect to individuals. They not only differ in characteristics such as knowledge, skills, attitudes, and values, but as we know from longitudinal studies, this variability increases across the life span. The interactions between different individuals with diverse environments may have a differential effect on persons within these environments as well as on the work environments. Given these circumstances, we agree with Farr that "there is a need for research that examines how organizationally-relevant variables (e.g. structures and practices) operate as environmental factors to influence older employees' performance, behaviors, and attitudes" (chapter 4, p. 146) and vice versa.

There are megatrends in the change of organizationally relevant features. According to Farr many organizations are currently shifting to more flexible designs, flatter structures, and strategies designed to promote innovations, job descriptions that include a wider range of tasks, work that is more often team based, as well as politics and practices designed to encourage active participation and continuous learning (chapter 4, p. 147). Continuous learning is in our opinion one strategic parameter that can be used to cope with these changes. However, referring to other researchers in this field, Farr argues that "organizational policies and reward practices frequently do not encourage employees to engage in skills-updating activities . . . especially older workers who ask for training. When older workers are provided with training, inappropriate methods are often used, which perpetuates the myth that older workers cannot be trained as successfully as younger workers" (pp. 154–155). Therefore, the core question remains: How should the workplace and the "appropriate" training be designed so that continuous learning will take place?

FACTORS INFLUENCING PARTICIPATION
IN ADULT LEARNING ACTIVITIES

Learning may be regarded as a dynamic interplay among knowledge, skill, and will. Referring to results in the field of adult education, the aspect of "will" seems to be the crucial point for participation in adult learning activities. Participation in adult training and learning seems to be influenced by the following variables: (a) self-evaluation, (b) attitudes toward education, (c) importance of goals and expectation that the goals will be met, (d) life transitions, (e) opportunities and barriers for learning, and (f) information about educational offerings (Cross, 1981).

The Farr, Tesluk, and Klein chapter and other research findings seem to imply a tendency for mature workers to have a lower self-concept of their abilities in general and of their learning abilities in particular. However, one may question whether this is an effect of the disuse-hypothesis, discussed in gerontology. A similar tendency can be found in mature workers' attitudes towards education. Both factors may be related to the valence of certain goals and the expectation of attaining these goals (Straka & Nenniger, 1995). Reengineering the work organization and as a consequence redesigning the workplace may have similar effects as in life transitions. These are times of coping with new demands and for creating a special sensitivity for learning in which "teachable moments" may be identified. Participation of mature workers in continuous vocational training may be related to information, barriers, and opportunities especially created by their supervisors (Straka & Kuwan, 1994).

CRITERIA FOR DESIGNING TRAINING

Deciding to participate in training is only one side of the coin, successfully completing the training program the other. The adult and older-adult training and retraining literature has documented numerous aspects for successful training programs. Sterns and Doverspike (1988) propose five central aspects:

1. *Motivation.* This is an important factor for every training success. However, the concerns are slightly different for mature trainees. Their desire to learn may be accompanied by a fear of failure or the fear of an inability to compete against younger, better educated trainees. Therefore, trainers have to keep trainees informed of their progress, to use positive feedback, and to encourage them repeatedly to continue and complete the program.
2. *Structures.* The training material should appear relevant, give positive feedback, eliminate fear of failure, and should be based on job analyses.
3. *Familiarity.* The training program should relate to existing skills, knowledge, and abilities of the trainees. The material should be meaningful from the perspective of the mature worker. Similarities and differences between the old and new task should be carefully demonstrated.
4. *Organization.* This aspect relates to strategies to organize learning, which should play an important role in training. Therefore, learning strategies and metacognitive strategies should be a central part of training, especially if the aim is to create a learning organization.
5. *Time.* It is one of the general "laws" that, given sufficient time, mature workers can perform as well as younger colleagues. Therefore, training programs should be designed to allow for variability in the time available to the trainee.

In addition to these five aspects, training designs have to be taken into consideration. The program itself should be surrounded by an organizational climate that rewards training and by an integrated career perspective (Sterns & Doverspike, 1988).

IMPORTANCE OF SELF-DIRECTED LEARNING

Continuous learning may occur between the poles of other- and self-direction. Rapid changes in the workplace, learning organizations, increasing the complexity of tasks faced by workers are some of the reasons why self-directed learning is getting greater attention in adult education (e.g., the 10th International Self-Directed Learning Symposium was held in West Palm Beach, FL, in March 1996), as well as in industrial training.

It seems that maintaining professional competence via self-direction in learning is attaining increasing importance for mastering the organization-technological changes of the workplace. For example, 454 employees who participated in a pilot study on individual change management reported that two-thirds of their professional qualifications were based upon their own initiatives. Company-organized efforts contributed to no more than one third of their professional competency. Furthermore, these results showed a slight increase in the individual's own initiative with chronological age (Straka, Kleinmann, & Stöckl, 1994).

Reviewed emphasis of training on the job and the constructivistic view of learning and training as a serious alternative to the instructional design approach, now dominating educational science, might be favorable for continuous training of mature workers. Such an approach emphasizes work experience and may be effective throughout the life span. For example, Tough (1979), one of the initiators of the discussion on self-directed learning, found that the average adult in North America spends 816 hours on eight learning projects each year. Many of these projects were job related.

FACILITATING SELF-DIRECTED LEARNING

Self-directed learning occurs "unconsciously," nonsystematically, and incidentally. For example, our employees were surprised about the importance of their self-qualifying activities in the past when they had answered the questionnaire. As it turned out, our respondents were actually practicing "moderated criteria-guided reflection" on their own process of self-qualification during work. According to our observations, mature workers are becoming more self-confident about their learning capabilities, and their motivation to learn is significantly increasing.

The importance of self-qualification connected with work raises questions about the external and internal conditions that support self-directed learning. Deci and Ryan (1991) specify three important conditions that support readiness for self-direction in learning: The individual's experience of autonomy, competence, and relatedness. These factors might become a challenge for organizational theory and practice to create work environments in which relevant experiences are possible. Dubin (1990) suggests further that the following aspects are involved: (1) job and work assignments, (2) supervisory-subordinate relationships, (3) organizational climate, (4) peer-colleague interactions, and (5) management policies and practices.

A variety of external and internal conditions or factors may contribute to the participation in adult continuing education activities, to successfully designed training for mature workers, and to self-directed learning in the process of work. However, we may ask whether these criteria directly and exclusively relate to chronological age and the mature worker?

Sterns and Doverspike (1988) argue that "designing an effective training program for the older worker is really much different from the principles for effectively designing any training program. In general, an effective training program for older workers will be effective for all workers" (p. 99).

Empirical findings continually confirm a negative correlation between chronological age and the participation in continuing vocational training. However, if additional variables such as level of general and vocational education, occupational status, and job function are included in the analysis, chronological age ceases to be the most important factor. Far more important is the amount of primary vocational training in general, followed by occupational status for nonprofessionals (Straka & Kuwan, 1994).

An evaluation of training programs for older workers revealed a nonsignificant relationship between chronological age and learning outcomes. However, there were significant relationships between domain-specific knowledge at the beginning and at the learning outcomes (Straka, Kleinmann, & Will, 1994).

An analysis of patterns of coping with technological change in the workplace showed that chronological age is not as important as it was assumed (Staufer, 1992). However, the perceived aspects of the work environment had a distinct influence on the coping patterns of mature workers.

These examples and many other research results in the area of life-span development verify that technological age is not as important as it seems at first glance. The deficit model derived from the study of dimensional relationships between chronological age and selected personal characteristics is generally falsified. This model is replaced by conceptions of difference and competence (Olbrich, 1987). As a consequence, the question may be raised: What are the criteria that justify the term "older worker"? What are the variables that determine the "older worker"?

LEGITIMATION OF CHRONOLOGICAL AGE

To obtain an answer to this question, let's make a brief detour to review some aspects of the theme of the "older worker" as it was discussed in the recent past—especially in Germany. In the 1960s and 1970s the focus was upon the competence of mature workers (Thomae & Lehr, 1973). In the 1990s the scientific discussion shifted to problems associated with preretirement (i.e., "new or young olds") and upon retirement. Now, the financial burden of preretirement on the Social Security system has come on the research agenda. In the political arena "the plundering of the Social Security system" or "human resources management of the private companies at the expense of the Social Security system" is a major theme of public discussion.

If one looks at the conditions of the labor market over time, reasons for the shift in viewing "older workers" become clear. During the 1960s and 1970s there was a shortage of workers. As a consequence, there was a search for reserves in the workforce. At that time older and even retired workers were regarded as a potential reserve for the workforce. During the 1980s policy makers became increasingly aware of the fact that the surplus of workers in Germany and Europe in general posed a basic structural problem. As a consequence, the focus shifted to segments of the labor force whose exclusion from the labor market was socially acceptable. The solution was early retirement—carried out by informal or even unspoken agreements among companies, unions and the government (Straka, Fabian, & Will, 1990). This policy is now increasingly threatening the capacity of the Social Security system and its political legitimacy, however. As a consequence, this informal agreement is becoming increasingly fragile.

In the recent past, older workers were persons near the end of their 50s. Currently, even persons in their late 40s are labeled "older workers." In this context it might be interesting to cast a retrospective glance at the days when the Social Security system was first introduced in Germany by Chancellor Bismark in 1871. At that time, the retirement age was 70 years even though only 4.6% of the population reached the age of 65 and more. Today over 16% of the German population is over age 65, and the actual average retirement age is around 58.

This brief historical retrospective suggests that the "older worker" is clearly a phenomenon. However, the dilemma or paradox is that other Germans who by chronological age make up this segment of the labor force cannot be defined with a limited number of meaningful variables. As we know, the older population is characterized by heterogeneity rather than by homogeneity. Research on social and psychological development has repeatedly confirmed that individual differences are increasing over the life span instead of decreasing. In the present context, the question might then be raised: What might be the potential contributions of social gerontology, adult education, and organizational theory as related to the phenomenon of the "older worker"? Our answer could be: Continuous falsification and abandonment of chronological age as a valid criterion for decisions in human resource management and in social policy. Given the background of global competition, fast innovation, increasing importance of human resources, and shifts from an industrial to an information society associated with demographic change in developed countries, a major challenge for organization theory for the third millennium will be to investigate the effect of the complex interactions between organizationally relevant variables and personality characteristics during the lifespan, with the ultimate aim to contribute to an age-irrelevant society (cf. Neugarten & Neugarten, 1986).

REFERENCES

Cross, P. L. (1981). *Adults as learners.* San Francisco: Jossey-Bass.

Deci, E. L., & Ryan, R. M. (1991). A motivational approach to self: Integration in personality. In R. Dienstbier (Ed.), *Nebraska symposium on motivation: Perspectives on motivation,* (Vol. 38., pp. 237–288). Lincoln: University of Nebraska Press.

Dubin, S. S. (1990). Maintaining competence through updating. In S. L. Willis & S. S. Dubin (Eds.), *Contemporary approaches to professional updating* (pp. 9–43). San Francisco: Jossey-Bass.

Neugarten, B. L., & Neugarten, D. A. (1986). Changing meanings of age in the aging society. In A. Pifer & L. Bronte (Eds.), *Our aging society* (pp. 35–51). New York: Norton.

Olbrich, E. (1987). Kompetenz im Alter [Competence in old age]. *Zeitschrift für Gerontologie, 20,* 319–330.

Staufer, M. (1992). *Ältere Beschäftigte und technischer Wandel* [Older workers and technological change]. Göttingen, Germany: Hogrefe.

Sterns, H. L., & Doverspike, D. (1988). Training and developing the older worker: Implications for human resource management. In H. Dennis (Ed.), *Fourteen steps in managing an aging work force* (pp. 97–110). Lexington, KY: Lexington Books.

Straka, G. A., Fabian, T., & Will, J. (1990). Berufsverbot mit 65? [No right to a job over 65?]. *Psychologie und Gesellschaftskritk, 14*(4), 63–80.

Straka, G. A., Kleinmann, M., & Stöckl, M. (1994). Self-organized job-related learning: An empirical study. In H. B. Long and Associates (Eds.), *New ideas about self-directed learning* (pp. 149–160). Oklahoma: Oklahoma Research Center for Continuing Professional and Higher Education of the University of Oklahoma.

Straka, G. A., Kleinmann, M., & Will, J. (1994). *Motivationale Wirkungen selbstorganisierten Lernens in der betrieblichen Weiterbildung* [Motivational effects of self-organized learning upon vocational continuing education]. Berlin: Bandesinstitut für Berufsbildung.

Straka, G. A., & Kuwan, H. (1994). Einflussfaktoren auf die berufliche Fort- und Weiterbildung von Arbeitnehmern/innen in der zweiten Hälfte des Erwerbslebens [Factors influencing vocational continuing education of workers in the second half of their working life]. In J. Abel (Ed.), *Berufliche Weiterbildung und neue Technologien* [Vocational continuing education and new technologies] (pp. 139–148). Munster: Waxmann.

Straka, G. A., & Nenniger, P. (1995). A conceptual framework for self-directed learning readiness. In H. B. Long and Associates (Eds.), *New ideas about self-directed learning* (pp. 243–257). Oklahoma: Oklahoma Research Center for Continuing Professional and Higher Education of the University of Oklahoma.

Thomae, H., & Lehr, U. (1973). *Berufliche Leistungsfähigkeit im mittleren and höheren Erwachsenenalter* [Professional competence in middle and old adult age]. Göttingen, Germany: Otto Schwartz.

Tough, A. (1979). *The adult's learning projects* (2nd ed.). Toronto, Canada: Institute for Studies in Education.

Commentary: The Older Worker and Organizational Restructuring: Beyond Systems Theory*

Victor W. Marshall

The chapter by Farr, Tesluk, and Klein summarizes a large literature on organizational structure of the workplace and its effects
on the older worker, using a systems theory approach for guidance. Useful as this framework is, all frameworks direct our gaze in one
direction, potentially diverting attention from other things. In my comments I want to partially reinforce some assertions made in the chapter
and to broaden our vision a bit beyond what the systems theory model
illuminates.

My comments on the chapter are informed by my own research
agenda at the University of Toronto, where I lead a multidisciplinary team
of researchers in a program called "Issues of an Aging Workforce." The
heart of our program is a set of firm-based studies in different sectors of

*Illustrative data in this chapter are from the project Issues of an Aging
Workforce, Victor W. Marshall, Principal Investigator, funded by the
Innovations Fund of Human Resources Development, Canada.

the economy. Two of these are in the United States, the remainder Canadian. We have completed case studies of: a Canadian life insurance company, Sun Life, and a matched study of Prudential in the United States; two case studies of the garment industry in Montreal and in New York City; a large gas pipeline utility and petrochemical manufacturer in Alberta (Nova Corporation); a medium-sized steel company in Hamilton, Ontario (Slater Steels); and a survey of over 2,000 retirees of Bell Canada. The case studies typically involve key informant interviews, focus groups, archival data gathering, a manager survey and a large employee survey. It will become evident that my perspective differs somewhat from that taken in the chapter under discussion (chapter 4), no doubt because my research grounding is in Canada and strongly influenced by European colleagues and scholarship, and because I start from a sociological rather than a psychological perspective.

VALUES, ATTITUDES, AND STEREOTYPES

Farr et al. (this volume) are quite convincing in arguing that organizational factors shape the relationship between age and work performance outcomes. Interestingly, many of the suggestions made to foster competence in the older worker—better lighting, sound ergonomics, enhancing control over work—are good for people of all ages. Moreover, most such innovations are not implemented explicitly to aid older workers. Their beneficial effects on older workers are unintended bonuses.

Organizational change is a broad term covering any "ways in which jobs are designed and work is organized" (O'Grady, 1993, p. 4). Organizational change can take many forms such as move toward teamwork or greater provision for flextime. It is closely tied to technological change. As chapter 1 emphasizes, recently it often means downsizing and a move toward leaner (some have said, "anorexic," some have said, "meaner") organizations. At Prudential, fully 71% of employees agree with the statement "Older workers can adapt to organizational change." However, older workers are significantly more likely to agree than younger workers (89% of employees aged 50+ but just 63% of employees aged less than 30 agree). A similar pattern is found regarding attitudes toward older workers, technology, and training. At Prudential, approximately two-fifths of respondents state that older workers do not want to be trained, are more difficult to train than younger workers, and cannot adapt to new technology. Again, while attitudes toward older workers in this domain are predominantly positive, they are less positive among younger workers than among older workers. These attitudes are not "hard"—for the most part, they are expressed by "slightly agree" rather than "strongly agree" response alternatives in a Likert format. However, adaptations to organizational change and to new technology seem to be the *only* areas in which reservations are expressed about older workers.

Here is where age norms and stereotypes can be a problem for the older worker. If managers with control over access to training activities or promotions think that older workers are not able to adapt to organizational change, this belief could well affect the career mobility or job security of older employees. Fortunately for older employees at most companies, those who have such control over the fate of other employees are more likely to be old. Moreover, it is essential to distinguish between attitudes and behavior. Farr and colleagues assert that "approximately three-fourths of all older workers believe that they have been discriminated against in some way in their employment." I suggest that this is an unrealistically high overestimate. In our case studies, we have found much lower rates in response to the direct question "Do you feel you have been discriminated against or favored, while working at (company)?; If yes, On what grounds?" For example, only 20% of employees at Prudential (of 784 surveyed) said they had experienced any discrimination. While older employees were more likely to say so, the percentage for workers aged 45 and older was only 25%. In total, 209 respondents of 784 employees surveyed claimed to have been discriminated against, but when these people suggested the basis of discrimination, only 7% of the reasons given were age. At Sun Life, in Canada, 18% of all employees, and a high of 32% for women aged 45 and older, claimed to have been discriminated against, but again, when we asked the basis, only 6% of the reasons given referred to age. Our other case studies show similar patterns.

One of the major findings of social psychology dating back for several decades, and perhaps rooted in attempts to assess the relationship between attitudes of racial prejudice and discriminatory behavior, is the finding that the relationship between attitudes and behavior is a tenuous one at best (Deutscher, 1973; LaPierre, 1935). Certainly, we should be alert to ageist attitudes and their possible translation into discriminatory behavior, but we should be equally alert to social and organizational patterns that might *unintendedly* have discriminatory effects on workers in one age group or another.

OLDER WORKER AS MENTOR

I want to reinforce the notion of the older worker as mentor to younger workers, as mentioned in chapter 4. In a Danish case study (Holm, 1994), older and younger workers in a cable manufacturing plant were trained together in new production technologies. Although the older workers were at first fearful of the new technology, they adapted well. The author of the study notes that, "The two groups of employees can learn from each other, which is resource-efficient: Older employees can transfer their work and life experience to younger employees and the company's stability is maintained" (Holm, 1994).

At Prudential, fully 88% of employees agree with the statement that "older workers serve as mentors for younger workers," and 73% agree that "older workers are respected." In our study at Nova, we dealt with employees whose work is potentially dangerous—workers in petrochemical plants and gas pipeline maintenance crews. Older workers in these environments are valued for the cautiousness that might be a basis of criticism or negative stereotyping in other environments. They were also valued for the knowledge they have by virtue of long-term employment. In one example, a work crew discussing a pipeline emergency situation was lauding an older worker. There was a danger of explosion. As a company that has acquired many small companies, Nova has not yet completed its program of developing a computerized engineering plan of its entire pipeline system. In this case, the records of the placement of shut-off valves were not terribly accurate, but the older worker knew where they were because he had helped to install them. I am reminded of the alleged basis for respect of elders in aboriginal society, rooted in their superiority in the oral tradition and knowledge of weather patterns and the migration habits of deer and elk. Although Nova Corporation has been downsizing its company for the past few years, early retirement is not the sole or primary mechanism. Senior management made a deliberate decision to avoid the loss of valued experience and mentoring potential of older workers.

CAREER, JOB, TASK

I would like to reinforce the view that "workers can no longer anticipate a career with a single company; rather, multiple careers and frequent job transitions are becoming the norm." One can argue that this development is positive or negative, and I am therefore disappointed at the tone of inevitability that runs through the chapter. Our employee survey provided responses from 986 Prudential employees to a question about how they obtained their current job. Only 30% said it was the result of a promotion, 21% said this was their first job, and 48% said their current job involved either a lateral move or a redefinition of their former job. Professionals were no more likely than administrative staff to say they attained their current job through a promotion. Just under a quarter of employees described their career histories as involving two or more jobs, moving up the organization; 56% saw themselves as having two or more jobs moving both up and across the organization; 11% described their careers as two or more jobs moving down and across the organization, and 10% as involving few, if any, job moves.

Younger employees are aware of the plateauing described in the chapter, and Prudential now discourages people from assuming they will have a career waiting for them. But the cause of concern is not merely the demographic factor of the large baby boom cohort. It is company downsizing. In our focus groups at Prudential, we ask people to talk about careers. One manager from the Human Resources Department said:

> The word career has been stricken literally from all Human Resources Development material. So after 23 years with a company, what do you have? You're not allowed to have a career any more because your job is, you know, could be eliminated tomorrow . . . you have a job and (are) grateful for it. . . . It is no longer a career . . . career is taboo, you can't even say the word when you're discussing it with someone, you cannot talk career; you cannot have the word career in documentation because there are no careers here anymore; and that's been very clearly spelled out to everyone.

If company policy no longer accepts the notion that the company provides careers, to its credit, Prudential carries through in support of its employees in this new modality. As one middle-aged male manager at Prudential put it:

> I think in the past I might have thought that a goal was to get promoted. But right now I think it might be better to take a rotational assignment to develop new knowledge or different skills that might help your ultimate marketability rather than going forward in a specific area where you have expertise. And Prudential does seem to be offering more and better training that's geared towards that type of activity.

Sociologists have customarily thought of a career as a property of the social structure of a firm (Sørensen, 1986); but companies like Prudential, Bell Canada, and Nova Corporation are either erasing the very concept or redefining it. At Nova, the term "career" is retained—the company has a "Career Resource Centre," for example. However, it fosters the notion that "you are your career." One of the slogans in this campaign to redefine the notion of career is, "Life is a highway and you are in the driver's seat." In company offices one can find full-length mirrors. Looking at yourself in the mirror you see the questions "Who am I? Where am I going?," with an invitation to the Career Resource Centre for guidance. Career in this milieu ceases to be a property of social structure and comes to be a property of the individual.

Not only the career, but the job is at risk with contemporary restructuring on a global scale. By job, I mean a short-term salaried position with at least some prospects for security in the near term. Such positions are in danger of disappearing as more companies switch to contracting out. Here the person is paid for the specific task or product rather than the time, or in such limited durations of work time that it could not be dignified by the term "job." In academia the distinction among career, job, and task are illustrated by the differences among the tenure-track professor, the limited contract professor, and the junior Ph.D. recruited to teach one course on a fill-in basis.

Chapter 4 provides strong insights into both the dangers and the importance of companies providing career management support to older workers to ensure their long-term viability and competitiveness within the organization and to ensure a fit to changing job characteristics (such as by providing desk jobs for older workers who are unable to maintain physical labor on the job). For the most part, age-related declines in *performance* are mythological, reflecting ageist stereotypes. On the other hand, there are some age-related decrements in perception, cognition, and strength that normally do not affect performance levels (Rix, 1990, pp. 62–63). Making adaptations without reinforcing negative stereotypes requires a finely tuned approach and more secure knowledge than we now possess.

A related point is the importance for companies to have a long-range view of their own human resources needs in relation to demographic changes in their workforces. Companies that have had no or few new hires for long periods of time will be demographically old, since most new employees tend to be young. If there are few younger employees, there is no one for the older employees to teach. Important skills and unwritten lore that are required for efficient production might be lost. We are finding this in our steel industry case study and know that it occurs in the Japanese steel industry as well, where new hires have been almost nonexistent. Similarly, companies that pursue aggressive, early retirement incentive programs risk losing too much of their expertise in a brief period of time.

THE SMALL FIRM IGNORED

One of the issues not addressed in chapter 4, and, indeed, not addressed in the literature, is the small firm. Most new jobs are created in small firms, suggesting that these might have demographically young structures. However, a contrary factor is that many small firms are family firms that might be more likely to retain older workers. And many displaced workers start their own small firms or become consultants—which might suggest the emergence of a new form of firm in age terms—the small firm of older workers. But I am speculating, as I know of no research literature in this area.

EXTENSIONS OF THE MODEL NEEDED

I would like to turn now to the formal systems model presented in the chapter by Farr and colleagues. The model presented as well as the review imply that corporate policies and programs are *explicitly* shaped by age norms, stereotypes about older versus younger workers, and cultural values and beliefs about aging. This is seen in the causal arrows within the second zone from the outside of Figure 4.1. These in turn are shaped by organizational structure, organizational design, and organizational strategies, as shown by the causal arrows pressing inward from the outer circle.

Our research suggests that the first premise concerning what shapes corporate policies and programs is not a strong one. In our experience, age is rarely *explicitly* considered by corporate management or by unions. Corporate policies and programs have differential effects on older and younger workers, but these are largely what sociologists call "unintended" consequences.

This is not to say that the corporate sector is unconcerned with demographic issues such as the shrinking number of entry-level applicants, their lack of experience and inadequate writing and verbal skills. However, in a Canadian version of the Towers Perrin Workforce 2000 Survey, 64% of the companies responding said that they were *not* concerned about the aging workforce. When it came to specific programs for older workers, while 42% said they use or plan to use retirees on special programs, only 3% of companies have a formal policy in this area; only 6% hire retirees as consultants; 5% have elder care counseling; 3% have gradual retirement; 4% have programs to retrain older workers (Towers Perrin, 1991). In the Canadian study, a questionnaire was sent to 1,500 senior managers in private- and public-sector organizations across Canada. The results should be viewed with caution since the response rate was only 29%.

The corporate logic, as I see it, is as follows: (1) any CEO who reads current advice on corporate reengineering will want to reengineer his or her corporation; (2) the most popular vehicle of reengineering today is downsizing the complement of employees; (3) the easiest way to downsize is through the early retirement incentive; (4) the early retirement incentive is most attractive to older workers, who have accumulated enough pension credits that (so they think or are led to believe) early retirement is a viable option.

There is an industry of academics who are very much aware of the effects of corporate downsizing on older workers, but this is of only incidental or passing interest to most corporate managers, with exceptions such as the case of the Ford Motor Company or the famous Days Inn experiment, which are described in chapter 4. (For some recent European cases, see Health Education Authority, 1994, and Snel & Cremer, 1994). In our research, Nova Corporation adopted an age-neutral policy for downsizing in explicit recognition of the value of older, experienced workers. But we academics hear about and write about those cases because of our own interests in the relationship between age and work. We should not delude ourselves into thinking that most corporations have age-sensitive policies. If nothing else, the difficulty we have had selling corporations on the value of participating in research in this area convinces me that for the majority of corporations, age is just not high priority. What I am saying here only underscores the importance of the authors' inference from the Ford case—that companies have to develop explicit "human resource practices that complement the types of changes initiated by the movement toward new organizational strategies and structures designed to face an increasingly competitive environment."

Although it is beyond the scope of this chapter, I would add that not only corporate policies, but also government policies in North America that have differential effects on younger and older workers are often not explicitly framed within the context of age. Rather, the age effects are consequences of policies intended for other purposes. An example would be government decisions about the mix of private and public pensions in a society, which are primarily motivated by concerns about the generation and control of pools of capital, and only incidentally concerned with the economic security of pensioners (Guillemard, 1991; Kohli, Rein, Guillemard, & van Gunsteren, 1991; Schmähl, 1989).

The systems theory model in the chapter holds that human resource policies and programs, the perception of such programs, and age norms, stereotypes, and beliefs are shaped by organizational structure, design, and strategies. But the model is, I suggest, incomplete. The chapter makes passing reference to global economic conditions, but these, I think, would be a major component in a model that paid more explicit attention to social structure.

Social structure is not reducible to norms and beliefs. It refers to relatively enduring, powerful, institutionalized patterns of social behavior that simultaneously express and shape these patterns. In contemporary society, and for these concerns, a dominant feature of social structure is the global socioeconomic system. And this global economy has a cultural dimension to it—a dimension that affects older workers differently than younger workers without explicitly considering age.

We cannot understand what is happening in the Montreal or New York garment industry without paying attention to the contracting out of many aspects of the manufacturing to India, China, or the southern United States, where wages are lower and benefits nonexistent. When these jobs are lost, semiskilled, middle-aged garment workers are displaced with very poor job prospects. At the same time, we cannot understand how the Montreal industry can survive in a global labor market, while continuing to pay wages much above world standards, without recognizing the importance of just-in-time delivery of products, the control over the industry by its large customers (the commercial retailers who buy its clothing), and the ability to ship clothing or parts of clothing by air cargo at low cost. All these things related to a global economy are beyond the scope of the model provided by Farr and colleagues in chapter 4. These issues are given brief mention in the text, in noting that "strategic initiatives of cost-effectiveness, total quality, customer service, and time-based competition require concurrent changes in design and structure . . . organizations are moving to flatter, more streamlined, decentralized structures organized around products, services, or customers, rather than functions." I might add, "rather than around employees."

As noted in the chapter, increasingly companies are trimming their core complements while relying on contractual labor to do more and more tasks. Nova Corporation, one of our case study sites, is actually giving contracts to new companies started by former Nova employees—companies that were started with Nova assisting employees who were taking an early exit option to write a business plan. And this downsizing program also has Nova giving substantial start-up grants to these employees who take its "entrepreneur program."

Another dimension of social structure that could be developed further is gender relations. Organizational changes that influence the timing of retirement will affect women and men differently because of historical differentials between men's and women's wages and their labor force histories. To illustrate anecdotally, I am told by colleagues working for the Canadian government civil service that a current major program of early retirement incentives is playing out very differently for male and female workers. In Ottawa, as would, I suppose, be the case in Washington, many dual-career families have husband and wife working in the public sector. Men typically have had more stable work histories at higher salaries than their spouses, who have suffered both gender discrimination in salaries and interrupted labor force histories due to child-rearing. They have accumulated too few pension credits and years of eligible service to earn attractive early retirement incentives. Their husbands are able to take early retirement while they continue to work.

CONCLUSIONS

The systems model has been useful in organizing a complex literature. I have directed my comments to reinforce some points made in the chapter, and to suggest that the notion of social structure can be developed further, to shed more light on this topic. I sense in the chapter a psychologist's emphasis on motivated behavior. While motivated behavior is obviously important, sociologists also direct their analytical gaze toward unintended consequences of social arrangements. Social structure can have effects independent of the motivated person whose behavior is constitutive of social structure. Organizational structures, policies, and programs can have unintended consequences that influence age-related phenomena. In particular, the large-scale reengineering and restructuring of work in both the public and private sectors that is now happening as a global phenomenon has occurred, I have suggested, with little if any explicit awareness of its age-sensitive effects. We should be attentive to both motivated behavior and unintended consequences in our quest for knowledge of the organizational structure of the workplace and its effects on the older worker.

REFERENCES

Deutscher, I . (Ed.). (1973). *What we say/what we do.* Glenview, IL: Scott Foresman.

Guillemard, A.M. (1991). International perspectives on early withdrawal from the labor force. In J. Myles & J. Quadagno (Eds.), *States, labor markets, and the future of old-age policy* (pp. 209–226). Philadelphia, PA: Temple University Press.

Health Education Authority. (1994). *Investing in older people at work. Contributions, case studies and recommendations.* London: Author.

Holm, G. (1994). Older employees' participation in organizational and technological changes—experience from a company undergoing changes. In J. Snel & R. Cremer (Eds.), *Work and aging: A European perspective* (pp. 283–291). London: Taylor and Francis.

Kohli, M., Rein, M., Guillemard, A.M., & van Gunsteren, H. (Eds.). (1991). *Time for retirement: Comparative studies of early exit from the labor force.* Cambridge: Cambridge University Press.

LaPierre, R. T. (1935). Attitudes vs. actions. *Social Forces, 13,* 230–237.

O'Grady, J. (1993). *Direct and indirect evidence on the extent of changes in work organization in Canada.* Report prepared for the Ontario Premier's Council on Economic Renewal. Toronto: Premier's Council on Economic Renewal.

Rix, S. E. (1990). *Older workers.* Santa Barbara, CA: ABC-CLIO.

Schmähl, W. (Ed.). (1989). *Redefining the process of retirement: An international perspective.* Berlin: Springer-Verlag.

Snel, J., & Cremer, R. (Eds.). (1994). *Work and aging: A European perspective.* London: Taylor and Francis.

Sørensen, A. (1986). Social structure and mechanisms of life-course processes. In A. B. Sørensen, F. E. Weinert, & L. R. Sherrod (Eds.), *Human development and the life course: Multidisciplinary perspectives* (pp. 177–197). Hillsdale, NJ: Earlbaum.

Towers Perrin. (1991). *Workforce 2000: Competing in a seller's market: A survey report on organizational responses to demographic and labour force trends in Canada.* Toronto: Author.

CHAPTER 5

Career Trajectories and the Older Worker

Aage B. Sørensen*

It is apparent, but not much noticed, that modern society does not need the economic participation of either end of the life course. Further, the needed middle part becomes smaller as the useless parts become larger. We store our children and youth for ever more years, and for ever more time in each of these years, in educational institutions, claiming that education is good for them and needed for their futures. We also store more and more older people, for ever more years, in a state called retirement, and tell them the state is good for older people and a reward for their past contributions to society. It is a development that costs society a great deal of money. The inactive parts of the life course need to be supported by someone. This someone is increasingly the state. More state involvement means a larger public sector. Therefore, the trend is also

---

* I am very grateful to the discussants, Ann Howard and Thomas Juster, and to Matin Rein, Matilda White Riley, K. Warner Schaie, and Annemette Sørensen for valuable comments and suggestions. I am grateful to Gina Hewes for editorial assistance.

associated with the growth and increasing importance of the welfare state (Kohli, 1994).

The shrinking of the economically active part of the life course has many explanations. The most common explanation points to the increasing complexity of the modern world and its rapid change. This is supposed to make educational preparation more important and work in old age more demanding. These explanations have merit, but the most direct and simple explanation for the shrinking active part of the life course is the increasing irrelevance of the old and the young to the rest of the population. The young become irrelevant, for we do not need our children to support us when we become old. We do not need the old, for they control little of economic interest to us. The consequences of the irrelevance of persons, at both ends of the life course, are not equal for the old and the young. Because we all hope and most expect to become old, we do want old people to have good lives. Further, the old possess a major resource, the vote, and they use this resource very effectively to extract benefits from the rest, in the manner of farmers and oil companies. We do not expect to become young again, and the young do not vote, so individuals in the first part of the life course suffer the greatest disadvantage.

Although the changes in the life course partly reflect changes in the relationship between work and age generated by changes in industrial structure, the irrelevance of old and young also reflects the very reduced role of intergenerational transfer in modern society.[1] The mechanism is straightforward. In former times, family ownership of property generated economic welfare above the minimum needed for subsistence. The main concern thus was to maintain the match between the family and property. In families owning property, the old controlled something of interest to the young, the property, and they could use it to extract care and subsistence in old age. The young controlled something of interest to the old, which is their ability and willingness to maintain and expand the family property. Investment in the young was therefore in the interest of the old. In other words, since economic welfare, including welfare for the ill and the disabled, depended on maintaining the match between property and the family, family strategies governed the major events across the life course.

In modern society, the match between family and property has become irrelevant for most of the population, and economic welfare and active participation in economic decision making can no longer be extracted from the younger generation by controlling succession. The old have become inactive and powerless in the economic sphere except as consumers.

This chapter will discuss how the loss of economic power of the old influences their working life. The irrelevance of youth for society deserves a separate treatment. It is a topic largely ignored although the signs of the irrelevance of youth are abundant—high unemployment, ever later age of marriage, and stopgap jobs, rather than real careers.

Careers are flows of income and other benefits over time, and we usually restrict the term to flows generated by employment. There are many types of careers, and they provide very different trajectories—some are stable and flat, others are irregular and unstable, others again provide increasing income and other job benefits through most of the life course. At the end of the life course, however, all careers provide mainly risks for losses and few opportunities for gain. The result is that as persons become older, they become increasingly vulnerable or attracted to entering the state of retirement and leave the world of work. Few of us will be asked to stay on. Many may be offered incentives to leave, or forced to leave, because we cannot recover our careers after a job loss. The old cannot structure their world to prevent these events, for it is common to all careers based on employment that they do not provide the kind of control over the lives of the young that property provides.

Career types differ with respect to how the career of the older worker unfolds, and it is the purpose of this chapter to identify these differences. The differences are created by the labor market structure in which the employment is located. The differences largely determine how the state of retirement is entered, in particular, whether the working career is ended voluntarily. Ironically, the best careers, that is, those providing the highest economic and social benefits, are exposed to the greatest risks for involuntary termination because these careers are most vulnerable to external shock and to structural and organizational constraints on employment. How these differences come about is the main topic for the discussion that follows.

How labor market structures shape careers is discussed next. The discussion will identify three main structures of career types. They are careers in open, unstructured *spot labor markets*; in structured *job competition jobs* with closed employment relationships; and in *promotion systems* in internal labor markets. Next follows an analysis of aging and the three main types of career trajectories, and finally, some ideas about the future.

EMPLOYMENT CONTRACTS AND CAREERS

Labor markets allocate persons to jobs giving them a certain level of income, social status, and other job rewards in return for work. The rewards will differ according to the effort and abilities of the person, and for a given level of performance the rewards will vary according to the particular type of employment. Both economics and sociology have created a large literature on labor markets, emphasizing how different segments and structures of these markets create different outcomes in terms of socioeconomic attainment and employment. The literature proposes many different ways to identify different labor market structures. For our purposes, an emphasis on the employment contract is particularly relevant. This contract (usually implicit) specifies how pay and other rewards from work are tied to individual performance, and it specifies the conditions governing the termination of the employment contract.

The simplest employment contract is an agreement about the execution of a single task such as mowing a lawn or removing a tooth. The task is well described and the execution well controlled by the worker. There are two questions to consider: how much pay is to be received for completing the task, and when does the employment contract end. The answers to both questions in this case are simple. The employment contract ends when the task is completed. The pay is the outcome of a competition among workers bidding to obtain the contract, or so theory suggests. The accepted bid, usually the cheapest, becomes the pay for the task. In other words, prices for work are determined as prices for other goods, and employment contracts are like sales contracts.

The scenario of employment contracts being like sales contracts means that labor markets are *spot markets*. Supply and demand will govern pay in the normal manner. Workers will receive pay, usually measured at the hourly wage, that for a given demand schedule reflects their productivity as governed by effort and ability. Workers will try to find the best employment, and employers the best workers, for the given wage rate. In equilibrium, equally productive workers will be paid the same, and firms can be indifferent to whom they employ and workers to who employs them.

For the present purposes, the major implication of this scenario is that people change wages only when market demand changes or when they change their abilities and efforts. Market demand is not something the individual worker can do much about, except perhaps move to a market segment with higher demand. Changes in abilities and efforts constitute changes in the worker's supply of work. It is useful here to conceive of a unit of measure, sometimes called an efficiency unit of work, and to conceive of effort and ability as governing the number of efficiency units supplied per unit time. Abilities are usually seen as partly innate and stable over time, partly as variable because of the acquisition or loss of skill. If the sales contract scenario describes labor markets, then changes in wages by age must come about because of age-related changes in productivity, that is, a change in the number of efficiency units supplied, or by age-related changes in mobility among market segments with different demands. Age-related changes in individual productivity are produced by acquisition or deterioration of abilities to perform tasks or by changes in effort. Ability changes are produced by biological changes in capacities, physical or mental, related to aging, or by the acquisition or loss of skills. We have a well-developed theory about changes in skills, the theory of human capital, and a fair amount of knowledge and ideas about age dependency in capacities. These ideas will be considered further in this chapter.

For given demand schedules, the sales contract, or open-employment scenario, means that equally productive workers will obtain equal wage rates. There is one modification of this assumption. Workers' preferences for tasks will decide the actual supply to tasks and cause a variation in wage rates that compensates for the variation in preferences. These compensating differentials are of relevance for aging processes if workers' preferences change with age, for example, their preference for physically demanding or unpleasant tasks.

The scenario of treating the sale of work as sale of other goods in spot markets is, of course, the conception of labor markets attributed to neoclassical economics. Nobody claims that labor markets are like this, except perhaps in a few unusual places like docks. The issue is whether it suggests a sufficiently realistic scenario for the standard price theory to offer a useful theory of labor markets. About this there is much disagreement and a large literature proposing other scenarios both from economics and sociology.

The simplest modification of the neoclassical scenario suggests that the market is differentiated into submarkets with different demand schedules. Workers with identical productivity obtain different prices for their labor, depending on which submarkets they are in. Within each submarket, the standard price theory applies, and changes in individual performance create changes in relative wage rates. Between submarkets there will be wage differences not related to individual productivity, but only to the location of individuals. In other words, there will be advantages and disadvantages not associated with individual ability and effort. These advantages and disadvantages are a type of rent provided by the specific submarket in which the individual is employed. I will refer to such advantages or disadvantages unrelated to individual productivity as *employment rents*. They can be both positive and negative in relation to what the individual would have obtained had there been no submarkets. If there is effective market competition, employment rents would be what Marshall (1949) calls *quasi-rents*, and would eventually be eliminated by the competition.

Workers paid less than they would in another submarket should move to better paid employment. It is, of course, to the advantage of employers that workers are paid less than they are worth elsewhere, so negative rents should be associated with monopsony—monopolization of labor demand by a single employer. This is a rare phenomenon, according to the conventional wisdom. The permanency of monopsony presumably is dependent on the employer's ability to control the movement of workers or the ability to take advantage of geography or other barriers to movement. Workers paid more than they would be paid elsewhere should try to stay where they are. Employers should try either to get rid of them or to lower their wages. The positive employment rents will disappear unless the worker obtains some degree of control over his or her employment. A protection against dismissal also protects against lowering of wages, for using the threat of dismissal is the most effective means to lower a worker's relative wage. The permanency of the worker's monopoly over the job thus depends on the degree to which the decision to end the employment relationship resides with the worker. In other words, the permanency of the employment rents depends on the degree to which the employment relationship is *closed* (in contrast to the sales contract employment relationship created for single tasks, where the employment relationship is completely *open*). The closed nature of the employment relationship can derive from many sources—collective action by unions or professional organizations, monitoring and other transaction costs making it efficient to grant workers job security, and certain training arrangements. I will discuss further these reasons for closed employment relationship in later parts of the chapter.

When employment rents are obtained in a single job and end when that job is left, the (closed) employment relationship can be said to cover this particular job. I will consider these employment relationships as employment relationships for single jobs and the job structure involved as *job-competition jobs,* using a term suggested by Thurow (1975). They are jobs in very flat career trajectories. They are typically skilled and craft, blue-collar jobs. Job incumbents typically keep the job until a better job becomes available, and, therefore, some growth in wages and other job rewards will often take place with age. A better job is available in closed employment relationships when the previous incumbents leave the job, or a new job is created. The allocation of persons to jobs in a closed employment relationship thus assumes that a vacancy exists and is governed by a process of *vacancy competition* (Sørensen, 1977, 1983). This is a different process from the process that allocates persons to tasks in the spot markets described previously. In particular, in vacancy competition, a change (growth) in wages is not necessarily associated with changes in individual performance. This has important consequences for the career trajectories in old age for workers employed in these job structures, as I will show next.

Job-competition jobs are often closed because of collective agreements negotiated by unions or because of the threat of unions. There is another major reason for closed employment: the firm has made an investment in the training of the worker, in the form of firm-specific on-the-job training and, therefore, has an incentive to keep the worker in the firm. This means keeping the worker also when he or she changes jobs and the firm has an incentive to extend the employment relationship to cover a sequence of jobs. For reasons explained later in this chapter, the sequence of jobs will be organized in a promotion schedule, and I therefore will refer to the job structures where employment relationships cover a sequence of jobs or a career as *promotion-system jobs.* These jobs are typically white-collar or managerial jobs, but job ladders that span the blue-collar/white-collar line are also frequent.[2] With these employment relationships, firms and workers may be conceived of as sharing employment rents generated by the particular match of a firm and a worker with skills specific to the particular firm. Marshall calls such rents *composite rents* (1949). The application of the concept to the analysis of labor market structures is discussed in Sørensen (1996).

Closed employment relations pose an incentive problem. In job-competition jobs, there are two main solutions to this problem (Sørensen, 1994): efficiency wages and output-based incentive systems. The very existence of the employment rent creates an efficiency wage that instills effort. The literature suggests a variety of mechanisms explaining how employment rents act as an incentive (Akerlof & Yellen, 1986). Two of these mechanisms assume that the employment relationship is not completely closed. One is the threat of dismissal that will result in a loss of the employment rent either as a result of unemployment or employment in the open spot market (Solow, 1979). The second is the threat of the loss of a relative advantage provided by the employment rent, suggested by reference group theory (Merton & Rossi, 1950). A third mechanism is consistent also with completely closed employment relationships. As suggested by Akerlof (1982), the employment rent may be seen as a gift, to be reciprocated with greater effort.

Another solution to the incentive problem is to create an output-based incentive system in the form of a piece rate or a commission system. Piece rate and commission systems in fact try to eliminate whatever rents are associated with closed employment relationships by reestablishing the direct link between pay and the execution of tasks. Workers know this and therefore establish norms to regulate effort. A variety of schemes, such as group incentive systems, try to overcome the obstacles to the full operation of output-based incentive systems. There is a vast literature on the social processes generated by output-based incentive systems, as well as on the possible misdirection of effort (disregard of quality issues) produced by incentive systems. I have reviewed this literature elsewhere (Sørensen, 1994).

Output-based incentive systems assume that output can be measured with some accuracy. When this is not so, or when the measurement of only some aspect of the output produces a misdirection of effort, input-based incentive systems emerge. These are incentive systems based on a measurement or rating of the worker's performance rather than on the results of this performance. Again, a variety of such systems exist. Common to all of them is that the performance evaluation results in some kind of increase in wages or other job rewards. This can come about because of a promotion to a better job, or from a merit pay increase within the current job. In either case, the career gain is cumulative if the worker remains with the same employer. As noted previously, the resulting promotion systems are often associated with specific on-the-job training arrangements, but other reasons for closed employment relationships could also produce these incentive systems.

Promotion and similar incentive systems provide career gains that will increase the size of the employment rent as the individual ages. This means that the employment presumably becomes ever more costly to the firm, reducing over time whatever other efficiency advantages these employment structures provide. The common solution to this problem is the establishment of career trajectories where the worker is paid less than his or her marginal productivity at the start of the career and more than his or her marginal productivity at the end of the career. This arrangement thus assumes an implicit contract between the worker and the firm, a contract that is vulnerable in two ways. The firm has an incentive to default on the contract for older workers. This incentive is clearly important for the career trajectories of older workers (cf. Lazear, 1979).

The various solutions to the incentive problems caused by the closed employment relationship reduce the employment rent, when incentives work as intended, either because workers work harder than they otherwise would have, or because positive employment rents in the latter part of the career are being countered by negative rents in the early part of the career. The reduction in employment rents means that these job structures are not necessarily disadvantageous to firms and that they may persist in competitive markets. However, the very existence of the closed employment relationship has an important consequence for the link between individual performance and career trajectories. The closed employment relationship creates "grid" (Douglas, 1982), which is the insulation of individuals from competition by others. The more closed the employment relations, the more grid created by job structures. Input- and output-based incentive systems may reduce the insulation, but, for a variety of reasons, they cannot reestablish open competition.

The establishment of an employment relationship is the establishment of an indefinite and possibly long-term relationship. A second important consequence of the closed employment relationship is that the prediction of future performance is the main consideration when hiring the worker. Incentive systems again modify this, so that prediction of performance is less important in effective output-based systems than in input-based incentive systems. The prediction of performance must be based on indicators the employer assumes are indicators of performance: employment history, education, race, gender, and age. The resulting vacancy competition will be based on rankings of candidates for the closed job, not on their absolute level of performance. Individual careers tend to become interdependent in closed employment relationships, the more closed the job structure and the smaller the firm.

A third consequence of the closed employment relationship is the dependence of employment on the organizational changes of individual firms. In open employment, the worker can be completely indifferent to the firm that employs him or her. In job-competition jobs, the fate of the worker is tied to the fate of the firm for the duration of the job. In promotion systems, the fate of the worker is tied to the fate of the firm for the whole career.

These three sets of consequences of closed employment are important for the career trajectories of older workers. I will now discuss these careers in more detail for the three main types of job structures considered in this chapter.

LABOR MARKET STRUCTURES AND AGING

The three types of employment relationships define three different types of labor market structures with very different mechanisms for how people are matched to jobs and the wage rates and other benefits they provide. These different mechanisms explain observed career trajectories over age and enable predictions about the shape of the careers. The predictions are all very similar, and consistent with empirical evidence about the shape of careers as age-earnings and age-status profiles. I will first show this and then describe the consequences for the trajectories of older workers for each segment.

Consider first the spot markets' characteristics of completely open employment relationships. With completely open employment relationships, age-related changes come about because of changes in individual productivity reflecting changes in general productivity or in specific abilities. Changes in specific abilities may, for example, be changes in physical strength. The other main source of change in careers, entry into submarkets providing employment rents, will not result in stable and systematic changes by the definition of open employment relationships. Where temporary rents are important because of labor market imperfections, the resulting careers will tend to be chaotic, a characteristic sometimes used to define secondary labor markets in the early dual labor market literature (e.g., Doeringer & Piore, 1971).

Systematic age patterns presumably reflect changes in mental and physical capacities due to the biological aging process or changes caused by specific training activities undertaken by the worker. The combined effect is a career pattern that shows an increase in earnings and other job rewards in the early years, a stabilization in the middle years, and a decline in later years. There is considerable empirical support for this pattern, and it is well explained by what we know or believe about biological aging processes and by the major theory for the age-related training processes, human capital theory. This theory argues that training will concentrate in the younger years because the period of obtaining returns on the investments will then be longest and because training costs will be lowest, because of lower levels of earnings forgone and perhaps because of more efficient learning because of higher ability and fewer distractions. In older years, skills become obsolete and physical and mental productive capacities decline.

The evidence is not as unambiguously supportive of spot labor markets and human capital theory, as is sometimes assumed. It is well known that part of the age patterns can be attributed to cohort differences. The decline in older years may reflect the general growth of the economy into the 1970s and the growth in younger years may also be caused by cohort differences—because of falling real wages in the United States from the late 1970s and onward. Nobody would attribute all of the changes to cohort effects, however. There is ample evidence, especially for the growth in the younger years, available from longitudinal data (see, e.g., Neumark & Taubman, 1995, for earnings, and Sørensen, 1978, for status).

The observed pattern of growth followed by stability and eventual decline is genuine, if somewhat exaggerated by cohort effects. However, very different mechanisms can explain the pattern than changes in productivity produced by biology and training. In job-competition jobs, job security normally allows workers to remain in their jobs until a better job appears. This produces a growth in earnings and other job rewards until the worker reaches the job that is the best he or she can hope to obtain. As the worker approaches this job, the rate of shifts declines and we obtain a career pattern that mirrors exactly the pattern predicted by Human Capital Theory (Sørensen, 1977). After reaching the best job, most job shifts will be involuntary. Such shifts usually produce a loss in wages and other job rewards. The career trajectory of the older worker is therefore one of stability or of decline. In contrast to open employment relationships, the entire career pattern in job-competition jobs can be explained by the age grading of opportunities for better jobs, without any changes in individual productivity.

Promotion systems create career patterns designed to provide a set of employment events, promotions, that provide incentives for competition and generate effort. The major organizational problem is to establish a promotion schedule that will generate a rate of promotion sufficient to make promotions available to all, but not to establish a rate so high that promotions are taken for granted. This is not a simple task when the basic organizational form is to be preserved. There are a number of ways to establish a system. Most firms establish differential rates of promotions where the different rates reflect assessments of performance. These rates may change differentially over time—in the extreme case so that some workers continue to be promoted as they age, while others cease to be promoted. Whatever the system, the promotion schedules taken together likely produce age profiles that correspond to the one typically observed: increases in younger years followed by average stability and eventual decline as workers are induced or forced to leave the system.

Although the empirical predictions about the shape of the career trajectory over the life course are the same for all types of employment structures, the different mechanisms that produce them create different economic and psychological consequences of aging. These consequences are outlined next, for each of the three types of employment structures.

Aging in Spot Labor Markets

In spot labor markets, individual productivity is the main determinant of wages and earnings, and changes in productivity are produced by physical and mental aging processes. The physical capacities presumably peak in young adulthood, but actual physical ability might well continue to increase for a while because of increased experience, even in the absence of any deliberate training activities. The physical capacities presumably decline in older years. The appearance of declining health may, of course, be misleading. Separating the incentive effect of retiring from the actual decline in health and physical capacities is difficult.

We do have evidence on the effect of physical decline from a system without incentives to retire. Ransom and Sutch (1995) calculate ages of peak productivity for journeymen (based on surveys in New Jersey) in the last century, using self-reports on when these workers felt they were in decline. They estimate the onset of decline to be the early 50's. Though it can be argued that these ages are earlier than they would be today, because of the better health of older people today, the bias is probably not major. Most of the decline in mortality is caused by reduction in infant and child mortality and by reduction in infectious disease as a cause of death and morbidity. Therefore, there was also more selection in the relevant ages in the last century.

The evidence for age-related changes in mental capacities is produced in particular by the pioneering use of cohort-sequential methods by Schaie (1979; see also Baltes, Dittmann-Kohli, & Dixon, 1984). The consensus seems to be that mental capacity or intelligence has two components, one called fluid, the other called crystallized. The crystallized intelligence, basically the amount of knowledge available to the person, seems to increase with age; fluid intelligence, or speed of operation, remains stable and then declines. Crystallized intelligence might often not be relevant for job performance in the employment sector considered here, but we know very little about these matters. Fluid intelligence may have relevance for task completion in open employment situations, at least with the ability to carry out different tasks. This suggests stable, if not declining, mental capacities with age. However, we also know that most older people have substantial mental reserve capacity to call on, so a prediction of a systematic decline in mental capacity to explain changing career patterns is not warranted (see, e.g., Baltes & Baltes, 1990). Among the biological aging processes relevant for productivity and wages in open employment relationships, physical capacity is likely the most relevant. This suggests declining wage rates with age, at least from the early 50's, especially pronounced for persons who start in physically demanding jobs and are forced by age into less demanding, and less well paying jobs. The same pattern, of course, will obtain, should workers prefer less demanding jobs with age, even if the capacities do not decline, for example, because their income needs decline as children leave home.

Training and schooling will modify the age trajectory in mental and physical capacities. However, training will not fundamentally change the predictions about the career pattern in old age. A decline in older years can also be justified by human capital theory because of the obsolescence of skills. The argument is popular, especially by those who make a living by training others, but we know little about the extent to which obsolescence actually occurs. Many other mechanisms can explain the decline, if it occurs. Those who attribute declines to obsolescence often advocate training programs as the cure for unemployment and early retirement. Human capital theory has a clear prediction about such retraining: the older the person, the lower the return on the training because the less time is left in the labor force and the more costly the training (due to earnings forgone and possibly lower rates of learning). According to theory, this means that the training must be subsidized to be undertaken at all. It may be argued that if skills rapidly become obsolete, the incentive to concentrate the training in younger years is reduced. However, the likely higher training costs in older age will continue to provide a disincentive to training older workers.

The economic consequences of aging in spot labor markets are clear-cut. The worker's own wage rate will likely decline or at best remain stable. A decline in wage rates will, by itself, reduce labor supply and therefore earnings, because of the substitution of leisure for work. So will a decline in income needs. Even without income substitutes to wages, we should therefore expect a decline in hours worked from middle age and onward. The availability of transfers magnifies the effect, especially transfers from public sources. The most important such transfers are public pensions—in the United States, Social Security—but there are many other transfers relevant for older workers. Unemployment benefits are one. Unemployment is not supposed to occur in the spot market. Nevertheless, when it occurs, theory predicts it should be search unemployment, as people quit their jobs in the search for higher wage rates. For older workers, theory may not be a very good guide, not even for workers employed in the open sector. Nevertheless, unemployment is probably less intimately involved in retirement decisions in the spot labor market than in the closed labor market structures to be discussed later. Other public transfers, especially disability pensions, are probably more importantly involved in the retirement decisions for older workers in the spot market sectors.

The overall career pattern for the older worker in open employment jobs is likely to be one of gradual reduction in labor supply as transfer payments become available. The availability of transfers is a matter of designing eligibility requirements and of taxation of earnings by the various programs. Current changes try to delay the reduction in labor supply, presumably with some success, as retirement rates have stabilized in the United States. This is taken by some to be evidence of the increasing healthiness of older workers. However, improvements in the benefits available from public pensions or deterioration of the economy, which lowers labor demand and wage rates, would probably cause a further decrease in the age of retirement.

The psychological and social consequences of retirement from careers in the open sector should be modest. People change their labor supply voluntarily, and they have some control over their lives and incomes as soon as alternative means of support from public pensions and the like are available. By the definition of "open sector," firms do not have attachments or investments in workers, and workers do not have attachments and investments in firms and coworkers. Retirement is unlikely to have much of a negative impact on health and psychological well-being, and, probably, usually a positive one—unless the leisure is too unmanageable. Some support for this proposition is provided by House et al. (1992). They show that although psychological self-efficacy is declining continuously for persons with high socioeconomic status from middle into old age, self-efficacy is increasing for persons with low socioeconomic status as they grow older, except in the very end of the life course. This pattern presumably reflects the career trajectories of older workers and the events leading to retirement.

Aging in Job-Competition Jobs

The most salient characteristic of job-competition jobs for aging processes is that they provide insulation from market competition. Changes in physical and mental capacities are less relevant for the career pattern. The main concern for the worker is to preserve the employment rent. A worker, therefore, will remain in his or her job until he or she decides to leave the job voluntarily or until he or she is forced to leave. A voluntary leave occurs if the worker finds a better job or decides that he or she is better off not working and being retired. An involuntary leave occurs when the job is eliminated, or if the job or the worker is covered by a mandatory retirement rule[3] or a pension rule that forces or strongly induces the worker to leave. Most workers are likely to obtain the best job they can hope to obtain by middle age. Job shifts after that time, if any, are likely to be involuntary. Since involuntary job shifts take place when the worker must find a job, they are likely to result in a loss of earnings. Unless the worker is covered by a generous private pension scheme, retirements are also likely to result in loss of income because the employment rents usu-ally mean that the earnings from work cannot be replaced completely by public pensions and transfers. Retirements are triggered by a job loss, or by a retirement rule. They will be abrupt and usually complete and not gradual as in the open sector.

Job losses are caused by the elimination of the job, because of a cur-tailment of production (or budget reduction in public sector jobs), or by ill health and incapacity. In both cases, the job loss will often be followed by a period of unemployment and/or disability. Unemployment in job-competition jobs results from a layoff is therefore often involuntary, in contrast to the voluntary search unemployment supposed to characterize careers in the open sector. It should be noted that there seems to be con-siderably more unemployment in the job-competition sector than one would expect from the number of permanent job losses. Temporary lay-off is a common method to regulate production by firms using these employment relationships. These layoffs are suspensions of jobs rather than permanent job losses. The job suspensions may result in some income loss for a period, but when the worker is recalled, the basic career pattern is resumed.

Permanent job losses, because of permanent elimination of the job and loss of rights to recall, or because of longer term illness or disability, result in spells of unemployment concluded either (1) by permanent withdrawal from the labor force, or (2) by entry into a job in the spot market, or (3) by regaining a similar job to the one lost in the closed sector. The latter out-come is usually the most favorable, but this outcome is difficult to achieve for the middle-aged and older worker. The reason is the mechanism for the allocation of people to jobs used in this employment sector.

As noted previously, in closed jobs persons are allocated to jobs in a process of vacancy competition. This means there has to be a vacancy available (either because the previous incumbent has left or because a new job has been created). Candidates for this vacancy are ranked by firms in terms of their predicted future performance because the match between the person and the job is difficult or impossible to undo, once it is made. Employers will use a variety of observable characteristics of the candidate to make this prediction, and age is likely to be one of them. Age may be believed to provide more employment stability and better work habits. However, age is also believed to give higher risks of illnesses and disability; the skills of the old are more likely to be obsolete; and the old simply will have less time left with the firm to recuperate costs of firm- and job-specific on-the-job training. Whether or not aging confers disadvantages in the competition for vacant jobs may depend on specific circumstances. Older age evidently is usually a disadvantage, however, for it can be shown that both length of unemployment spells and withdrawal from labor force after a spell of unemployment is highly related to age. In Europe, unemployment is the major route to early retirement (Kohli & Rein, 1991), and job-competition jobs are probably more important in European labor markets than in the United States.

The choice between (early) retirement and a job in the spot market after a job loss in the closed sector is obviously dependent on the availability of a pension. A worker not covered by a private pension enters the spot market for jobs and then decides if and how much to work. For workers with a private pension, this additional pension will be important and when available should lead to higher rates of retirement. About half (52%) of full-time workers in the private sector have private pensions, and almost all in the public sector have pensions (Turner & Beller, 1992). These pensions are presumably provided to workers involved in closed employment relationships in job competition and promotion-system jobs. There are two main reasons for such pensions. One is that firms have an incentive to keep workers attached to the firm because of a wish to capture the returns on investments in on-the-job training. The other is collective agreements between workers and firms, typically created by unions, or the wish to avoid unions. In job-competition jobs, collective agreements are the typical reason for the pension schemes. The reason for pension schemes in this case is that training arrangements are less important for the emergence of closed employment relationships and firms have less investment in workers.

Pensions in job-competition jobs may be used by firms to ease the consequences of job losses for workers when a reduction in labor force is desired. This is a pattern that is widely believed to have been followed by firms in Germany and elsewhere in Europe with a highly skilled labor force (Jacobs, Kohli, & Rein, 1991). A similar pattern presumably exits in the United States involving manufacturing firms with job-competition jobs.

Even when they are not used to justify job destruction and the creation of early retirements, private pension schemes typically produce less than completely voluntary retirements because of retirement rules. The effect of the pension depends on whether it is a defined-benefit pension or a defined-contribution pension. With defined benefits, there are often more disincentives to work (Burkhauser & Quinn, 1994), and separation from the firm, therefore, often will be abrupt and result in an abrupt exit from the labor force. With defined contributions, there is less or no penalty for working. However, the gradual adjustment of labor supply expected from defined-contribution pensions is much less likely to occur when employment is in job-competition jobs than in spot market jobs, because the indivisibility of the former jobs makes it difficult to work part time. Defined contribution pensions will produce gradual retirement rates only if the worker shifts into the open employment sector.

In job-competition jobs, careers of older workers may produce gains in earnings and other job rewards without any increased effort and skill by the worker, if vacancies in better jobs emerge and the older worker becomes ranked higher than other candidates for the job. This is not a likely outcome since most workers will have reached the best job they will ever attain by middle age. However, jobs in this sector will still protect the worker from falling attainments even when performance declines because of the insulation from competition. The price to be paid for these advantages is that external events, unrelated to the worker's individual performance, can destroy the worker's career unexpectedly. Even when the job termination is anticipated, the exit from employment may be abrupt and complete, whatever the intellectual and physical capacity of the worker.

The economic consequences of aging in job-competition jobs are much less predictable than with spot market jobs. Careers of older workers in these employment structures are especially vulnerable to business downturns and disability, because economic and health events have much more dramatic consequences than such events in the open sector, where gradual adjustments are more feasible. The firms magnify the business cycle effect on the job. In periods of upturn, firms have an interest in keeping workers to reduce hiring costs and help in the training of new workers. In downturns, firms often have a direct interest in shedding older workers.

Public transfers are relevant for the careers of older workers in the job-competition jobs as an income alternative when they have lost their jobs and are forced to move into the spot market sector. Disability pensions also are important for workers who have lost their jobs because of ill health or accidents and are unable to regain access to job-competition jobs.

Workers are likely to form strong attachments to their jobs in the job-competition sectors and the jobs may become important sources of identity. The psychological consequences of career events are therefore likely to be different and stronger in the job-competition sector than in the spot market sector. Job losses produced by destruction of jobs by the business cycle or by ill health govern changes in careers, and this means that the career seems to be outside the control of the individual. The insulation from competition means that the individual cannot avoid or mitigate a career loss by working harder or acquiring new skills. Career events are thus likely to produce a feeling of lack of control and to result in depression and resignation. In contrast, open sector workers, even if worse off economically, can maintain a sense of control and adapt to the changes in their employment prospects and attainments.

While careers of older workers in the job-competition sector are very much dependent on the events in the external market produced by the business cycle, the careers of older workers in promotion system jobs are also intimately tied to events in the organization. These events may be independent of the behavior of the larger market. These careers are discussed next.

Aging in Promotion Systems

Promotion systems, being closed employment systems covering the whole career, provide insulation from competition from workers from outside the firm. However, they are often designed to create competition within the firm among a cohort of workers at the same career stage. The competition can be more or less direct. Systems that rely on ratings of performance for salary increases and other career changes often do not explicitly compare a specific set of workers, or when such comparisons are required, often provide everyone very high ratings. Systems that primarily rely on changes in job titles and assignments for career changes usually do select a winner out of a specific pool of candidates. In other words, a rank order tournament is created. The latter is likely the most effective incentive system and is the system I shall concentrate on here.

The incentive effect of tournaments depends on the size of the price to be obtained from the contest, that is, the gain in earnings and status resulting from the promotion. The salient measure of the gain is the gain compared to the gains of others of about the same career age. This relative gain depends on the rate of promotion. If the rate of promotion is very high, everyone can expect to gain, and the relative advantage offered by a contest will be modest. The incentive effect should be correspondingly modest. If the rate of promotion is very low, the expected relative gain is so low that trying for the price may not seem worth the effort. Further, when the rate of promotion is low, work groups are stable, and it is therefore more likely that collective agreements to control effort will be effective (see Sørensen, 1994, for an elaboration of this argument). The incentive effect of the career changes is again modest.

At the firm level, the rate of promotion will be determined by the rate at which vacancies occur at the various job levels. This rate is governed by two components: the shape of the organization and the rate at which new vacancies are created by people leaving the system and by new jobs being created (Sørensen, 1977). The shape of the organization is governed by the relative size of the various job levels and the number of levels. The more jobs there are at each level and the more levels there are, the more opportunities for promotion in the system. The second component to the rate of promotion is the rate at which new vacancies emerge. This component is governed by the age and seniority distribution of the firm's workforce, which will determine the rate of exits, and by the growth of the firm, which will determine the rate at which new vacant jobs appear.

Effective promotion rates or opportunity structures require that the firm can control the rates. The determinants of the rates are controllable to varying degrees. The shape of the organization is clearly strongly influenced by firm size. Though some variation can be created at a given size, there are obvious constraints on what is possible in smaller firms. In smaller firms, it may thus be very difficult, if not impossible, to design an effective promotion system. The rate at which new vacancies appear is also largely not controlled by the firm. It depends on the rate of growth. Rate of growth, in turn, depends on product markets, and if there is no increase in demand, firms are unlikely to create new jobs. If there is an increase, firms, of course, can adjust more or less fully to the opportunity for expansion. The factor that is most fully under the firm's control is the rate of exit from the firm. This fact is clearly of major importance for the lives and careers of older workers.

The firm's need to have control over the rate of exit combines with the employment rent provided older workers to create the main forces shaping their careers. Given the typical career, firms have a strong incentive to default on the implicit contract, which means younger workers are paid less than they are worth and older workers are paid more. The main constraint on the firm's ability to appropriate the employment rents for older workers is the need not to create too high promotion rates for younger workers. A second constraint is possibly also the firm's concern for its reputation.

Older workers have most likely been promoted for the last time, except possibly those in higher managerial positions. Since older workers are not involved in rank order tournaments anymore, their performance may be irrelevant for their careers. Their careers are much more strongly affected by the usefulness of their departures from the firm for the careers of younger workers than by the usefulness of their abilities and efforts.

The specific path taken out of the working career depends on the job level achieved by the worker. Middle and lower level workers, involved in promotion systems, end their careers much like workers in job-competition jobs, that is, through job elimination. They move directly into retirement or into the open employment sector. The move may be preceded by a period of involuntary unemployment or disability. Private pensions are very likely to be available for this group of workers, since this is one method for the firm to maintain the attachment of the worker to the firm.

For upper-level management, direct job elimination may be unfeasible (every firm needs a president). This does not reduce the need for the firm to control the exit rates for top level management. Their departures have cascading effects down the organization, and the employment rents to be gained by the firm may be very substantial. The solution is to give these workers inducements for departure. These inducements can be considerable, especially for the highest level and highest paid positions, where the employment rents forgone by departure are largest.

Much sociological literature on the labor market uses authority as a major independent variable and finds that it has a substantial effect on earnings (e.g., Wright, 1979). Presumably this effect reflects the importance of power in firm labor markets. One might therefore ask why managers do not use their power to keep their jobs and obtain the maximum benefits from their employment. Perhaps they try to, but they are not very successful. While older managers may have more decision-making power than other workers, they are also more vulnerable to the organizational processes that govern the careers of older workers in promotion systems. Indeed, their higher earnings are more likely to be a cause of their vulnerability than a result of their alleged power. The organizational forces governing career events are so important that top level managers rarely have the power to shape their own careers. At most, they can influence the sizes of the bribes given to end their careers.

The economic consequences of aging in promotion systems for middle-level workers are likely to be similar to the consequences of aging in job-competition jobs, probably often a bit better because of better pensions. For top level workers, career ends usually do not produce significant declines in income, though opportunity costs of retirement of course may be substantial.

The psychological consequences of aging in promotion systems are likely to be even more varied and dramatic than in job-competition jobs. As workers in job-competition jobs are likely to derive their identities from their jobs, workers in promotion systems are likely to be attached to firms and derive their identities from these firms. The careers of older workers in these systems may, however, put strong pressures on firm loyalties and attachments. The combination of business cycle and organizational processes that generate job events in promotion systems may cause frustration and a sense of powerlessness. As noted earlier, the pattern of changes in self-efficacy around the time of retirement supports these predictions (House et al., 1992). The structure of competition in rank order tournaments such as promotion systems creates interdependencies in the careers of workers so that the career gain of one worker reduces the chance for a similar gain for another. These interdependencies create intrigue and strategic behaviors, and these outcomes should be especially likely and frustrating toward the end of the career, when most of the salient career events are negative or potentially negative.

CONCLUSIONS

Older workers lose power over their careers because they lose earning power in the open employment sector, or because they lose the ability to recuperate from job losses in job-competition jobs, or because even when workers have considerable managerial power, they cannot overcome the organizational forces that make the conclusion of their careers desirable. The career of the older workers is a game with a predetermined outcome, retirement. This outcome is least problematic for workers in the job structures providing the least to lose, the spot labor markets, and most problematic in those structures where individual performance has the least impact and organizational and economic forces the most, the promotion systems.

Retirement rates depend on two variables: workers' needs for retirement and their ability to obtain a satisfactory replacement of their earnings from work. The mechanisms for ending the careers described here will generate retirements in proportion to the overall distribution of workers between labor market sectors and the effect of business cycles and organizational demographics on the careers within each of the sectors. The ability to replace earnings from work depends on the provision of replacement income from public and private pensions and other transfers. It is of considerable interest to know which of the two components has had more effect on retirements. It is well known that retirement rates have been increasing. This should then be a result of better pensions and other transfer or of a greater need for retirement.

There has been considerable change in the labor markets of industrialized countries in the last few decades. The industrial composition has changed with considerable growth in service industries and decline in manufacturing. There has been a marked increase in earnings inequality, and there is much discussion of considerable industrial restructuring. These trends may suggest that there has been an increase in the proportion of the labor force employed in spot markets and an increase in the proportion of those employed in promotion systems. The increase in proportion employed in spot markets appears to be especially pronounced for young workers (Burtless, 1990). The much commented upon industrial restructuring should produce job destruction in both the job competition and the promotion system sectors. In the United States, many of the displaced workers are presumably absorbed by the open employment sector. In many European countries, where labor markets are considerably less flexible—that is, more closed—unemployment has remained very high now for a long period of time. Overall, it appears that there should be some increase in the need for retirement.

Pension benefits have increased since about 1975 because Social Security has been expanding both benefits and coverage more than other transfer programs, and because private pension benefits also have become more generous (Burkhauser & Quinn, 1994). The combined effect of an increased need for retirement and more generous benefits suggests increasing rates of retirement, which is indeed what we find. The exception might be the United States, where age of retirement has stabilized and where there is some increase in labor force's participation rates for older men, aged 65 to 69 (Treas & Torrecilha, 1995), a result, probably, of changes in Social Security regulations. The labor force participation of older men appears to be very responsive to the business cycle, suggesting that we are seeing spot market employment as older men adjust their labor supply to the changing employment opportunities. For women, there is virtually no trend as increased labor force participation is countered by earlier retirement. In European countries the trend to earlier retirement has continued.

Recent scholarship on these topics presents a picture of societal changes that have created a paradox of an increasingly healthier older labor force being forced into retirement at increasingly younger ages (Kohli, 1994; Riley, Kahn, & Foner, 1994). The paradox has been described by Riley and her associates as a structural lag, where society has been unable and unwilling to adjust to the increasing health and longer lives of older people. The line of reasoning is very persuasive. However, attributing the phenomenon to recent trends in health may be misleading. It is clearly the case that the capacities of older people have little to do with their careers in important segments of the labor market. The analysis presented in this chapter shows that the organizational and structural forces governing the careers of the older worker make it very difficult for some older workers to maintain control over their careers, regardless of how healthy they are. Ironically, however, these organizational and structural forces impinge most on careers of workers insulated from competition from others, where health is the least relevant factor for one's career.

The loss of control of careers for older workers in job-competition jobs and promotion-system jobs is not a new phenomenon, but a larger proportion of birth cohorts now live to experience the loss of control over their career endings. It should be noted that this increase in the number of persons reaching middle and old age is not primarily a result of increased healthiness of older people, but primarily a result of more people surviving birth and childhood. The increase in life expectancy at, say, age 40 in this century is modest for men, although more substantial for women (Treas & Torrecilha, 1995). The lives for the larger number of survivors into adulthood are perhaps not healthier, except for the elimination of infectious diseases (Crimmins, Saito, & Ignegneri, 1989).

The structural "lag" is therefore a persistent feature of industrial society. It is not primarily a recent result of increases in health both because health is less relevant for careers where the loss of economic power is most important and because the increase in health for the workers reaching older ages is less pronounced. The "lag" may in fact become smaller as the importance of the spot labor market continues to increase. This trend will allow older workers to gain more control over their careers, although not in employments that are very desirable.

The economic powerlessness of older workers does not translate into political powerlessness. As more people age, they gain power. The early retirement is a testimony to this increasing power more than to changes in the labor market. Older workers have made it increasingly possible to avoid the problems of career losses by gaining, from the taxes of younger workers, economically more rewarding alternatives to work.

NOTES

[1] There are, of course, transfers of goods, money, care, and support between parents and children, also in modern times. But these transfers are not insititutionalized bases of well-being and welfare for the old.

[2] There is considerable cross-national variation in the occurrence of such job structures. They are found less often in Germany with its heavy reliance on highly skilled and autonomous workers than in France and the United States. The variation seems to be unrelated to production technology (Maurice, Sellier, & Silvestre, 1983).

[3] Mandatory retirement based on age criteria are no longer allowed in the United States, but mandatory retirement based on other contracts and criteria replaces them. The very existence of the employment rent is the reason for these rules. The abolishment of mandatory retirement might be seen as providing the old

with more economic power, thus reversing the trend toward powerlessness described previously. However, the effect is probably modest.

REFERENCES

Akerlof, G. A. (1982). Labor contracts as partial gift exchange. *Quarterly Journal of Economics, 97,* 543–569.

Akerlof, G. A., & Yellen, J. L. (1986). Introduction. G. A. Akerlof & J. L. Yellen (Eds.), *Efficiency wage models of the labor market* (pp. 1–21). New York: Cambridge University Press.

Baltes, P. B., & Baltes, M. M. (1990). Psychological perspectives on successful aging: The model of selective optimization with compensation. In P. B. Baltes & M. M. Baltes (Eds.), *Successful aging: Perspectives from the behavioral sciences* (pp. 1–34). New York: Cambridge University Press.

Baltes, P. B., Dittmann-Kohli, F., & Dixon, R. (1986). Multidisciplinary propositions on the development of intelligence in adulthood and old age. In A. B. Sørensen, F. E. Weinert, & L. R. Sherrod (Eds.), *Human development and the life course: Multidisciplinary perspectives* (pp. 467–598). Hillsdale, NJ: Erlbaum.

Burkhauser, R. V., & Quinn, J. F. (1994). Changing policy signals. In M. W. Riley, R. L. Kahn, & A. Foner (Eds.), *Age and structural lag* (pp. 237–262). New York: Wiley.

Burtless, G. (1990). Introduction and summary. In G. Burtless (Ed.), *A future of lousy jobs?* (pp. 1–30). Washington, DC: Brookings Institution.

Crimmins, E., Saito, Y., & Ignegneri, D. (1989). Changes in life expectancy and disability-free life expectancy in the United States. *Population and Development Review, 15,* 235–267.

Doeringer, P. B., & Piore, M. J. (1971). *Internal labor markets and manpower analysis.* Lexington, MA: Heath Lexington Books.

Douglas, M. (1982). Cultural bias. In M. Douglas (Ed.), *In the active voice* (pp. 184–253). London: Boston, Routledge & Kegan Paul.

House, J. S., Kessler, R. C., Herzog, A. R., Mero, R. P., Kinney, A. M., & Breslow, M. J. (1992). Social stratification, age and health. In K. W. Schaie, D. Blazer, & J. S. House (Eds.), *Aging, health behavior and health outcomes* (pp. 1–37). Hillsdale, NJ: Erlbaum.

Jacobs, K., Kohli, M., & Rein, M. (1991). Germany: The diversity of pathways. In M. Kohli, M. Rein, A. M. Guillemard, & H. van Gunsteren (Eds.), *Time for retirement: Comparative studies of early exit from the labor force* (pp. 181–221). New York: Cambridge University Press.

Kohli, M. (1994). Work and retirement: A comparative perspective. In M. W. Riley, R. L. Kahn, & A. Foner (Eds.), *Age and structural lag* (pp. 80–106). New York: John Wiley.

Kohli, M., & Rein, M. (1991). The changing balance of work and retirement. In M. Kohli, M. Rein, A. M. Guillemard, & H. van Gunstern (Eds.), *Time for retirement: Comparative studies of early exit from the labor force* (pp. 1–35). New York: Cambridge University Press.

Lazear, E. P. (1979). Why is there mandatory retirement? *Journal of Political Economy, 87,* 1261–1284.

Marshall, A. (1920/1949). *Principles of economics* (8th ed). London: Macmillan.

Maurice, M., Sellier, F., & Silvestre, J. J. (1983). The search for a societal effect in the production of company hierarchy: A comparison of France and Germany. In P. Osterman (Ed.), *Internal labor markets* (pp. 231–269). Cambridge, MA: MIT Press.

Merton, R. K., & Rossi, A. K. (1950). Contributions to the theory of reference group behavior. In R. Merton & P. Lazarsfeld (Eds.), *Continuities in social research* (pp. 40–105). New York: Free Press.

Neumark, D., & Taubman, P. (1995). Why do wage profiles slope upward? Tests of the general human capital model. *Journal of Labor Economics, 13,* 736–761.

Ransom, R. L., & Sutch, R. (1995). The impact of aging on the employment of men in American working-class communities at the end of the nineteenth century. In D. I. Kartzer & P. Laslett (Eds.), *Aging in the past: Demography, society and old age* (pp. 303–327). Berkeley, CA: University of California Press.

Riley, M. W., Kahn, R. L., & Foner, A. (Eds.). (1994). *Age and structural lag.* New York: John Wiley.

Schaie, K. W. (1979). The primary mental abilities in adulthood: An exploration in the development of psychometric intelligence. In P. Baltes & O. G. Brim (Eds.), *Life-span development and behavior* (Vol. 2, pp. 67–115). New York: Academic Press.

Solow, R. M. 1979). Another possible source of wage stickiness. *Journal of Macroeconomics, 1,* 79–82 .

Sørensen, A. B. (1977). The structure of inequality and the process of attainment. *American Sociological Review, 42,* 965–978 .

Sørensen, A. B. (1978). Causal analysis of cross-sectional and over time data: With special reference to the study of occupational achievement. In W. Wesolowski, K. M. Slomczynski, & B. W. Mach (Eds.), *Social mobility in comparative perspective* (pp. 111–129). Warszawa: Ossolineum.

Sørensen, A. B. (1983). Processes of allocation to open and closed position in social structure. *Zeitschrift für soziologie, 12*(2), 203–224.

Sørensen, A. B. (1994). Firms, wages and incentives. In N. J. Smelser & R. Swedberg (Eds.), *Handbook of economic sociology* (pp. 504–528). Princeton, NJ: Princeton University Press.

Sørensen, A. B. (1996, March). The structural basis of social inequality. *American Journal of Sociology, 101,* 1333.

Thurow, L. C. (1975). *Generating inequality.* New York: Basic Books.

Treas, J., & Torrecilha, R. (1995). The older population. In R. Farley (Ed.), *State of the union: America in the 1990s* (Vol. 2, pp. 47–92). New York: Russell Sage Foundation.

Turner, J. A., & Beller, D. J. (1992). *Trends in pensions: 1992.* Washington, DC: U.S. Government Printing Office.

Wright, E. O. (1979). *Class structure and income determination.* New York: Academic Press.

Commentary: New Careers and Older Workers

Ann Howard

S ørensen (chapter 5, this volume) offers a useful distinction among three types of employment contracts—spot market, job competition, and promotion system—with different implications for older workers. These contracts illustrate the ebb and flow of employment during the last century, but they are likely to undergo revisions in future labor markets.

Spot labor markets grew in the United States with the rise of industrialization. People left farming to more capable machines and sought work in factories. At the turn of the 20th century, this work was simple and readily available to the uneducated, to immigrants who spoke little English, even to children. Sørensen rightly notes that firms could be indifferent to whom they employed. Some foremen threw apples to the throngs waiting at the factory gates and hired those lucky enough to catch one (Jacoby, 1985). Employment contracts were economic transactions, usually short term. The arbitrary foremen just as readily fired as hired with no necessity to justify their actions.

Job competition and promotion system jobs arose with the bureau-cracies that characterized most of the 20th century. By 1950, blue-collar manual laborers—mostly skilled laborers with flat careers—constituted about two-fifths of the U.S. labor market, and white-collar and manage-rial workers, presumably in promotion systems jobs, counted for nearly an additional two-fifths (U.S. Bureau of the Census, 1975). Both of these groups had relational employment contracts. They were expected to stay with their firms throughout their careers, and their relationships with their companies were both economic and socioemotional. Unlike the open sys-tem of spot markets, their labor market was internal and closed.

As the new millennium approaches, corporations are reevaluating these closed employment systems. Automation is displacing blue-collar workers, and information technology is revamping and replacing the role of middle managers. Now facing intense global competition, firms seek greater efficiencies through programs such as process reengineering, which typically reveals excess labor. Organizations that once considered their closed market systems a competitive advantage increasingly view them as liabilities.

CLOSED EMPLOYMENT SYSTEMS

As Sørensen notes, closed employment systems create problems for firms that use them, and these in turn affect older workers. Organizations today are taking new approaches to meeting these challenges, but difficulties remain.

Problems with Closed Systems

Incentives

Workers in closed systems are insulated from competition from outsiders, observes Sørensen. Organizations have sought ways to motivate workers despite this protection and comfort. One early solution, the piece rate sys-tem, was undermined by what industrial engineer Frederick Taylor called "soldiering"—group norms that regulated effort (Taylor, 1911). Today, organizations try to use group norms as a positive spur to continuous improvement and other team-based productivity enhancements. Some firms use group incentive systems, particularly as rewards for relatively stable self-directed teams. Yet the increasing need for quickly assembled and disassembled teams makes implementing these rewards difficult.

The alternative, merit pay, accumulates over time if workers remain with the same employer. Sørensen reports that this creates an incentive for the firm to default on older workers' contracts. Some current merit pay plans try to diminish this effect by giving proportionally larger merit increases to those at lower ends of the pay distribution (Rogers, 1996). Nevertheless, only bonus plans avoid the accumulation of rewards by older workers, and these are also on the rise.

Selection

If employees are expected to remain with the same employer, notes Sørensen, there is a premium on being able to predict future performance. The field of industrial psychology forged ahead during the 20th century with the challenge of providing tests and other assessment tools for this purpose. The management assessment center, for example, successfully predicted rising in the telephone company hierarchy over a period of 25 years (Howard & Bray, 1988). Skills and abilities, job knowledge, motivation, and work preferences have been successfully measured and used to forecast later work performance. Contrary to Sørensen's contentions, however, using race, gender, or age as selection criteria is illegal in the United States. One could argue, of course, that these criteria would not have been banned if they were not used.

A precursor to development of personnel selection batteries is an analysis of the job for which the person is being selected. As work becomes more fluid and changeable, this bounded entity called a "job" is beginning to disappear (Bridges, 1994). Predicting future performance in unknown jobs is problematic, to say the least. Instead, some employers seek workers with competencies considered essential throughout the organization (such as having a customer focus) or hire people who are highly adaptable (Howard, 1995).

It is unclear how older workers will fare against a criterion of adaptability. On one hand, they will have more experiences to draw from and the emotional stability that comes from meeting and surmounting life's challenges. On the other hand, it may be difficult for aging workers to stay up-to-date in a rapidly changing environment.

Vulnerability to External Events

In a closed relationship, observes Sørensen, the fate of the worker is tied to the fate of the firm. This problem takes on new urgency as organizations are destabilized by rapid technological change and global competition. Corporations often downsize to reduce their costs, and dispensing with older workers rids them of proportionally greater costs. To make this practice more palatable, many firms offer older workers a financial incentive to retire early. Employees accustomed to the security of a closed system, however, may lack the psychological and financial resources to adjust comfortably to this unexpected turn of events.

Retirement from Closed Systems

Sørensen states that workers base their retirement decisions on their ability to replace earnings and "need to retire." Each of these criteria warrants further exploration.

Early Retirement

A study of telephone company managers who had been promoted over the years from the blue-collar ranks (Howard, 1988) provides some insights about early retirement decisions. When offered a "golden handshake" to retire early, 85 managers accepted the offer and 52 decided to continue working. Extensive longitudinal data on these managers revealed that several factors differentiated the two groups.

Retirees and stayers had comparable levels of ability and work performance, but they differed in motivations and attitudes. The retirees placed less value on the primacy of work and had lower work standards. They were less identified with the telephone company than those who stayed. From about age 40, the retirees became more dissatisfied with their jobs and supervisors than those who opted to continue their employment.

Values and interests also differentiated the two groups. The early retirees had more avocational, recreational, and social interests and were more interested in travel and maintaining their homes. Those who rejected early retirement were more religious, perhaps inspired by the Protestant work ethic or similar religious teachings that equate hard work with spiritual virtue.

The early retirees were also better off financially. They had fewer money concerns than those who stayed and were less motivated to continue to enhance their net worth. This affirms the importance of being able to replace earnings as a significant determinant of the decision to retire.

Pensions

The telephone company managers in the 1980s were, of course, more fortunate than many workers today. Their closed employment system included generous private pensions, beefed up over the years by union negotiations. But unions have lost considerable clout in the U.S. labor market. They represented one-fourth of workers in 1950, but are projected to cover no more than 7% by the year 2000 (Seligman, 1995).

Sørensen argues that corporations have also provided pensions to keep employees attached, but many organizations today are not at all sure they want those kinds of attachments. With the external environment full of surprises and future work ambiguous, they do not want to be tied to too many workers or to those with the wrong skills. The popularity of the idea of portable pensions is testimony to the fact that both employees and employers desire more flexibility. As organizations turn to more contract and peripheral workers, the availability of' private pensions may be additionally compromised. Pension coverage has been best for jobs that are becoming increasingly scarce—full-time careers, unionized jobs, and jobs in government and large corporations (Peterson, 1996).

Retirement income and other benefits are also provided by the welfare state, which Sørensen claims is increasingly important. But there are many signs that the welfare state may have reached its limits. Even though older people have political power that currently intimidates politicians, Americans will eventually have to confront the impending bankruptcy of the Medicare and Social Security systems. Socialized European countries are also rethinking the welfare state as unemployment remains high and firms have difficulty competing in a world economy. Germany, for example, just reduced by 20% mandatory corporate obligations to provide sick leave.

Retirement from closed employment systems can be comfortable as long as workers can plan when to retire and the system includes a reliable pension. As both of these conditions become more tentative, older workers may be threatened. Although people forced out of their jobs may still seek other employment in the spot market, those unprepared by tradition and culture to manage their own careers may have great difficulty doing so.

Organizations that downsize are breaking the psychological contract of lifetime employment in a closed system. At the same time, they are experimenting with new employment arrangements that offer employees different kinds of careers.

EMERGING EMPLOYMENT SYSTEMS

Advancing technology, dependence on knowledge and information for competitive advantage, and global competition are promoting major changes in the world of work (Howard, 1995). Sørensen points to more use of the spot market, growth of services, decline of manufacturing jobs, and earnings inequality. These are only some of the factors that signal the overhaul of closed employment systems.

The Boundaryless Organization

Organizations are beginning, to tear down internal and external boundaries that have made them inflexible for an information economy. Organizational structures have evolved in tandem with advancements in computer technology in the following manner:

1. Early computers were mainframes, and people used cards or dumb terminals to communicate with a centralized management information system. Similarly, mid-century bureaucracies were controlled centrally, and workers communicated through tall hierachies of management.
2. Once scientists discovered how to put the processor on a chip, the computer was born. As employees gained access to important information at their own desktop, organizations began to empower frontline employees to make decisions and handle responsibilities formerly restricted to managers. Internal vertical boundaries of the organization thus began to disappear.

3. Personal computers were networked, and organizations found that teams could assume joint responsibilities. Internal horizontal boundaries came down as cross-functional teams shared information and solved problems together.
4. Computer users then discovered they could link to others outside of organizational boundaries using the Internet. This served to lower external horizontal boundaries between an organization and its customers and suppliers. It was no longer necessary for a firm to produce everything in-house in order to maintain coordination and control. Thus was born the boundaryless or virtual organization, which forms pertnerships outside its own borders.

The boundaryless organization is an open system. To respond quickly to fast-paced technological shifts and eager competitors, it values flexibility more than stability. Such organizations are not bureaucracies but adhocracies, formed and disbanded as the situation demands.

New Employment Contracts

Some employees will serve "boundaryless" and adaptive organizations for long periods of time. They will be adaptable workers who perform core functions; organizations can outsource noncentral functions like human resources. Organizations need to retain these core employees for continuity and long-term corporate memory, but their numbers will be relatively small. It has been predicted that organizations will function with half the people who receive twice the pay, but are three times as productive as those in the past (Handy, 1990).

To remain flexible, adaptive organizations will supplement their core managers, technicians, and professionals with contractors—specialized people and firms replacing outsourced functions. They will also have a part-time and temporary contingent labor force that serves as a buffer for external events. A recent Conference Board survey of multinational corporations found that more than one-third expect contingent workers to make up at least one-tenth of their workers within the next 5 years (Koretz, 1996). These three types of workers—core, contractor, and contingent—will have widely different employment contracts.

Rousseau and Wade-Benzoni (1995) forecast further that there will be long-term and short-term insiders and outsiders. In Sørensen's terms, the spot market comprises short-term outsiders, and job competition and promotion system jobs encompass long-term insiders. But a significant number of insiders will be short term, with loyalty to their profession rather than to specific firms. And both contractors and contingent workers can be outsiders with long-term contracts with core firms.

As these trends continue, organizations may need to reevaluate their responsibilities to outsiders. But increasingly, they are modifying their contracts with insiders away from guaranteed employment and toward employability, as the next section describes. Insiders are expected to have multiple careers, not necessarily with the same firm.

New Careers

Some career researchers suggest that the time has come for a new paradigm. Early studies, in the tradition of Robert Merton, Donald Super, and John Holland, focused on matching the person to the occupation. The next phase of career research, which evolved in the context of' personnel selection, matched the person and the job. Later researchers focused on matching the individual and the organization; consistent with closed systems, they emphasized organizational commitment and career stages. The new paradigm calls for matching the individual to his or her life's work. This emphasis reflects the decline of the long-term career in one closed system and the emerging need for workers to develop a portable portfolio for an open market (Hall & Mirvis, 1995).

Movement across jobs and organizations is likely to accelerate. Workers will add value through the knowledge and experience they bring to their jobs, but they must continually refresh their skills to stay competitive. New careers represent "the end of work as marriage" (Calabresi, Van Tassel, Riley, & Szczesny, 1993) and the beginning of "careers as lifelong learning" (Hall & Mirvis, 1995).

Many organizations now encourage people to take charge of their own self-development and careers. Given the unpredictable nature of work, firms no longer feel able to plan employees' long-term careers. Rather, the emerging employment contract calls for organizations to provide systems, tools, and work assignments for training and development, but for employees to assume primary responsibility for acquiring the skills and competencies they need. Workers will do so with the anticipation that they will not necessarily remain with their present employers and that they must prepare themselves to step into the open market.

OLDER WORKERS IN A NEW AGE

On the Job

As Sørensen recounts, the typical career pattern is one of increasing earnings and rewards early in the career, stabilization in the middle years, and decline in the later years. If new careers are characterized by learning, adaptation, and change, people could go through a cycle of establishment, maintenance, and disengagement many times rather than just once. This pattern detaches the aging cycle from the career cycle. People would age over several career cycles while acquiring new skills and industry knowledge (Hall & Mirvis, 1995).

Such a career could be advantageous to the older worker. Continuous retraining might take the edge off human capital theory's projection that it is not worthwhile for organizations to train older workers. Moreover, older workers may add value as mentors and coaches for workers trying to master new skills. Consistent with such value enhancement, a recent study found that older managers were rated more highly than younger managers by their subordinates and peers, even though supervisors made no such differentiation (Brutus, McCauley, & Fleenor 1996).

Decline and Retirement

Older workers also have serious liabilities as work and the workplace change. Handy (1990), for example, predicts that core employees will have short and hard careers. In the light of intense competition and rapid change, their jobs will be fast paced and high pressured. He predicts that workers will retire from these jobs at about age 50, not coincidentally the same approximate age that Sørensen cited as the onset of physical decline among journeymen. Besides feeling their own needs to seek relief from pressure, older workers will be pushed from behind by workers who are younger, more energetic, and more up-to-date.

Decline, even among knowledge workers, may come earlier than age 50. For example, peak performance for professionals is in the 20's to 40's (Ericsson & Charness, 1994), and great software developers do their best work before age 30 (Deutschman & Tetzeli, 1994). Declines at earlier ages will pose a particular problem for women, whose most productive work years will overlap with their childbearing years.

Sørensen assumes that retiring workers will have public pensions, a questionable proposition in the United States, unless the impending bankruptcy of the Social Security system is rectified. The surplus of tax revenues over outlays will turn negative as early as 2013 (Peterson, 1996). Although a public retirement system may remain, chances are high that benefits will be smaller, come later in life rather than earlier, and be subject to a means test.

Prospects will not necessarily be grim for older workers pushed out by a younger generation. If they grow up with and expect a more open labor market, reasonable people will take steps to manage their careers rather than leaving them to fickle employers. As Sørensen noted, the psychological and social consequences of retirement from careers in the open market are modest because people change their labor supply voluntarily and have control over their lives and incomes. Older workers who keep their work portfolios current, their savings accounts flush, and their options open will be better prepared for the environmental surprises that have cost the jobs and self-esteem of so many unprepared, downsized workers during the last decade.

Older workers may decide to have a phased retirement, as in Japan, moving in their 50's from core employee to contractor or contingent worker. Or if they plan well, they may join the not-too-religious, recreation-loving former telephone company managers on the golf course.

REFERENCES

Bridges, W. (1994). *JobShift: How to prosper in a workplace without jobs.* Reading, MA: Addison-Wesley.

Brutus, S., McCauley, C. D., & Fleenor, J. D. (1996). Age and managerial effectiveness: Some interesting trends. *Issues & Observations, 16* (1), 5–6.

Calabresi, M., Van Tassel, J., Riley, M., & Szczesny, J. R. (1993, November 22). Jobs in an age of insecurity. *Time,* pp. 32–39.

Deutschman, A., & Tetzeli, R. (1994, July 11). Your desktop in the year 1996. *Fortune,* pp. 86–98.

Ericsson, K. A., & Charness, N. (1994). Expert performance. *American Psychologist, 49*(8), 725–747.

Hall, D. T., & Mirvis, P. H. (1995). Careers as lifelong learning. In A. Howard (Ed.), *The changing nature of work* (pp. 323–361). San Francisco: Jossey-Bass.

Handy, C. (1990). *The age of unreason.* Cambridge, MA: Harvard Business School Press.

Howard, A. (1988). Who reaches for the golden handshake? *Academy of Management Executive, 11*(2), 133–144.

Howard, A. (Ed.). (1995). *The changing nature of work.* San Francisco: Jossey-Bass.

Howard, A., & Bray, D. W. (1988). *Managerial lives in transition: Advancing age and changing times.* New York: Guilford Press.

Jacoby, S. M. (1985). *Employing bureaucracy: Managers unions, and the transformation of work in American industry, 1900–1945.* New York: Columbia University Press.

Koretz, G. (1996, January 15). U. S. Labor gets flexible . . . Long-term jobs are waning. *Business Week,* p. 22.

Peterson, P. G. (1996, May). Will America grow up before it grows old? *Atlantic Monthly,* pp. 55–86.

Rogers, R. W. (1996, October). *Linking performance management to compensation.* Paper presented at the Maximizing Performance Client Networking Conference, Development Dimensions International, Pittsburgh, PA.

Rousseau, D. M., & Wade-Benzoni, K. A. (1995). Changing individual-organization attachments: A two-way street. In A. Howard (Ed.), *The changing nature of work* (pp. 290–322). San Francisco: Jossey-Bass.

Seligman, D. (1995, December 11). The Kennedy-Goldberg labor movement. *Fortune,* pp. 236–237.

Taylor, F. W. (1911). *The principles of scientific management.* New York: Harper & Row.

U. S. Bureau of the Census. (1975). *Historical statistics of the United States: Colonial times to 1970* (Vol.3, Pt. 1). Washington, DC: U. S. Department of Commerce.

Commentary: Career Trajectories and the Older Worker

F. Thomas Juster

Sørensen's chapter (chapter 5 of this volume) attempts to explain some of the salient features of labor supply behavior in later life, when workers begin to choose among continuing work with a current employer, continuing work with a different employer or a different job, or leaving the workforce wholly or partly in favor of greater leisure. The chapter also addresses issues relating to the change over time in incentives to leave the workforce, resulting from changes in the structure of competition, in public pension schemes, and in private pension arrangements.

OVERVIEW

Sørensen's chapter is based on a set of perceptions about life-course changes in work and leisure, both at younger ages and at older ages. He argues that the active part of the life-course is shrinking, in that we keep our children longer in school than we used to, and we pressure our old into spending an increasing amount of time in an inactive life course phase called retirement. He argues that both the young and the old are increasingly irrelevant to society's functioning, and that this is especially true for the young, because they lack the political power that the old accumulate. The argument is that, as we all expect to get old, we want to have a good life for older people generally, because we will one day be in that state, but because we do not expect to get young, we care less about what happens to children, as we will not be in that state again. Finally, Sørensen argues that we need state support to make the system work effectively, because private-sector incentives are presumed to be unable to cope with a society in which larger numbers of young and old serve no useful economic function but need to be maintained at some satisfactory level of living standard.

This is a very pessimistic view about modern society, work, and aging. One can quarrel with Sørensen's view that present circumstances place severe disadvantages on children because those with power in society do not expect to become young, although they do expect to get old. The problem with that argument is that, although it is certainly true that we do not expect to be young again, we do have children and grandchildren who are young and whose welfare we are apt to be concerned with. Hence while the young may be disadvantaged, I do not think it is because those with economic power do not expect to be young again and are, therefore, unwilling to adopt policies that help the young: any such disadvantage presumably accrues to our own children and grandchildren. Moreover, the old still have a major effect on what happens overall in society, not only because they tend to vote with greater frequency than other population segments and therefore have more political power than other groups, but also because the old continue to control most economic resources— something on the order of three-quarters of our total national wealth is owned by households headed by people 45 years of age and older. Thus not just political power, but also economic power, is characteristic of the old in our society.

The major part of Sørensen's chapter is concerned with analysis of the three types of labor markets into which he divides the world. This is a well-worked literature, in which many contributions have been made by Sørensen himself in other papers. The employment world, in Sørensen's view, is divided into spot labor markets, job-competition markets, and career job markets. Spot labor markets, by definition, represent markets in which a worker is hired for a particular job at a particular time, but where there is no continued attachment of the worker to the firm or vice versa. Wages are determined by worker productivity in such a market, and can be expected to have the variation with age that one expects to find as a function of changes in skill. Wage rates should be low when people are young because they are investing in skills, and they should be low when people are old because their skills are diminishing as a consequence of physical or cognitive frailties.

Job-competition markets are ones in which a worker stays with a particular firm in a particular job; wage rates are not necessarily determined by competitive forces but by organizational constraints, such as union power. Employees in job-competition jobs keep the job they have until a better job opens up, in which case they are free to apply for it and may or may not be successful For that reason, wage rates tend to rise on average as workers age, since some of them will be chosen for the more attractive jobs that have opened up in the firm.

Finally, there is a career job pattern in which people are hired with the expectation that they will spend a lifetime with the firm in a series of jobs, with promotion opportunities becoming available as workers acquire skills and experience. Pay is conditioned on the expectation that workers will be paid less than their productivity warrants early in their careers, higher than warranted by productivity late in their careers—the so-called implicit contracts view that is so popular in the job market literature. For these jobs, the fate of the worker is tied to the firm (as it is also with job-competition jobs), but wage rates are equal to productivity because, over the lifetime, average wages are related to average productivity, and thus there are no employment "rents" available to the worker.

It is perfectly reasonable to structure this view of the job market as Sørensen does, and to suggest that these three types of jobs face different kinds of pressures as workers age. What I find lacking is any recognition of the fact that workers continue in jobs not solely because of the income available from work relative to the rewards available from nonwork, but also because work, for many people, constitutes a major part of their active life and represents a major source of social contacts in the nonwork phase of their lives. Sørensen's argument about wage rate, labor supply, and retirement decisions takes the usual view among labor economists—that workers make decisions about work hours at the margin by choosing between work that yields a combination of money income and disutility (because work is presumed to be unpleasant), and leisure, which does not yield income but which yields positive utility because leisure is pleasurable. The problem with that argument is that there is evidence that work is one of the most intrinsically valued activities that people do, and that part of the returns from work have nothing to do with income but with the social interactions associated with the work environment. In previous studies, I have called the value attached to the intrinsic satisfactions from the work environment the "process benefits" from work, and have observed that the process benefits from work tend to be ranked above the process benefits from most leisure activities (Juster, 1991).

If the intrinsic benefits from work constitute an important reason to continue working, analysis of labor supply decisions needs to recognize that loss of work means not just loss of income, but also loss of the flows of utility associated with the nonmarket rewards from work.

In describing the incentive structures that go along with spot market jobs, job-competition jobs, and career job promotion ladders, Sørensen notes that one of the key features of the job structure as it relates to the retirement decision has to do with the nature of the pension plans associated with various jobs. For a variety of reasons, private pensions are more likely to be associated with job-competition jobs and career jobs than with spot market jobs. While it is certainly true that private pension schemes are apt to have early retirement incentives built into the structures of their returns, it is also true that the relation between work and pensions applies only to work at the particular firm from which one is expecting to draw a pension, and does *not* apply to the relationship between work generally and pensions. That is, the fact that a pension provides substantial incentive for a worker to leave a firm at ages like 60 or 62 does not mean that this arrangement provides any incentive for workers not to become attached to some other firm at age 60 or 62. In effect, nothing prevents a worker from taking advantage of the pension incentives contained in his or her arrangements with Firm A by leaving Firm A, taking the pension, then going to work for Firm B. Except for the kinds of forces noted by Sørensen in the analysis of employer incentives to hire workers at younger or older ages, as far as I can see, there is nothing to prevent workers from taking advantage of the pension option on their career job, leaving that job, but going to work for some other firm in a different job.

There is, incidentally, a bit of recent empirical evidence that indicates the importance of this phenomenon—leaving a job with a substantial pension but not leaving the workforce. In the Health and Retirement Study (HRS), now under way at the University of Michigan and designed as a continuing panel study, we ask respondents whether they have been offered early-out windows—options to leave the firm with a relatively more attractive pension benefit than contained in the original pension plan. Of those workers who took advantage of such an early-out window, about half chose to stay in the workforce, shifting to a different job with a different employer, often at lower wage rates and typically with somewhat fewer hours (Brown, 1993).

One of the interesting features of labor supply decisions as workers age is the degree to which workers choose to move from full-time to part-time work as they age, rather than from full-time work to zero work hours. It would certainly be expected, based on standard economic analyses of labor supply decisions, that workers would tend to shift from full-time work to some amount of part-time work rather than shifting directly from full-time work to zero work hours—the function relating utility to work hours and leisure hours surely does not fall off the cliff at some age like 62 or 65, but rather contains incentives for people to shift some hours from work to leisure as they age, rather than shifting abruptly from some 2,000 hours per year to zero.

While most workers do not go from full-time to part-time work before moving eventually to zero work hours, there is some evidence that the reason is the absence of market opportunities for part-time work, not the preference of workers. It is not at all clear why this is true. It may be that the inability of many people to find appropriate part-time work when they age is due to the fact that part-time work is economically inefficient, and employers can only afford to offer extremely low wage rates to part-time workers. But it is also possible that employers provide relatively few part-time work opportunities because they have always tended to think in terms of a full-time workforce, and have got into the habit of supposing that the only realistic options are fulltime hours or zero hours.

Finally, it seems useful to ask whether Sørensen's tripartite job classification (spot market jobs, job-competition jobs, and career jobs with promotion ladders) is likely to be characteristic of the future as it seems to have been of the past. Sørensen suggests in his chapter that spot market jobs may be growing in frequency relative to the other two types of jobs. That sounds right to me. It may also be true that structural shifts in competition, particularly those relating to competition from overseas suppliers, have been forcing employers to adopt competitive modes that have been much less common in the past than they are now or will be in the future. In particular, lifetime job security with a single firm—the traditional vision of many large manufacturing firms in the United States and elsewhere—may be a sharply declining labor market characteristic. Whether the tripartite division of jobs described in chapter 5 will continue to serve as a useful organizing framework is not at all clear, although it is also fair to say that I do not have any suggestion as to how to enrich that menu of job types.

Overall, Sørensen has done us a good turn by presenting the issues in a constructive and thoughtful chapter. It represents an admirable starting point for thinking about job markets and labor supply in the future.

REFERENCES

Brown, C. (1993). *Early retirement windows: Windows of opportunity? Defenestrations? (And even refenestrations?* Health and Retirement Study Working Paper Series 94-014, University of Michigan.

Juster, F. (1991). Rethinking utility theory: A summary statement. In A. Etzioni & P. Lawrence (Eds.), *Toward a new synthesis.* Armonk, NY: M. E. Sharpe.

CHAPTER 6

Age, Work, and Mental Health

Peter Warr

F or most adults below middle age, having a paid job provides clear psychological, social, and material benefits. However, there has been relatively little research into these benefits, specifically at older ages. This chapter examines the role of paid work in terms of the broad notion of "mental health," with particular reference to older individuals. Under what circumstances is paid employment psychologically valuable for older people?

First, I will seek to unpack the concept of mental health, differentiating among six main aspects. Second, I will review what is known about the psychological effects of employment, unemployment, voluntary nonemployment, and retirement, irrespective of age. Third, age patterns in the principal aspects of mental health will be summarized, and possible explanations of those patterns explored. Finally, nine important features of any environment (whether in a job or elsewhere) will be introduced, with the argument that it is the levels of these features that makes for better or worse mental health. A principal conclusion will be that good mental health at older ages does not depend upon having a job or not having a job; the key requirement is the availability of a mix of beneficial features, from whatever source they arise.

THE NATURE OF MENTAL HEALTH

There are many different views about the components and processes of mental health. It is generally accepted that the concept is heavily value-laden, so that a universally agreed definition is unlikely to be attained (e.g., Jahoda, 1958). "Health" is not merely the absence of ill health, in an either-or manner. We also need to think in terms of continuous dimensions from poor to good health, such that people can be described in respect of the degree to which they are or are not healthy.

That approach will be taken here. Rather than focusing on *ill health*, identified in specific disorders, diseases, or syndromes of clinically significant symptoms, investigations will be reviewed that look at differences between people in terms of different degrees of healthfulness. This does not in any way deny the value of the clinical classification of individuals who are ill, in respect to schizophrenia, manic-depression, depressive psychosis, or other medical conditions. Such classifications require separate causal treatments, and the majority of the population is excluded from them.

One possible perspective on gradations in mental health for the population as a whole, as the concept is applied in Western societies, is through six principal dimensions. These may be labeled (1) Affective Well-Being, (2) Positive Self-Regard, (3) Competence, (4) Aspiration, (5) Autonomy, and (6) Integrated Functioning (Warr, 1987).

Affective Well-Being

The first component, affective well-being, is usually taken to be a principal indicator of good or bad mental health. This feature has sometimes been measured in a rather undifferentiated way, roughly from feeling bad to feeling good. However, several authors have identified two separate elements, which can be incorporated usefully into more sophisticated forms of measurement: these may be referred to as "pleasure" and "arousal" (e.g., Mackay, Cox, Burrows, & Lazzerini, 1978; Matthews,

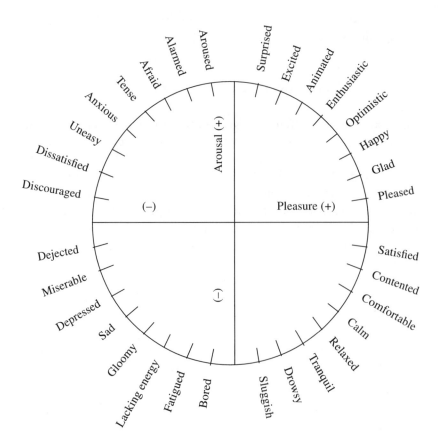

Figure 6.1 Three axes for the measurement of affective well-being.

Jones, & Chamberlain, 1990; Russell, 1980; Thayer, 1989; Watson & Tellegen, 1985). Feelings of pleasure and psychological arousal may be treated as independent of each other, as illustrated in Figure 6.1.

We can view any affective state in terms of its location on these two dimensions. For example, depressed feelings are characterized by low scores on each dimension, being placed in the bottom left-hand corner; and anxiety may be described in terms of a low score on pleasure and a high score on arousal, in the top left-hand quadrant. Although higher

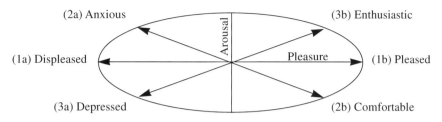

Figure 6.2 Two-dimensional view of affective well-being.

levels of affective well-being are in general associated with the right-hand side of the figure, it is clear that mentally healthy people also experience feelings in the left-hand sectors. A person as it were moves around in the two-dimensional space.

For the measurement of affective well-being, a derivative of the basic framework is set out in Figure 6.2. As previously depicted, pleasure is shown horizontally with psychological arousal as the vertical dimension. However, two diagonal axes are now included, through contrasting quadrants. Variations in psychological arousal, uncorrelated with the pleasure axis, are not considered on their own to be an indicator of well-being. There are thus three main axes to be examined in measuring affective well-being: pleasure, anxiety-to-comfort, and depression-to-enthusiasm.

In discussing well-being (and other components of mental health), it is essential to distinguish between two different levels of abstractness. First, we can examine the concept in general, without restrictions to a particular setting; let us call that "context-free" well-being. Or we can study "context-specific" well-being, in one limited situation, such as the family environment or in respect of jobs. *Job-related affective* well-being is the context-specific form that is of particular interest in this chapter.

Context-free affective well-being (concerned with life in general) has been measured very well. There are several established inventories of distress, life satisfaction, anxiety, depression, and so on, that can tap the three axes in an overall, context-free sense. Job-related well-being has most commonly been studied along the horizontal axis, in terms of job satisfaction, but some scales have tapped aspects of job-related tension or anxiety. Those cover feelings in the top left-hand quadrant of Figures 6.1 and 6.2, but the bottom right sector appears to have been largely ignored in occupational research. That is a pity, since that area is particularly important in respect to low-arousal, resigned feelings; people in that quadrant may not explicitly complain about their jobs, but they tend to be apathetic and uninvolved.

Positive Self-Regard

Although affective well-being is central to mental health, also important are feelings about oneself as a person. These feelings are less directed at features of the environment than is affective well-being; they might be labeled in terms of degree of positive self-regard. Such feelings have often been examined in terms of self-esteem, self-acceptance, self-worth, and associated concepts, and it is clear that positive self-regard and affective well-being overlap both conceptually and empirically (e.g., Ryff, 1989a; Ryff & Keyes, 1995).

Having positive feelings about oneself is a central characteristic of good mental health at all ages, but the nature and sources of these feelings can vary among different life stages. For instance, Birren and Renner (1981) have drawn attention to the need for older individuals to gain an understanding and acceptance of their past lives to date, coming to feel that their time has been spent in ways that are personally appropriate, worthwhile, and meaningful. This retrospective review is dependent upon a recognition that one's position and role relationships have changed with the passing years; acceptance of those changes is often necessary for older people to feel positively about themselves (Ryff, 1989b).

Older people's interpretative review of their previous activities occurs in respect both of context-free and context-specific mental health. This means that, as well as for context-free well-being, retrospective reviews are also important for the job satisfaction of older employees (an aspect of *job-specific* well-being). For older individuals, job satisfaction derives strongly from a review of previous job and career successes and failures, "adding up where one has been rather than a preoccupation with what will be achieved" (Birren & Renner, 1981, p. 248). Positive self-regard at older ages (both context-free and job-specific) thus derives in part from people's perceptions of their past. This aspect deserves greater attention in studies of older people's mental health than it has received so far.

Competence

The third feature of mental health, here referred to as "competence" (e.g., Smith, 1968), has been emphasized by many writers (e.g., Bradburn, 1969; Jahoda, 1958). Terms have included effective coping, environmental mastery, self-efficacy, effectance motivation, and so on. This feature covers a person's ability to handle life's problems and act on the environment with at least a moderate amount of success.

Low competence is not always a sign of low mental health, however; everyone is incompetent in some respects. The key factor is a link with generalized low well-being. It is clear that an inability to cope with important environmental demands is often associated with negative feelings of low well-being and self-regard (e.g., Nezu, 1985), but that is not the case for activities that are not salient to the individual. For these nonsalient activities (for example, my inability to play the piano), low competence is not normally a sign of low mental health.

Note also that we can think in terms of either "subjective" or "objective" competence, as viewed by the person in question or by observers of that person; and that subjective and objective views do not always coincide with each other. It is difficult to measure in quantitative terms either form of competence, since one has to cover the link with generalized well-being; that link is central if competence is to be viewed as an aspect of mental health.

Aspiration

There are also difficulties in the measurement of aspiration, the fourth aspect of mental health. The healthy person is often viewed as someone who establishes realistic goals and makes active efforts to attain them (e.g., Herzberg, 1966; Maslow, 1973). Such people show an interest in the environment, they engage in motivated activity, and seek to extend themselves in ways that are personally significant. For example, Csikszentmihalyi (1975) emphasized the importance of endeavors that involve "a going beyond the known, a stretching of one's self toward new dimensions of skill and competence" (p. 33). On the other hand, low levels of aspiration are seen in apathy and acceptance of the status quo, no matter how unsatisfactory they are.

To characterize people in these terms in a context-free, general manner is difficult, since a person's aspirations can have many different targets. However, a broad-ranging scale of goal-directedness has been shown to be significantly related to affective well-being and positive self-regard among older employees and retired persons (Payne, Robbins, & Dougherty, 1991; Smith & Robbins, 1988). Goal continuity, defined as "the overall ability to set goals, the presence of a clearly established purpose, and the energy to take concerted action" (p. 21), has also been found to have both direct and indirect effects on life satisfaction among early retirees (Robbins, Lee, & Wan, 1994). In occupational settings alone, where the interest may be in purely *job-related* aspiration, it is sometimes appropriate to use questionnaires that cover aspects of intrinsic motivation or growth-need strength (e.g., Warr, Cook, & Wall, 1979; Warr, 1990b). Those questionnaires record the degree to which a person seeks out challenging goals in his or her job, a process that can be viewed as central to job-related aspiration.

Autonomy

The fifth factor, autonomy, has been emphasized more by Western than by Eastern writers. For example, in the United States, Angyal (1965) identified the tendency to strive for independence and self-regulation as a key aspect of mental health, and Loevinger (1980) included in her account of personal development a high-level "autonomous stage." Mentally healthy people are usually considered able to resist the influence of environmental features and determine their own opinions and actions. However, many theorists have pointed out that too much as well as too little autonomy can be undesirable. We should thus think in terms of a continuum of personal autonomy, ranging from extreme dependence on other people all the way to extreme counterdependence, with both interdependence and independence located between the extremes. It is a balance between interdependence and independence that reflects good mental health of this kind.

Integrated Functioning

The final aspect of mental health, integrated functioning, concerns the person as a whole and the relationships between other components. People who are mentally healthy exhibit several forms of balance, harmony, and inner relatedness (e.g., Lazarus, 1975). Different writers have their own preferred theoretical perspectives on integrated functioning, but those theories rarely include consideration of processes associated with paid employment. Integrated functioning is an important aspect of mental health, but in view of its conceptual complexity and difficulties of measurement, it will not figure greatly in this chapter.

General Issues

To be mentally healthy is more than merely not being ill. Healthy people experience to varying degrees positive states of the kinds illustrated previously. Futhermore, they often experience strain or anxiety in coping with their environment, and, indeed, they may *create* situations that turn out to be stressful as they identify and pursue difficult targets. Researchers have often given the impression that the presence of, for instance, anxiety is always a sign of low mental health. However, that is only the case if the anxiety is particularly severe, or if it lasts for a long period of time. In other cases, feelings of anxiety can in fact be associated with a high level of mental health.

The intermittent experience of anxiety by people who are mentally healthy is linked to the fact that the separate components of mental health are not always positively intercorrelated. Positive associations are usually present (e.g., Ryff, 1989a; Ryff & Keyes, 1995), but there are exceptions. For example, proactive, risk-taking people may be considered healthy in terms of competence, aspiration, and autonomy, but their difficult relations with the environment may also make them anxious for a considerable proportion of time. High aspirations in those circumstances can be accompanied by low affective well-being.

Differences are also present in the associations between a person's job level and his or her affective well-being on the two diagonal axes illustrated in Figure 6.2. People in higher level jobs report significantly *less* job-related depression than workers in lower level jobs, but also significantly *more* job-related anxiety (Birdi, Warr, & Oswald, 1995; Warr, 1990b; Warr, 1992); both higher and lower well-being occur at higher occupational levels, depending on the facet examined. Another way of describing this pattern is in terms of the dimension of psychological arousal; individuals in higher level positions experience greater arousal, in terms of both diagonal axes in Figure 6.2.

More generally, the aspects of mental health summarized here act both as continuing attributes extending from the past and also as outcomes from new environmental conditions. There is considerable evidence that high levels of mental health contribute to effective handling of life problems as well as to continuing mental health itself (e.g., Antonovsky, 1980; Warr, 1987). The causal process is thus a multiple one, with prior mental health influencing behavior, and both behavior and prior mental health influencing subsequent mental health.

EMPLOYMENT STATUS AND MENTAL HEALTH

What is known about the impact of a person's employment status upon his or her mental health? A consistent finding is that people who are involuntarily unemployed tend to be psychologically harmed in a range of ways. The relevant comparison is in terms of context-free mental health, as introduced previously, and most research has covered affective well-being or self-regard of this context-free kind. It is clear that lower well-being and more negative self-regard are widespread among the unemployed at all ages (e.g., Feather, 1990; Wooten, Sulzer, & Cornwell, 1994), but it is noteworthy that older unemployed individuals exhibit less distress than those in their 30s and 40s (Warr, Banks, & Jackson, 1988). This age difference appears to be associated with several factors, such as perceptions of reduced employment opportunities at older ages, fewer financial and family pressures, a tendency to view oneself as "retired" rather than "unemployed" (avoiding the social stigma attached to unemployment), and sometimes the receipt of welfare benefits for physical disability and an accompanying acceptance of the sick role.

The psychological costs of enforced joblessness are greater among those who have the greatest commitment to paid employment (Warr et al., 1988); unemployed people with little desire for a job exhibit relatively good mental health. Associated with that relationship, persons who prefer to remain outside the labor market, perhaps in the roles of homemaker and child-minder, typically exhibit mental health at a level comparable to those in jobs. Conversely, some people are employed in work settings that can be more psychologically harmful than some states of unemployment, either because their job conditions are greatly aversive

(Warr, 1987) or because family demands in combination with difficult job conditions make for low well-being (Lennon & Rosenfield, 1992).

In comparing people of different employment status, it is thus often important to think in terms of the detailed content of the roles that people hold, rather than merely specifying the status itself (e.g., "employed" or "unemployed"). This point will be developed later, as well as examining variations within the status of being "retired" from the labor force.

Retirement itself takes many different forms, has a range of different causes, and is experienced differently according to the values and attitudes of the persons in question. Reasons for the decision to retire may be grouped as individual, family, or institutional. In the first case, relevant individual factors include a person's financial position, health, age, sex, perceived ability to work effectively, attitudes about paid work and leisure, and so on (e.g., Feldman, 1994). Family influences include the need to care for aged parents and the possibility of synchronizing retirement with that of one's spouse (e.g., Ruhm, 1996). Institutional factors affecting the decision to retire include the availability of a satisfactory company or government pension, organizational and societal norms and pressures to retire early, and the presence of suitable work opportunities (e.g., Hanisch, 1994; Talaga & Beehr, 1989; Taylor & Shore, 1995).

In view of these potential variations, it is not surprising that in general the mental health of retired persons is not significantly different from that of individuals in paid work. In some cases, retired people exhibit better mental health, in other cases the reverse is observed, and often there is no difference. Most research has examined forms of affective well-being (the first aspect of mental health introduced previously), and the general equivalence is particularly clear after statistical controls for age, physical health, and other factors that might confound the comparison based upon retirement status alone (e.g., Midanik, Soghikian, Ransom, & Tekawa, 1995; Palmore, Burchett, Fillenbaum, George, & Wallman, 1985; Salokangas & Joukamaa, 1991). There is some evidence that retirement is associated with greater well-being on the second axis in Figure 6.2; context-free anxiety may decline after exit from the labor market, as the hassles of employment are removed (Bosse, Aldwin, Levenson, & Workman-Daniels, 1991; Campbell, 1981; Midanik et al., 1995).

Despite the in-general absence of mental health differences between the retired and the not-retired, one group of retired persons has been identified as clearly at risk. Some individuals retire earlier than is usual.

Decisions to do that appear to have two main sources, which differ in their nature and likely implications. In some cases, early retirement is forced upon a person, for example, by a company closure or by declining health. In other cases, a person chooses retirement positively, in a setting of adequate income and opportunities for a fruitful and enjoyable period of nonemployment.

Individuals who are forced to retire early tend to exhibit lower well-being than others (e.g., Bosse, Aldwin, Levenson, & Ekerdt, 1987; Palmore et al., 1985). Associated with the fact that in general, poor physical health is accompanied by poor mental health (e.g., Goldberg & Williams, 1988), involuntary early retirement based upon declining physical health tends particularly to be accompanied by poorer mental health (e.g., Feldman, 1994; Hardy & Quadagno, 1995). Sometimes this is linked to the fact that physical decline continues in postretirement years. On the other hand, for people who choose retirement voluntarily and positively, there is no reason to expect harmful effects, especially if they remain healthy and have an adequate income.

The labor force participation rate for older men has declined substantially in recent years in many countries, such that the proportion of men who may be termed "retired" has increased accordingly. However, in many cases retirement does not mean the complete cessation of paid employment; it is often partial, especially at younger ages. A large minority of retired people (between one-quarter and one-half) take up at some point either full-time or (more usually) part-time paid work, possibly on a temporary or intermittent basis (Elder & Pavalko, 1993; Hayward, Crimmins, & Wray, 1994; Myers, 1991; Palmore et al., 1985). In most cases, postretirement jobs involve a reduction in prestige and income (Palmore et al., 1985), consistent with the more general fact that jobs designated for older (nonretired) people tend to embody relatively unattractive characteristics (Warr & Pennington, 1994).

Are there mental health differences between retired persons who take up subsequent employment and those who remain completely outside the labor market? One study observed no differences between retired individuals with part-time and no employment (Bosse et al., 1987), but there is a need for more extensive examination of this issue. Remaining in (or taking up) a job beyond normative retirement age can occur for either negative or positive reasons, and mental health effects would be expected to vary accordingly. For instance, a person may have pressing needs for money obtainable only through paid work, or he or she may value and enjoy a continuing employed role without any financial concern. More generally, in view of the recent increase in employment among those who retire at early ages, patterns of work during retirement may now be associated with some motivations and outcomes that differ from those at the time of earlier investigations.

AGE DIFFERENCES IN MENTAL HEALTH

Next, let us explore the pattern of mental health at different ages. (Recall that the present focus is upon gradations in healthfulness among the population as a whole, rather than upon clinically significant disorders experienced by a minority.) Findings about context-free mental health will first be reviewed, followed by those concerning job-specific mental health. Having defined the age patterns in both forms of mental health, it will be important to consider possible explanations. In keeping with the present focus upon paid employment, I will look primarily at possible interpretations of the observed age-gradient in *job-specific* mental health.

In practice, most quantitative research has examined one of the first two components of mental health summarized previously: affective well-being or positive self-regard. Some confusion has arisen from the fact that studies often differ from each other in ways that significantly affect results. Five inconsistencies are as follows:

1. Investigators have not always distinguished among different facets of mental health, for example, along the lines suggested previously, so that reviewers are not always comparing like with like.
2. The measures used have varied considerably across studies, even between instruments labeled in identical terms.
3. Samples have varied in their age range and age composition.
4. Studies have differed in their degree of control of potentially important factors. For instance, some studies have examined responses from national or community samples as a whole, without regard for differences in employment status or domestic circumstances at different ages; other investigations have been restricted to employed respondents or to individuals of a specific marital status.

5. Researchers have varied in their attention to either linear or curvilinear patterns of association. In most cases, research results are presented in terms merely of the linear component of an association, for example, summarized as a product-moment correlation with age. However, there is increasing evidence for curvilinear associations between age and aspects of mental health. This review will emphasize findings supportive or otherwise of a curvilinear association. Such a pattern is particularly important for interpretations in terms of life-cycle variations, and its presence would suggest that accounts of an age effect in terms of cohort differences are at best limited. These points will be taken up again later.

Given these several differences among investigations, it is not surprising that results differ somewhat among them. However, the following pattern has been found fairly consistently.

Age and Context-Free Mental Health

The first axis of context-free *affective well-being* in Figure 6.2 (positive or negative feelings irrespective of arousal level) has often been measured in terms of life satisfaction. This has been shown to increase cross-sectionally with age to a significant but modest degree (e.g., Campbell, 1981; Judge & Watanabe, 1993).

In contrast, there is a small cross-sectional decline in the aroused forms of well-being in the top-right quadrant of Figure 6.2; reported happiness becomes less with advancing age (e.g., Andrews & Withey, 1976; Campbell, 1981). One way of interpreting this difference in the direction of age-gradient between axes 1 and 3 is that older people may become more satisfied in a low-aroused way; their feelings of well-being may tend to become more positive, but they move from 3b in the diagram (away from happiness of an active kind) toward 1b (more satisfaction of a relatively passive kind).

Regarding the left-hand pole of axis 3, concerned with feelings of depression, research attention has often focused upon the possibility of a curvilinear association with age. There is considerable evidence for a U-shaped (or more precisely a J-shaped) pattern, such that among the population as a whole feelings of depression first decline up to the mid-40s and then increase up to higher average levels among people in their 80s (associated with impaired physical health and reduced personal control) (Mirowsky & Ross, 1992; Neumann, 1989); see also Ryff (1989a). For example, in a national U.S. sample contacted in a telephone survey by Mirowsky and Ross (1992), depression scores declined by about 25% between the ages of 20 and 45 and increased by about 30% between 20 and 80.

Incidentally, the fact that age in some investigations is found not to be related to depression among older people is likely to be due to sampling variations at different ages (e.g., Rabbitt, Donlan, Watson, McInnes, & Bent, 1995). It may be that older people who choose to take part in relatively arduous research tasks are characterized by high activity levels, good health, high motivation, and fewer depressed feelings than are nonparticipants of the same age. Procedures for representative sampling are clearly of major importance in this area.

For the second axis of affective well-being in Figure 6.2 (from anxiety to comfort), there is also evidence of curvilinearity, but in the opposite direction. The top-left quadrant of Figure 6.2 has often been tapped with the General Health Questionnaire (GHQ) (Goldberg, 1972; Goldberg & Williams, 1988). This is a self-report measure to index nonpsychotic psychiatric disorder, with questions that cover the left-hand portion of Figures 6.1 and 6.2, especially feelings of anxiety (2a). Respondents are asked about sleep loss through worry, feelings of strain, finding life a struggle, being unable to face up to problems, and other aspects of distress.

The GHQ has been administered in a large national survey in Britain (the British Household Panel Study), and the overall age pattern from 1991 data is shown in Table 6.1. It can be seen that distress scores increase (cross-sectionally) from low values among teenagers up to a maximum around the age of 40. Distress is then successively lower up to the early 60s, then scores tend to increase again. That later increase is presumably associated with increasing health problems for oneself and one's spouse. Incidentally, although the findings in Table 6.1 cover both men and women, the age pattern is the same in separate analyses. However, as is usually found, women in this sample report higher distress than men at all ages.

In a study of employed respondents in that survey, Clark, Oswald, and Warr (1996) observed that GHQ distress scores were low among

**TABLE 6.1 Distress Scores (GHQ) as a Function of Age:
Representative Sample of the British Population, 1991**

Age	Mean GHQ Score	Number of Cases
Less than 20	9.41	667
20–24	10.46	840
25–34	10.75	2,011
35–44	11.13	1,808
45–54	10.98	1,476
55–59	10.90	580
60–64	10.21	553
65–69	10.77	588
70–74	10.97	471
75–79	11.36	324
80 and above	11.50	295
All ages	10.86	9,613

employed 16- to 19-year-olds, but that they increased up to age 38, before declining to particularly low levels among employed people in their 60s. This age pattern is consistent with findings of greater family, financial, and occupational pressures in the middle years (Folkman, Lazarus, Pimley, & Novacek, 1987); below and above those years, distress is less pronounced. Using another measure of context-free anxiety with employed people, Warr (1990b) also observed a cross-sectional decline after the middle years; Campbell (1981) reported the same pattern in a sample of nonemployed as well as employed respondents, as did Warr et al. (1988) in samples of unemployed individuals.

The opposed curvilinear patterns for anxiety and depression may be interpreted in terms of greater psychological arousal in the middle years of employment (see Figure 6.2). Around the age of 40, people tend to experience more anxiety (higher arousal, in the terms of the figure) and less depression (also more arousal, at higher levels on the diagonal axis). In later years, environmental demands and daily hassles are likely to decline somewhat for most people, resulting in reduced psychological arousal linked both to less anxiety (2a) and to more depression (3a).

What about the second component of context-free mental health, *positive self-regard?* Ryff (1989a) compared groups aged on average 20, 50, and 75 years on (intercorrelated) measures of self-esteem and self-acceptance.

No significant age differences were found in either case. In a separate investigation, Ryff and Keyes (1995) replicated this finding in respect to self-acceptance. It seems likely that positive self-regard is in general maintained at a high level for two reasons. First, as people grow older they experience and value new positive changes in themselves and their behavior. Second, self-evaluations are subject to age-related shifts in comparison standards. At all ages, people tend to compare their behavior and attainments with those of other people and with themselves at younger ages. Although objective performance may decline with age, assessments of self-worth often remain constant, since comparison standards in terms of other people and of reasonable levels of attainment are also reduced.

Judgmental adaptation is also likely in respect to other components of mental health. For instance, subjective *competence* and *autonomy* (the third and fifth features introduced previously) were found by Ryff (1989a) to be significantly greater at age 50 than at 20; both remained high at age 75, despite probable declines in some aspects of objective competence and autonomy; see also Ryff and Keyes (1995). This stability appears likely to be associated with changes in the perceived importance of certain goals and attributes. It may be that the experienced significance of certain aspects of competence or autonomy is reduced when these features objectively decline (perhaps accompanied by an increase in importance attributed to remaining or new features); by modifying personal importance in this way, perceptions of oneself can be maintained at acceptable levels.

Brandstädter and Rothermund (1994) illustrated this process longitudinally in a sample aged initially between 30 and 59. Noting that there is no evidence for a general age-related decline in people's assessments of their autonomy, they reasoned that "personal control and well-being in later life critically hinge on accommodative processes that keep goals and ambitions commensurate with personal resources and situational constraints" (p. 266). Over an 8-year period, it was found that a reduction of control in a particular goal domain tended to affect a person's sense of personal control to a lesser degree if that domain was downgraded in importance. A similar finding was obtained for depressive tendencies; see axis 3 of affective well-being, described previously. It appears that, although some aspects of functioning do indeed decline at later ages, people can be psychologically buffered against those declines by making mental adjustments to their perceived importance.

Finally, what is known about age patterns in context-free *aspiration*, the fourth aspect of mental health introduced previously? Ryff (1989a) observed no difference in people's reported purpose in life between the ages of 20 and 50, but a significant cross-sectional decline between the ages of 50 and 75. This later decline (also found by Ryff and Keyes, 1995) is consistent with a general reduction in opportunities and potential with increasing years. As with competence and autonomy, however, there remains a need for additional investigations.

In overview, the association between context-free mental health and age depends upon which component of mental health is examined. For context-free affective well-being, there tends to be a cross-sectional increase with age on axis 1 (in terms of greater life satisfaction), and curvilinear associations for axes 2 and 3, with more anxiety and less depression in the middle years. Positive self-regard appears to remain constant on average; context-free subjective competence and autonomy seem to increase to the middle years and then remain stable; and context-free aspiration tends to decline somewhat in later years, after an early period of stability.

It is now essential to identify causal mechanisms underlying observed age-gradients. For example, differences in domestic circumstances at different ages are associated with different levels of depression (e.g., Mirowsky & Ross, 1992). However, life-stage models of aging have typically paid only limited attention to specific characteristics of employment, unemployment, or retirement that alter with age and that may underlie shifts in context-free mental health. A change of emphasis in these models would now be desirable.

The patterns outlined in this chapter provide a background against which to consider age patterns in *job-specific* mental health. Context-free and job-specific well-being are positively interrelated and mutually influencing (Judge & Watanabe, 1993; Tait, Padgett, & Baldwin, 1989), and some similarity in age patterns at the two levels of mental health would be expected.

AGE AND JOB-SPECIFIC MENTAL HEALTH

Investigations into job-specific mental health have been (excessively) concentrated on the first component, affective well-being. Furthermore, there has been almost exclusive focus on the first axis in Figure 6.2, in terms of measured job satisfaction.

We may identify three levels of specificity of job satisfaction, and it is desirable to examine separately age patterns of each kind. The most general approach is in terms of "overall job satisfaction," the extent to which a person is satisfied with his or her job as a whole. More focused "facet-specific" satisfactions concern different aspects of a job, such as one's pay, colleagues, supervisors, working conditions, job security, promotion prospects, the company, and the nature of the work undertaken. The last of these is particularly strongly correlated with other facet-specific satisfactions and with overall job satisfaction.

At an intermediate level of abstractness is the distinction between "intrinsic" and "extrinsic" job satisfaction. "Intrinsic" job satisfaction covers satisfaction with features inherent in the conduct of the job itself: opportunity for personal control or with the utilization of skills, amount of task variety, and so on. "Extrinsic" job satisfaction concerns aspects of a job that form the background to work activities themselves: satisfaction with pay, working conditions, job security, industrial relations procedures, and so on.

It is regularly found that overall job satisfaction is significantly higher among older workers (e.g., Abraham & Hansson, 1995; Clark, Oswald, & Warr, 1996; Rhodes, 1983; Warr, 1994a), although the positive correlation is not high, usually falling between +.10 and +.20. Consistent with the findings from a number of investigations, the conventional view is that this association is purely linear, with no significant curvilinear component of the kinds illustrated previously.

In that respect, there is a discrepancy between the most common contemporary view and earlier findings. After reviewing evidence up to the mid-1950s, Herzberg, Mausner, Peterson, and Capwell (1957) suggested that "in general, morale is high among young workers. It tends to go down during the first few years of employment. The low point is reached when workers are in their middle and late twenties, or early thirties. After this period, job morale climbs steadily with age" (pp. 5–6). That decline from a raised level immediately after entry into the labor market is plausible in terms of young people's initial enthusiasm for the adult role followed by a gradual discouragement in the face of routine activities with few opportunities for change. Such a J-shaped pattern of overall job satisfaction scores was found in an early British study (Handyside, 1961), and has recently been observed in a sample of British employees ($N = 5,192$) (Clark et al., 1996) and in a multinational study ($N = 4,356$) (Birdi et al., 1995). Overall job satisfaction was found to be at its minimum at 31 and 26 years of age, respectively, in the latter two studies, and in both cases there were hints of greater curvilinearity among male employees than among women.

The J-shaped and the linear patterns differ only in respect to the youngest employees. Job satisfaction is relatively high for them in cases where a J-shaped association is observed; however, in a purely linear pattern, the youngest respondents are the least satisfied. Discrepancies between findings for the youngest individuals seem likely to arise for the following reasons:

1. differences in sample composition (e.g., the number and age of young respondents; whether or not students working part time are included in a study);
2. differences in labor market characteristics, perhaps between studies conducted at different times (e.g., young jobholders may feel particularly positive when jobs are extremely scarce, but less so when jobs are plentiful);
3. differences in job content (e.g., young jobholders in dead-end jobs may experience a greater decline in job satisfaction than those receiving training and advancement).

This issue is interesting, but it is not central to the present chapter. Note, however, that a curvilinear association with age is inconsistent with a cohort explanation of age differences, if that, argues that an older cohort is always more satisfied than a younger one. This point will be developed later.

Facet-specific job satisfactions are associated in different ways with variations in employee age. Satisfaction with the work itself tends to be greater at older ages, but a significant age-gradient is often absent in relation to satisfaction with promotion opportunities, coworkers, and supervisors (Rhodes, 1983; Warr, 1994a). This does not preclude the possibility that significant relationships are present in some settings, and findings about facet satisfaction are likely to depend on the nature of the sample, the organization, and the measures applied. For example, *negative* correlations with age were reported by Morrow and McElroy (1987) in respect to satisfaction with promotion opportunities and with pay; however, the latter was significantly positively age-related in studies by Oliver (1977), Lee and Wilbur (1985), and Clark et al. (1996). At the intermediate level of abstractness identified previously, intrinsic job satisfaction appears more likely to be significantly positively correlated with age than is extrinsic satisfaction (e.g., Schwab & Heneman, 1977).

What about the second axis of affective well-being shown in Figure 6.2, from feelings of anxiety to comfort? Job-related anxiety and feelings of strain have been found to be significantly curvilinearly associated with employee age by Warr (1992) and Birdi et al. (1995), with greatest job anxiety in the middle years. A similar but less pronounced pattern was found for axis 3 (depression to enthusiasm) in the study by Warr (1992), with employees in the middle-age groups reporting most job-related depression. (Note that this pattern is the converse of that found for *context-free* depression, where *lowest* levels are found in the middle years.)

In a study of employees aged 40 to 69, Abraham and Hansson (1995) found that older individuals reported less job-related anxiety and depression than did younger ones. There is thus consistent evidence that all three aspects of job-related well-being increase cross-sectionally with age. In addition, several recent investigations (all outside the United States) have suggested that the pattern is curvilinear, with raised well-being also at the youngest ages. How might the generally observed increase after the age of about 30 be explained? Six interpretations have been offered, and it is likely that more than one of those is appropriate for any set of data.

Transitions to Better Jobs

With increasing age, many people move into jobs that have more desirable characteristics, as a result of which they might be expected to be more satisfied (e.g., Janson & Martin, 1982; Kalleberg & Loscocco, 1983; Wright & Hamilton, 1978). Older employees (often with longer tenure) tend to occupy jobs with more positive intrinsic characteristics (opportunity for control or skill utilization, for instance) and better extrinsic features, such as income. A variant of this possibility is seen in models of person-environment fit (e.g., Dawis & Lofquist, 1984), which suggest that individuals move into positions that are consistent with their needs and skills. Role transitions of this kind are sometimes examined in terms of different career stages, For instance, Morrow and McElroy (1987) observed significantly greater intrinsic job satisfaction in the stage identified as primarily concerning career "maintenance" than in the earlier "trial" stage.

Nevertheless, after statistically controlling for differences in key job attributes, a significant age difference in job-related well-being is typically retained (Birdi et al., 1995; Clark et al., 1996; Glenn, Taylor, & Weaver, 1977; Kalleberg & Loscocco, 1983; Pugliesi, 1995; Warr, 1992). Movement into more attractive jobs thus cannot completely account for the positive age-gradient in job-related well-being across the later years. It may be that variables included in analyses of this kind have been insufficiently comprehensive, however, and an overall categorization of key environmental features will be suggested in the next section.

One important issue that has received very little research attention concerns the impact of specific job characteristics upon different components of mental health. Given that older people tend to move into jobs with features that are different from younger people's jobs, we need to define which particular transitions affect different aspects of, for instance, job-related well-being.

It appears that job-related anxiety (axis 2 in Figure 6.2) is predominantly affected by levels of job demand and overload, whereas axis 3 (from depression to enthusiasm) is more influenced by variations in decision latitude (Warr, 1990a). It is important now to examine more precisely the specific shifts in job content that might lead to differences in aspects of job-specific well-being at older ages (cf., Birdi et al., 1995).

Shifts in Specific Work Values

There is evidence that older employees have specific work values that lead them to rate certain job characteristics as more important than do younger people. In some circumstances, that differential weighting may contribute to different levels of well-being at different ages.

For instance, Wright and Hamilton (1978) and Kalleberg and Loscocco (1983) (in secondary analyses of the same data) found that the rated importance of many job features was stable across ages, but that income level and promotion opportunities were of relatively less concern to older employees. As a result of that difference in work values at different ages, jobs with relatively low pay or opportunities for promotion would be expected to be evaluated particularly negatively by younger employees (since they view these features as more important to them). This process of judgmental adaptation was illustrated for *context-free* mental health in the previous section.

The age patterns observed in specific work values vary somewhat from study to study, in part because of different measurement procedures. A cross-sectional decline in the perceived importance of income and promotion opportunities (above) is consistently found. In addition, O'Brien and Dowling (1981) reported that less skill utilization and variety were desired at older ages. However, Birdi et al. (1995) found that the rated importance of independent work activities and of helping others were greater at older ages. Possible changes with age in a range of specific work values will be considered in a later section.

Several investigators have examined statistically whether differences in measured values of these kinds can account for the cross-sectional increase in job satisfaction with age. As with job characteristics, discussed previously, it is found that differences in work values can statistically account for some of the age pattern. However, the independent effect of age is typically retained in multivariate analyses even after the introduction of controls for specific work values (e.g., Birdi et al., 1995; Clark et al., 1996; Kalleberg & Loscocco, 1983; Warr, 1992).

Changed Standards of Comparison

It seems probable that older workers will come to lower their expectations in ways that affect their job-related well-being. High expectations are likely to be modified after substantial experience of routine jobs, coming to be set lower in later years. Reduced comparison standards are likely to generate more positive evaluations of work, as the perceived gap between actual and expected work characteristics becomes smaller. If older people come to expect less from any possible job, then comparative assessments of their own positions relative to other possibilities will give rise to more positive feelings about their own jobs. Clark and Oswald (1996) have provided evidence that this comparative process operates in respect to people's satisfaction with their income levels, but it is difficult to investigate in relation to other aspects of well-being. However, the longitudinal approach described by Brandstädter and Rothermund (1994) (examining context-free mental health; see the previous discussion) has promise in this area.

Variations in Nonjob Mental Health.

Another possible explanation of the greater job well-being of older employees is in terms of nonjob variations. Cross-sectional increases in life satisfaction and decreases in context-free anxiety with age have been described earlier, and it has been pointed out that life satisfaction and job satisfaction are interdependent. It is likely that job-related well-being in part reflects *context-free* mental health.

Differences in context-free affect are associated with variations in family composition (for instance, in respect to dependent children) and with differences in financial position and demands, self-concept, personal and normative expectations, and social roles at different ages. In practice, it is difficult in large-scale surveys to measure the less public aspects of self-concept and personal aspirations, and attention so far has mainly been focused on surface variables such as marital status and number of dependent children. Controls for those factors do not remove the significant influence of age (Clark et al., 1996; Kalleberg & Loscocco, 1983; Warr, 1992). The age-gradient in job satisfaction thus has not been explained through the limited life-stage variables that have been included in analyses to date.

A direct approach to the overlap between job-specific and context-free well-being was taken by Clark et al. (1996). Into multivariate analyses of age and overall job satisfaction they introduced individuals' scores on the GHQ (GHQ, a measure of context-free distress; see the previous discussion). It was shown that GHQ score was itself a significant predictor of job satisfaction, even after inclusion of a range of other variables. However, the J-shaped relationship of job satisfaction with age remained almost unchanged despite control for GHQ score. Even though the same curvilinear relationship may be present between age and both job-specific and context-free well-being, age-related variations in the former cannot be explained in terms of the latter.

Cohort Differences

The positive age-gradient might also be explained in terms of cohort differences. The members of older generations in a study may always have been more satisfied with their jobs. To examine this possibility directly, it is desirable to compare individuals or surveys over a period of years. Such comparisons are not widely available, but in general, the evidence for cohort differences in job satisfaction is not strong (e.g., Janson & Martin, 1982).

Glenn and Weaver (1985) examined differences in U.S. national surveys carried out between 1972 and 1982, concluding that "we cannot be absolutely certain" but that "the best available evidence indicates a long-term intercohort trend toward a lesser tendency to be satisfied with work, with a distinct difference between persons born in 1945–1964 and those born in the previous 20 years" (p. 106). However, this issue appears not to have been examined recently. It is now possible to study larger numbers of individuals born in a longer run of years after World War II. It would be valuable at this time to analyze findings from consecutive national surveys over more lengthy and recent periods.

Two sets of findings make it unlikely that the positive age-gradient in job satisfaction can be explained in terms of a progressive cohort difference (assuming that currently older people have always been more satisfied than currently younger ones). First, it is usually observed that older groups have lower nonfinancial employment commitment. When asked whether they would choose to continue in employment if they had no financial need to do so, older individuals tend to respond more negatively than younger people (e.g., Hanlon, 1986). A cohort explanation would need to account for both more positive and more negative employment orientations among older cohorts. Second, the presence of a curvilinear relationship with age in several studies (see the previous discussion) would require an interpretation in terms of some reversal of previous cohort differences; the youngest group is in some studies found to be more satisfied than the cohort currently in middle age.

Varying Subsample Composition

Finally, some of the observed differences among age groups might be accounted for by varying composition of particular subsamples at different ages. For example, chronic physical disability tends to lead to relatively early exclusion from the labor force. More generally, the rate of labor force participation is progressively lower in older groups. Whereas between the ages of 25 and 54, more than 90% of British or American men are economically active at present, only around two-thirds of men between 55 and 64 are in the labor market; for women, these values are about 75% and 40% in Britain and 75% and 49% in the United States (e.g., Ellison, Melville, & Gutman, 1996; Fullerton, 1995; Organisation for Economic Co-operation and Development, 1995). Older employees are therefore somewhat less representative of their overall age group in comparison to younger ones. It is possible that, through greater self-selection into the sample, they have more positive average work attitudes than do those of the same age who are no longer employed.

Nevertheless, that self-selection effect, if it occurs, is unlikely to be large. Some older people outside the labor force have in practice been excluded against their will; conversely, others remain employed only reluctantly. Furthermore, the explanation is less relevant to early investigations into age and job satisfaction, since older people's participation in the labor force declined substantially only in the 1970s and 1980s. Differential subsample composition was of less concern prior to that period, but a positive age-gradient has been found at all times.

However, possible differences in subsample composition at different ages have become of increasing importance recently, in view of the tendency for retired persons to undertake part-time or temporary employment (see the earlier discussion). Merely examining full-time workers (the common practice) appears inappropriate at a time when the labor market is increasingly differentiated. Separate analyses are needed for different categories of workers, especially in their later years. For instance, it is desirable to examine separately the job-related well-being of full-time and part-time workers defining themselves as "retired," as well as "nonretired" people in those two categories; differences in age-gradients between men and women, and between employees and self-employed individuals, also deserve attention. To date, variations in the proportion of an age group in employment have not been shown to determine the age pattern in job-related mental health, but this issue deserves further investigation.

In overview, it seems likely that each of the six sets of features outlined previously may contribute something to the positive association between age and overall job satisfaction. Nevertheless, individual investigations have so far rarely accounted for all the age-satisfaction variance, despite inclusion in analyses of up to several dozen other variables. Furthermore, an overall empirical examination of the relative importance of the six possible explanations is still awaited. The issues examined here clearly warrant further research attention.

AGE, JOB CHARACTERISTICS, AND SPECIFIC WORK VALUES

There is a particular need to develop the first two possible explanations outlined previously: with increasing age, many people move into jobs that have more desirable characteristics; and the importance attached to specific job features may change. In this section, I will draw together findings from research carried out by industrial and organizational psychologists into the job characteristics that (irrespective of age) affect the mental health of people at work. After suggesting an overall categorization of key factors, I will consider some aspects of each feature that might be influential at older ages. In doing that, it will be essential to examine also the second possible explanation of age patterns suggested previously: shifts in specific work values. From that analysis, I will seek to define those aspects of job transitions that are most likely to determine the observed age-gradients in mental health and those that appear to be unimportant in that respect.

The studies by industrial/organizational psychologists that underpin this review have rarely considered age as an influential variable, so the discussion that follows will be a mix of speculation as well as a research report. Conversely, there is very considerable evidence for the general importance (irrespective of age) of the factors discussed; full references in respect of each one will therefore be omitted here (see, e.g., reviews by Kahn & Byosiere, 1992; Warr, 1987).

Nine features will be identified that are important in any environment, both within jobs and also outside jobs. The nine environmental features deserve attention whether a person is unemployed, retired, or not concerned with the labor market (e.g., as a homemaker). However, this presentation will refer primarily to jobs, since paid work is the principal focus of the chapter.

The nine features of jobs and other environments that underlie mental health may be described as follows. In each case, a primary descriptive term is followed by other labels or more specific illustrations from the literature in industrial/organizational psychology.

1. *Opportunity for control:* discretion, decision latitude, independence, autonomy, job control, self-determination, personal control, absence of close supervision, participation in decision-making, absence of routinization.

2. *Opportunity for skill use:* skill utilization, utilization of valued abilities, application of skills and abilities, required skills.
3. *Externally generated goals:* job demands, task demands, quantitative or qualitative workload, environmental demands, structural imperatives in a job, time structure, time demands, role responsibility, work traction, time pressure at work, required concentration, conflicting demands, role conflict, job-induced goals, normative requirements.
4. *Variety:* variation in job content and location, nonrepetitive work, varied roles and responsibilities, skill variety, number of different job operations.
5. *Environmental clarity:* three aspects: (a) information about the consequences of behavior, availability of feedback, task feedback; (b) information about required behavior, low role ambiguity, clarity of role requirements; (c) information about the future, absence of job future ambiguity, absence of job insecurity, low uncertainty about the future.
6. *Availability of money:* income level, amount of pay, moderate or high standard of living, absence of poverty, material resources.
7. *Physical security:* absence of danger, low physical risk, good working conditions, ergonomically adequate equipment, adequate health and safety conditions, safe levels of temperature and noise, absence of continuous heavy work.
8. *Opportunity for interpersonal contact:* two aspects: (a) quantity of interaction, absence of isolation, friendship opportunities, contact with others, social density, adequate privacy; (b) quality of interaction, good relationships with others, social support, coworker support, emotional support, instrumental support, good communications.
9. *Valued social position:* three aspects: (a) cultural evaluations of status, social rank, occupational prestige, or social stratification; (b) more localized social evaluations of in-company status or job importance; (c) personal evaluations of task significance, valued role incumbency, meaningfulness of job, or self-respect from the job.

There is considerable evidence that, at least up to moderate levels, increases in these factors in a job are psychologically desirable. It is extremely improbable that the associations are purely linear, however. For example, if that were the case, we would expect that for every increment of a certain size in money received (no. 6) there would be a standard increase in affective well-being all the way across the range of values. Yet it seems plausible that a given unit of increase in income will have greater benefits at low-income levels than for people already receiving large sums. A nonlinear association may thus be present in most cases: increased levels of a job feature are desirable, but not continuously so. This point is developed by Warr (1987, 1994b).

Furthermore, we can easily envisage the possibility of *too much* of some desirable characteristics. For example, although a moderate level of externally generated goals (no. 3) is important in providing targets for action, with associated possibilities of reward and self-validation, extremely high levels and numbers of goals can become overloading and stressful. In general, at very high levels an environmental "opportunity" becomes an "unavoidable requirement," coercing rather than permitting action. For example, the negative effect of excessively high levels of control has been identified in laboratory as well as occupational situations (Burger, 1989; Xie & Johns, 1995). In addition, extremely high levels of some desirable features tend to be empirically associated with other characteristics that are themselves undesirable. For instance, managers whose jobs contain unremittingly high control opportunities (no. 1) have to make decisions continuously and accept personal responsibility, in some cases being subject to relentless overload (no. 3).

Possible Changes with Age

Given that these nine types of job characteristics are important for mental health at all ages, what can be said specifically about the jobs of older workers? Let us consider each feature in turn, to explore two aspects: possible changes with age in the amount of a characteristic available (that is, in exposure to the feature) and possible changes in the way it is viewed (thus incorporating the second possible explanation of age differences introduced previously: shifts in specific work values).

1. *Opportunity for control.* As they grow older, many people gain greater discretion over their work activities, such that they can

better control activities and events. This may arise from promotion to more senior jobs or from increased tenure in a single job, or it may be associated with norms about the treatment of older workers. This aspect of job content has been shown consistently to influence several aspects of mental health among workers as a whole. Furthermore, variations in job control can account for a portion (but not all) of the positive age-gradient in job-specific well-being (e.g., Warr, 1992).

Is there any evidence that people's desires for job decision latitude change with age? The question has rarely been posed specifically for this single job feature, but from somewhat circumstantial evidence, it appears that its rated importance remains high across the years of employment (Eichar, Norland, Brady, & Fortinsky, 1991; O'Brien & Dowling, 1981; Warr, 1992; Wright & Hamilton, 1978). Indeed, there is no obvious reason why older employees might come to value decision latitude in their jobs less than younger ones. Autonomy and positive self-regard (components of mental health introduced previously) depend upon self-determination and the ability to control one's own fate to at least a moderate degree. In addition, the opportunity for personal control is of general significance for mental health, because control permits an individual to manipulate some or all of the other eight factors; one can use this feature to turn other features of an environment to personal advantage.

2. *Opportunity for skill use.* The opportunity to use valued abilities has also been shown to be crucial to the job-related mental health of people at work. This aspect of an environment feeds into a person's subjective competence and positive self-regard, and is regularly reported by employees to be much desired in their work. As with opportunity for control (discussed previously), this feature of a job is likely to increase at least up to the middle years of a working life.

However, many workers in their 50's and above may have only a limited chance to use high levels of skill. This can arise through gradual obsolescence, especially as formal learning is relatively unlikely for older people in organizations (e.g., Warr, 1994a). As a result, some older employees may find it necessary to accept lower-quality positions with reduced opportunity for skill use.

Recognizing this diversity among individuals, it seems probable that on average opportunity for skill use at work first increases with age and then remains stable.

What about the age pattern in rated importance of this feature? From the few investigations available, it appears that older individuals are somewhat less concerned than younger ones about their potential to make use of high levels of skill (O'Brien & Dowling, 1981; Wright & Hamilton, 1978). Explanation of this finding is difficult; perhaps older workers place their emphasis elsewhere. Overall, we may surmise that the perceived importance of skill use increases somewhat up to middle age, but that this feature is somewhat less valued at older ages. However, published supporting evidence is very limited.

3. *Externally generated goals.* It is firmly established that moderate levels of job demands, responsibilities, and challenges are important for worker mental health. At very high levels, however, this feature may be viewed in terms of quantitative or qualitative overload (either excessive amount or excessive difficulty of goals), being associated with poorer rather than better mental health.

Does this job feature vary with worker age? Goals in employment can arise from many different sources, and their level depends both upon the targets set by an organization and a person's own initiatives and responses to outside opportunities and pressures. Although for some people work demands are likely to decline over the years, the opposite is the case for others. In the absence of systematic evidence, it appears appropriate to suggest that the amount of this job characteristic does not in general vary significantly between age groups.

However, there do appear to be differences in the degree to which work demands are considered important at different ages. As with other features, evidence is somewhat indirect, since measures of job-related values tend to be rather general, but it does appear that the desire for substantial challenge and high targets tends to be lower at older ages (Kalleberg & Loscocco, 1983); this may be especially the case among blue-collar rather than white-collar employees (Wright & Hamilton, 1978).

Why should this specific work value decline with age? Three possible reasons are habituation, reduced expected utility, and declines in energy as people grow older. In the first case, individuals become accustomed to recurring environmental stimuli of all kinds, such that their potential to reward or punish becomes less; in work settings, this adaptation may be seen in a reduction in enthusiasm for recurring job tasks as "the novelty wears off." An overlapping explanation is in terms of a decline in the expected utility of meeting external demands; the personal valence of achieving familiar goals may become less with age. Third, for a proportion of people, physical and/or mental energy declines somewhat with age. These people become less able to cope effectively with the magnitude and variety of demands that were acceptable or attractive at younger ages, so that high levels of externally generated goals are no longer desired.

4. *Variety.* Variation in job content and location has been shown to be positively correlated with job-specific well-being, but it appears that no studies have examined this feature in jobs held by people at different ages. Although wide differences occur in the amount of variety experienced in different jobs, it may be that on average, this feature is reduced for older workers, as their activities and skills become increasingly specialized. In respect to the rated importance of job variety, one study has indicated a reduction among older persons (O'Brien & Dowling, 1981).

5. *Environmental clarity.* This feature concerns the degree to which an environment is experienced as clear and comprehensible. Three aspects of clarity were listed earlier, and age patterns in these appear to vary somewhat.

   First is the availability of information about the consequences of behavior, often described as the presence of feedback about performance. No studies have been located about the age pattern in this feature in jobs, and it seems reasonable to assume it remains on average stable with age. However, it is likely that younger individuals rate feedback more highly than older ones, since they have a more limited exposure to different work situations; older employees, with greater experience of employment activities, might be better able to estimate and evaluate the outcomes of their behavior and thus have a lower concern about this form of clarity.

   Second is the presence of information about required behavior, sometimes referred to as "role clarity" or low "role ambiguity."

Once again, there appears to be a lack of published information about the age-gradient in this respect. However, it seems likely that on average, older workers have greater role clarity because of their greater experience and knowledge of relevant jobs and forms of job behavior. In terms of rated importance, there appears to be no reason to expect a difference with age.

A third form of environmental clarity is information about the future and an absence of job insecurity. One might expect some older persons' jobs to be more insecure because of advances in new technology and their relative lack of skills in new areas of work. Furthermore, steady careers have recently been replaced for many older people by a succession of short-term jobs of uncertain duration (e.g., Hall & Mirvis, 1995). Conversely, some older employees are protected against potential job loss because of their seniority in the organization. It therefore seems likely that on average, this feature is constant across ages, although between-job variations will be considerable.

However, a significant difference in rated importance across age has been identified for this feature (no. 5c in the present model). Older employees have been found to be more concerned about having a secure position than are younger ones (Wright & Hamilton, 1978). This specific work value is expected to influence feelings about a job at all ages, but especially among older workers. For example, an absence of job security will yield particularly low well-being among older people.

6. *Availability of money.* In general, income levels for full-time employees increase up to the 40s, after which they level off or tend to decline (e.g., Department of Employment, 1994, Table E125). There is considerable evidence that younger, middle-aged persons have the greatest need for income, deriving from family and other demands. Associated with that pattern of financial need, current level of income and the opportunity to increase income through promotion are considered relatively less important by older individuals (Birdi et al., 1995; Kalleberg & Loscocco, 1983; Oliver, 1977).

7. *Physical security.* Poor working conditions and high physical risk have significant negative effects on job-related mental health at all ages. However, it appears that variations in the presence of this

feature are uncorrelated with age (Warr, 1992). As for rated importance as a function of age, it seems possible that older people will
see physical security as more important than younger ones, associated with a greater cautiousness and some reduced physiological effectiveness; however, no evidence has been located.

8. *Opportunity for interpersonal contact.* Social interaction at work
   may be viewed in terms of either the quantity or quality of interaction. In the first case, emphasis is upon the opportunity to meet
   people and to avoid social isolation; second, qualitative differences
   are seen in terms of variations in friendliness and social support
   from colleagues. There is no evidence that, in general, the jobs of
   older and younger people differ significantly in either of these
   respects.

   What about the importance attached to job-related social contact
   at different ages? Wright and Hamilton's (1978) analyses suggest
   that no differences exist, but the issue has rarely been examined
   empirically. On balance, it would appear that the average level and
   rated importance of this job characteristic remain stable across
   employee age, but additional data are clearly required.

9. *Valued social position.* The final feature listed previously concerns
   personal and societal evaluations of the value and prestige of a job.
   Age-patterns in this respect vary considerably according to the
   nature of a person's employment. For example, successful managers tend to experience an increase in valued social position
   through promotions across the years, whereas skilled workers who
   lose their jobs and take up a more limited role shift in the opposite direction. Although there are undoubtedly large changes in
   individual cases, no overall age pattern in level or rated importance
   is likely to be observed.

This tentative set of findings and interpretations is summarized in
Table 6.2. Columns 2 and 3 summarize the material presented previously,
and implications for the positive age-gradient in job-related mental health
are suggested in the right-hand column. It can be seen from column 2 that
for most job features no increase with age is expected (only in respect to
opportunity for control, opportunity for skill use, role clarity, and availability of money); conversely, there may be some decline with age in the
amount of variety in people's jobs. The age pattern in rated importance
(tentatively suggested in column 3) can for the population as a whole only

TABLE 6.2 Probable Effect of Key Job Characteristics and Associated Specific Work Values on the Positive Age-Gradient in Overall Job Satisfaction for the Population As a Whole

Characteristics	Probable average age-pattern: Amount of the job feature	Probable average age-pattern: Rated importance of the job feature	Probable average effect on the observed age gradient
1. Opportunity for control	Increasing	Stable	Positive
2. Opportunity for skill use	Increasing then stable	Increasing then decreasing	Slightly positive then neutral
3. Externally generated goals	Stable	Decreasing	Neutral
4. Variety	Decreasing	Decreasing	Slightly negative
5. Environmental clarity:			
a. Feedback	Stable	Decreasing	Neutral
b. Role clarity	Increasing	Stable	Positive
c. Job security	Stable	Increasing	Neutral
6. Availability of money	Increasing then stable	Increasing then decreasing	Slightly positive then neutral
7. Physical security	Stable	Increasing	Neutral
8. Opportunity for interpersonal contact	Stable	Stable	Neutral
9. Valued social position	Stable	Stable	Neutral

Note: Empirical evidence is limited in these respects, so that assessments of probability are sometimes uncertain.

influence the age-gradient in mental health for those features where an age difference in average amount is indicated in column 2 (numbers 1, 2, 4, 5b, and 6). Differences in a particular work value are of no relevance to that mental health gradient for the entire population if no average difference in amount is indicated in column 2.

After adjusting age-related shifts in amount by possible age-related differences in specific job values, it appears (see column 4) that job characteristics 1, 2, 5b, and 6 are the ones most likely to contribute to the positive age-gradient in overall job satisfaction for employees in general, but that this gradient may be attenuated somewhat by a reduction with age in job variety (feature no. 4). Six other features, such as externally generated goals or job security, do not seem to contribute to the positive age-gradient for the population as a whole, since on average exposure (column 2) does not vary with age. However, there remains a great need for more evidence about these specific job characteristics and age, for people in general and for specific subgroups in terms of gender, ethnic background, employment sector, and so on.

We are already at the outer limits of research evidence about age and job satisfaction, and almost no information is available about the factors influencing age-gradients in other components of mental health. Some findings about job-feature influences upon either axes 2 or 3 of Figure 6.2 were summarized earlier, but these were irrespective of age (Warr, 1990a). For example, it was noted that differences in decision latitude (feature 1 in Table 6.2) were particularly important for well-being in terms of axis 3, from depression to enthusiasm. It may therefore be expected that increases with age in opportunity for control in jobs may contribute to the positive age-gradient in that respect. However, empirical knowledge is very sparse at this level.

The findings and speculations in Table 6.2 have another relevance to the content of this chapter. The rated importance of different job features at different ages (column 3) suggests which factors are most likely to affect the job-related mental health of older (and younger) workers. Those job features whose perceived importance increases with age (job security and physical security) are particularly likely to have a great impact on, say, job satisfaction at older ages. Conversely, those features whose rated importance decline with age (numbers 3, 4, and 5a) are likely to be more predictive of job satisfaction among younger people. Empirical tests of these predictions would now be of great interest.

DIFFERENCES BETWEEN ENVIRONMENTS AND BETWEEN PERSONS

The nine-category framework of environmental features can be applied to create profiles descriptive of the settings of individuals. Rather than taking as our unit of analysis a broad job title (a "computer operator"or a "manager") or a person's employment status ("unemployed," "retired," and so on), it is often more fruitful to characterize the nature of a person's situation in the nine terms summarized previously.

Questions about the occupational bases of older people's mental health can be of two kinds. On the one hand, we might ask in general terms about between-status differences (for instance, "Is mental health generally worse in retirement than in employment?"). On the other hand, we can ask more specifically about the relevant causal factors in individual settings (e.g., "Are the factors in this person's retirement better for his or her mental health than would be the factors in employment?"). Although retired people in general exhibit similar well-being to comparably employed people, there are wide between-person differences in both groups. Mental health is affected by the nine environmental features, rather than by a general employment status itself.

Paid employment is thus beneficial for older people only in cases where the mix of the nine environmental characteristics is favorable. The features in many older people's life space can support a high level of mental health without any involvement in the labor market at all (e.g., as a homemaker or a retired person), whereas for others a job is crucial to provide income or social contact. Conversely, some older people outside a job may experience considerable overload (too many externally generated goals in the present framework), for instance, because of the need to care for elderly parents, whereas the demands impinging on other nonemployed individuals can be less extreme.

It is thus often valuable to ask about the availability of the nine sources of psychological benefit or stress in a person's environment, taking an individual's situation as the unit of analysis, irrespective of whether he or she is employed, unemployed, retired, or whatever. Indeed, profiles of a life space can cover the full set of a person's employment and nonemployment roles, describing as a whole both work and home characteristics (e.g., Lennon & Rosenfield, 1992; Warr, 1987). Generalizations might then be sought in terms of the features in a person's environment rather than through overall statements about a particular employment status.

Creating individual profiles in the terms outlined above appears to be valuable at all ages, but this approach does need to be supplemented in respect to older people. Two other individual attributes need also to be examined: physical health and cognitive competence.

First, variations in mental health are strongly associated with differences in physical health (e.g., Goldberg & Williams, 1988), and physical health deteriorates more rapidly for some people when they reach older ages. It follows that, in seeking to explain and predict mental health among older individuals, the nine-factor model of environmental characteristics outlined here needs to be supplemented by information about a person's current and anticipated physical health. What is the level of the individual's physical health, as well as of the nine key characteristics of his or her life space?

Second, for some older people mental health is also likely to be increasingly affected by declines in cognitive competence. If cognitive competence is clearly low, a person is liable to have particular difficulty in dealing with events and environmental pressures. In seeking to explain differences in mental health in older individuals, it is thus important to consider cognitive competence as well as physical health, within a framework of the nine environmental factors described here. Nevertheless, the effect of cognitive competence (if it is found) may only be important at very low levels of cognitive functioning. Across a wide range of moderate to high values, people's cognitive effectiveness is unlikely to influence mental health, since relations with the environment tend to be acceptable across a broad band of competence.

An associated possibility in need of examination is that for some people being employed at older ages may sustain their cognitive functioning. It is known that (irrespective of age) complex work environments can contribute to employees' intellectual flexibility across a period of years (Kohn & Schooler, 1983). This general effect may have specific relevance around the age of retirement: cognitive functioning might decline more rapidly for those leaving the labor market than for those who remain employed.

This issue is, in general, very difficult to investigate, requiring longitudinal research, full details of a person's employment characteristics across the period examined, and information about his or her nonjob environments. Furthermore, it may that the complexity of many people's environments would not change much on retirement (e.g., because of a low initial level), so that the effect may overall be a small one. It would also be important to control for other factors such as changes in physical health. Investigations into possible cognitive changes associated with retirement, and into the more general overlap between cognitive competence and mental health, are greatly needed.

There is also a growing requirement to examine relationships between an individual and the environments he or she enters in the course of a career. The traditional career, typically focused on upward movement in a single organization, is becoming replaced by more variable exposure to different environments (e.g., Hall & Mirvis, 1995). This greater variability (and its accompanying uncertainty) can place more emphasis on the need for strong self-direction and the maintenance of a clear self-identity. In studying the association between features of a current job and the mental health of an older person, it is thus often important to explore the location of that job in a career of previous activities and possible achievements or disappointments.

A final point concerns interindividual differences more generally. The present concern has been for broad generalizations about stability or change across years of age. Such an approach means that differences between individuals are necessarily deemphasized. Between-person variation may be particularly important in respect to older people, however.

In many gerontological investigations, it has been found that interindividual variation tends to be greater at older ages. This observation has principally been made in respect to cognitive or physiological processes (e.g., Fozard, Vercruyssen, Reynolds, Hancock, & Quilter, 1994; Morse, 1993), but it may also apply to the nine environmental characteristics examined here. Some individuals proceed successfully through a career, being exposed to job features that are widely desirable. Others have intermittent or poor-quality jobs, primarily experiencing negative aspects of the features identified here. This bifurcation might be expected to increase with age, so that general statements about average exposure to, say, opportunity for control at work (column 2 of Table 6.2) may become increasingly inappropriate as the variance in exposure becomes progressively greater. The possibility of increased differentiation at older ages has not been examined in respect to the topics covered in this chapter; it now deserves serious attention.

More generally, research into older people has so far inadequately addressed occupational contributions to the mental health of that group. We need considerably more investigations into job features and their consequences for older individuals. And future research should extend beyond affective well-being alone, to examine the other aspects of mental health described in this chapter.

REFERENCES

Abraham, J. D., & Hansson, R. O. (1995). Successful aging at work: An applied study of selection, optimization, and compensation through impression management. *Journal of Gerontology: Psychological Sciences, 50B,* P94–P103.

Andrews, F. M., & Withey, S. B. (1976). *Social indicators of well-being: Americans' perceptions of life quality.* New York: Plenum.

Angyal, A. (1965). *Neurosis and treatment: A holistic theory.* New York: John Wiley.

Antonovsky, A. (1980). *Health, stress, and coping.* San Francisco: Jossey-Bass.

Birdi, K., Warr, P., & Oswald, A. (1995). Age differences in three components of employee well-being. *Applied Psychology, 44,* 345–373.

Birren, J. E., & Renner, V. J. (1981). Concepts and criteria of mental health and aging. *American Journal of Orthopsychiatry, 51,* 242–254.

Bosse, R., Aldwin, C. M., Levenson, M. R., & Ekerdt, D. J. (1987). Mental health differences among retirees and workers: Findings from the Normative Aging Study. *Psychology and Aging, 2,* 383–389.

Bosse, R., Aldwin, C. M., Levenson, M. R., & Workman-Daniels, K. (1991). How stressful is retirement? Findings from the Normative Aging Study. *Journal of Gerontology, 46,* P9–P14.

Bradburn, N. M. (1969). *The structure of psychological well-being.* Chicago: Aldine.

Brandstädter, J., & Rothermund, K. (1994). Self-percepts of control in middle and later adulthood: Buffering losses by rescaling goals. *Psychology and Aging, 9,* 265–273.

Burger, J. M. (1989). Negative reactions to increases in perceived personal control. *Journal of Personality and Social Psychology, 56,* 246–256.

Campbell, A. (1981). *The sense of well-being in America.* New York: McGraw-Hill.

Clark, A. E., & Oswald, A. J. (1996). Satisfaction and comparison income. *Journal of Public Economics, 61,* 359–381.

Clark, A. E., Oswald, A. J., & Warr, P. B. (1996). Is job satisfaction U-shaped in age? *Journal of Occupational and Organizational Psychology, 69,* 57–81.

Csikszentmihalyi, M. (1975). *Beyond boredom and anxiety.* San Francisco: Jossey-Bass.

Dawis, R. V., & Lofquist, L. H. (1984). *A psychological theory of work adjustment.* Minneapolis: University of Minnesota Press.

Department of Employment. (1994). *New Earnings Survey.* London: HMSO.

Eichar, D. M., Norland, S., Brady, E. M., & Fortinsky, R. H. (1991). The job satisfaction of older workers. *Journal of Organizational Behavior, 12,* 609–620.

Elder, G. H., & Pavalko, E. K. (1993). Work careers in men's later years: Transitions, trajectories and historical change. *Journal of Gerontology, 48,* S180–S191.

Ellison, R., Melville, D., & Gutman, R. (1996). British labour force projections: 1996–2006. *Labour Market Trends, 104,* 197–213.

Feather, N. T. (1990). *The psychological impact of unemployment.* New York: Springer Publishing Company.

Feldman, D. C. (1994). The decision to retire early: A review and conceptualization. *Academy of Management Journal, 19,* 285–311.

Folkman, S., Lazarus, R. S., Pimley, S., & Novacek, J. (1987). Age differences in stress and coping. *Psychology and Aging, 2,* 171–184.

Fozard, J. L., Vercruyssen, M., Reynolds, S. L., Hancock, P. A., & Quilter, R. E. (1994). Age differences and changes in reaction time: The Baltimore longitudinal study of aging. *Journal of Gerontology, 49,* P179–P189.

Fullerton, H. N. (1995). The 2005 labor force: Growing but slowly. *Monthly Labor Review, 118*(11), 29–42.

Glenn, N. D., Taylor, P. A., & Weaver, C. D. (1977). Age and job satisfaction among males and females: A multivariate, multisurvey study. *Journal of Applied Psychology, 63,* 189–193.

Glenn, N. D., & Weaver, C. N. (1985). Age, cohort, and reported satisfaction in the United States. In Z. S. Blau (Ed.), *Current perspectives on aging and the life-cycle* (pp. 89–109). Greenwich, CT: JAI Press.

Goldberg, D. P. (1972). *The detection of psychiatric illness by questionnaire.* Oxford: Oxford University Press.

Goldberg, D. P., & Williams, P. (1988). *A user's guide to the General*

Health Qestionnaire. Windsor: NFER-Nelson.

Hall, D. T., & Mirvis, P. H. (1995). The new career contract: Developing the whole person at midlife and beyond. *Journal of Vocational Behavior, 47,* 269–289.

Handyside, J. D. (1961). Satisfaction and aspirations. *Occupational Psychology, 35,* 213–243.

Hanisch, K. A. (1994). Reasons people retire and their relations to attitudinal and behavioral correlates in retirement. *Journal of Vocational Behavior, 45,* 1–16.

Hanlon, M. D. (1986). Age and commitment to work. *Research on Aging, 8,* 289–315.

Hardy, M. A., & Quadagno, J. (1995). Satisfaction with early retirement: Making choices in the auto industry. *Journal of Gerontology: Social Sciences, 50B,* S217–S228.

Hayward, M. D., Crimmins, E. M., & Wray, L. A. (1994). The relationship between retirement life cycle changes and older men's labor force participation rates. *Journal of Gerontology, 49,* S219–S230.

Herzberg, F. (1966). *Work and the nature of man.* Chicago: World Publishing Company.

Herzberg, F. I., Mausner, B., Peterson, R. O., & Capwell, D. R. (1957). *Job attitudes: Review of research and opinion.* Pittsburgh, PA: Psychological Service of Pittsburgh.

Kohn, M. L., & Schooler, C. (1983). *Work and personality: An inquiry into the impact of social stratification.* Norwood, NJ: Ablex Books.

Jahoda, M. (1958). *Current concepts of positive mental health.* New York: Basic Books.

Janson, P., & Martin, J. K. (1982). Job satisfaction and age: A test of two views. *Social Forces, 60,* 1089–1102.

Judge, T. A., & Watanabe, S. (1993). Another look at the job satisfaction-life satisfaction relationship. *Journal of Applied Psychology, 78,* 939–948.

Kahn, R. L., & Byosiere, P. (1992). Stress in organizations. In M. Dunnette & L. M. Hough (Eds.), *Handbook of industrial and organizational psychology* (Vol. 3, pp. 571–650). Palo Alto, CA: Consulting Psychologists Press.

Kalleberg, A. L., & Loscocco, K. A. (1983). Aging, values, and rewards: Explaining age differences in job satisfaction. *American Sociological Review, 48,* 78–90.

Kohn, M. L., & Schooler, C. (1983). In collaboration with J. Miller, K. A. Miller, C. Schoenbach, & R. Schoenberg. Work and personality: An inquiry into impact of social stratification. Norwood, NJ: Ablex.

Lazarus, R. S. (1975). The healthy personality: A review of conceptualizations and research. In L. Levi (Ed.), *Society, stress and disease* (Vol. 2, pp. 6–35). Oxford: Oxford University Press.

Lee, R., & Wilbur, E. R. (1985). Age, education, job tenure, salary, job characteristics, and job satisfaction: A multivariate analysis. *Human Relations, 38,* 781–791.

Lennon, M. C., & Rosenfield, S. (1992). Women and mental health: The interaction of job and family conditions. *Journal of Health and Social Behavior, 33,* 316–327.

Loevinger, J. (1980). *Ego development: Conceptions and theories.* San Francisco: Jossey-Bass.

Mackay, C., Cox, T., Burrows, G., & Lazzerini, T. (1978). An inventory for the measurement of self-reported stress and arousal. *British Journal of Social and Clinical Psychology, 17,* 283–284.

Maslow, A. H. (1973). A theory of human motivation. *Psychological Review, 50,* 370–396.

Matthews, G., Jones, D. M., & Chamberlain, A. G. (1990). Defining the measurement of mood: The UWIST mood adjective checklist. *British Journal of Psychology, 81,* 17–42.

Midanik, L. T., Soghikian, K., Ransom, L. J., & Tekawa, I. S. (1995). The effect of retirement on mental health and health behaviors: The Kaiser Permanente Retirement Study. *Journal of Gerontology, 50B,* S59–S61.

Mirowsky, J., & Ross, C. E. (1992). Age and depression. *Journal of Health and Social Behavior, 33,* 187–205.

Morrow, P. C., & McElroy, J. C. (1987). Work commitment and job satisfaction over three career stages. *Journal of Vocational Behavior, 30,* 330–346.

Morse, C. K. (1993). Does variability increase with age? An archival study of cognitive measures. *Psychology and Aging, 8,* 156–164.

Myers, D. A. (1991). Work after cessation of career job. *Journal of Gerontology, 46,* S93–S102.

Neumann, J. P. (1989). Aging and depression. *Psychology and Aging, 4,* 150–165.

Nezu, A. M. (1985). Differences in psychological distress between effective and ineffective problem solvers. *Journal of Counseling Psychology,*

32, 135–138.

O'Brien, G. E., & Dowling, P. (1981). Age and job satisfaction. *Australian Psychologist, 16,* 49–61.

Oliver, R. L. (1977). Antecedents of salemen's compensation perceptions: A path analysis interpretation. *Journal of Applied Psychology, 62,* 20–28.

Organisation for Economic Co-operation and Development. (1995). *Employment outlook.* Paris: OECD.

Palmore, E. B., Burchett, B. M., Fillenbaum, G. C., George, L. K., & Wallman, L. M. (1985). *Retirement: Causes and consequences.* New York: Springer Publishing Company.

Payne, E. C., Robbins, S. B., & Dougherty, L. (1991). Goal directedness and older-adult adjustment. *Journal of Counseling Psychology, 38,* 302–308.

Pugliesi, K. (1995). Work and well-being: Gender differences in the psychological consequences of employment. *Journal of Health and Social Behavior, 36,* 57–71.

Rabbitt, P., Donlan, C., Watson, P., McInnes, L., & Bent, N. (1995). Unique and interactive effects of depression, age, socioeconomic advantage, and gender on cognitive performance of normal healthy older people. *Psychology and Aging, 10,* 307–313.

Rhodes, S. R. (1983). Age-related differences in work attitudes and behavior: A review and conceptual analysis. *Psychological Bulletin, 93,* 328–367.

Robbins, S. B., Lee, R. M., & Wan, T. T. H. (1994). Goal continuity as a mediator of early retirement adjustment: Testing a multidimensional model. *Journal of Counseling Psychology, 41,* 18–26.

Ruhm, C. J. (1996). Gender differences in employment behavior during late middle age. *Journal of Gerontology: Social Sciences, 51B,* S11–S17.

Russell, J. A. (1980). A circumplex model of affect. *Journal of Personality and Social Psychology, 39,* 1161–1178.

Ryff, C. D. (1989a). Happiness is everything, or is it? Explorations on the meaning of psychological well-being. *Journal of Personality and Social Psychology, 57,* 1969–1081.

Ryff, C. D. (1989b). In the eye of the beholder: Views of psychological well-being among middle-aged and older adults. *Psychology and Aging, 4,* 195–210.

Ryff, C. D., & Keyes, C. L. M. (1995). The structure of psychological well-being revisited. *Journal of Personality and Social Psychology, 69,* 719–727.

Salokangas, R. K. R., & Joukamaa, M. (1991). Physical and mental health changes in retirement age. *Psychotherapy and Psychosomatics, 55,* 100–107.

Schwab, D. P., & Heneman, H. G. (1977). Age and satisfaction with dimensions of work. *Journal of Vocational Behavior, 10,* 212–220.

Smith, L. C., & Robbins, S. B. (1988). Validity of the goal instability scale (modified) as a predictor of adjustment in retirement-age adults. *Journal of Counseling Psychology, 35,* 325–329.

Smith, M. B. (1968). Competence and "mental health": Problems in conceptualizing human effectiveness. In S. B. Sells (Ed.), *The definition and measurement of mental health* (pp. 100–114). Washington, DC: Department of Health, Education, and Welfare.

Tait, M., Padgett, M. Y., & Baldwin, T. T. (1989). Job and life satisfaction: A re-evaluation of the strength of the relationship and gender effects as a function of the date of the study. *Journal of Applied Psychology, 74,* 502–507.

Talaga, J., & Beehr, T. A. (1989). Retirement: A psychological perspective. In C. L. Cooper & I. Robertson (Eds.), *International Review of Industrial and Organizational Psychology* (pp. 185–211). London: John Wiley.

Taylor, M. A., & Shore, L. M. (1995). Predictors of planned retirement age: An application of Beehr's model. *Psychology and Aging, 10,* 76–83.

Thayer, R. E. (1989). *The biophysiology of mood and arousal.* Oxford: Oxford University Press.

Warr, P. B. (1987). *Work, unemployment, and mental health.* Oxford: Oxford University Press.

Warr, P. B. (1990a). Decision latitude, job demands and employee well-being. *Work and Stress, 4,* 285–294.

Warr, P. B. (1990b). The measurement of well-being and other aspects of mental health. *Journal of Occupational Psychology, 63,* 193–210.

Warr, P. B. (1992). Age and occupational well-being. *Psychology and Aging, 7,* 37–45.

Warr, P. B. (1994a). Age and employment. In H. C. Triandis, M. D. Dunnette, & L. M. Hough (Eds.), *Handbook of industrial and organizational psychology* (Vol. 4, pp. 485–550). Palo Alto, CA: Consulting Psychologists Press.

Warr, P. B. (1994b). A conceptual framework for the study of work and mental health. *Work and Stress, 8,* 84–97.

Warr, P. B., Banks, M., & Jackson, P. (1988). Unemployment and mental health: Some British studies. *Journal of Social Issues, 44,* 47–68.

Warr, P. B., Cook, J., & Wall, T. D. (1979). Scales for the measurement of some work attitudes and aspects of psychological well-being. *Journal of Occupational Psychology, 52,* 129–148.

Warr, P. B., & Pennington, J. (1994). Occupational age-grading: Jobs for older and younger nonmanagerial employees. *Journal of Vocational Behavior, 45,* 328–346.

Watson, D., & Tellegen, A. (1985). Toward a consensual structure of mood. *Psychological Bulletin, 98,* 219–235.

Wooten, K. C., Sulzer, J. L., & Cornwell, J. M. (1994). The effects of age, financial strain, and vocational expectancies on the stress-related affect of adult job losers. In G. P. Keita & J. J. Hurrell (Eds.), *Job stress in a changing workforce* (pp.165–180). Washington, DC: American Psychological Association.

Wright, J. D., & Hamilton, R. F. (1978). Work satisfaction and age: Some evidence for the "job change" hypothesis. *Social Forces, 56,* 1140–1158.

Xie, J. L., & Johns, G. (1995). Job scope and stress: Can job scope be too high? *Academy of Management Journal, 38,* 1288–1309.

Commentary: Age, Work, and Well-Being: Toward A Broader View

James S. House

P eter Warr (chapter 6, this volume) has provided us an impressive overview of empirical regularities and conceptual possibilities in the study of age, work, and well-being, which he has defined here in terms of mental health. He points to a number of ways in which being older, as a worker and more generally, is salutary rather than problematic. I leave it to my colleague Jay Turner, who is far more expert than I in the area of mental health, to comment in more detail on Warr's conceptualizations of mental health and other aspects of his review of empirical regularities in the relation of age to mental health. First, I will note some ways in which Warr's analysis of the relationships among age, work, and well-being coincide with work of myself and others, providing another illustration of the type of convergence of theory and findings that Schooler (chapter 1, this volume) has pointed to as a sign of progress in this or any other field. At the same time, I will note the need for further research to better confirm or deepen our understanding of these important convergences. Then I would like to suggest more briefly several directions in which we need to expand our analyses of age, work, and well-being—directions that Warr's chapter hints at but does not develop, whether for lack of will or simply lack of time and space.

AGE PATTERNS IN MENTAL HEALTH
AND WELL-BEING: GENERAL AND JOB RELATED

Warr provides a quite masterful summary and synthesis of what he, we (e.g., Kessler, Foster, Webster, & House, 1992), and many others have learned about the relation of age to psychological well-being or mental health over several decades—a summary and synthesis that could not have been made with equal validity or assurances even 5 to 10 years ago. Though several caveats about his summary are in order, suggesting valuable lines for future research, the major parameters of his conclusions are not likely to be altered substantially by this further work, even if they are refined.

First, it should be noted that most of the work he summarizes has not addressed carefully and systematically the issues of individual or group differences that Sherry Willis raised during the conference's discussion. We know that most indicators of psychological well-being tend to increase with age, especially after age 40 or so in the total population, with possible downturns in later old age. Possible gender differences in these relationships have been most often examined, and appear not to be great, but are worthy of further scrutiny. Much less is known about possible racial-ethnic or socioeconomic differences in these areas, but limited evidence suggests greater potential for individual or group differences or variation in these domains. For example, in data first presented at an earlier conference at Penn State in 1990, we found that a measure of self-efficacy, combining items from Rosenberg's self-esteem scale (SES) and Pearlin's mastery scale, varies differently with age depending on socioeconomic status. At younger adult ages, as might be expected, upper socioeconomic strata manifest much higher levels of self-efficacy. But as age increases, self-efficacy declines modestly at higher socioeconomic levels, especially around the ages of retirement, while at lower SES levels, self-efficacy tends to rise with age, again most notably in the postretirement years, so that at ages 65+, socioeconomic differences in self-efficacy are quite small (House et al., 1992).

This finding plausibly reflects the different experience and meaning of retirement at different socioeconomic levels. For those at the higher level, retirement often entails the loss of a position and role that carried with it esteem, autonomy, self-direction, and other valuable attributes or opportunities. At lower SES levels, in contrast, retirement often means escaping from a position and role characterized by the absence of these positive attributes and experiencing opportunities to enter into new work (e.g., self-employment) or leisure roles that are much more conducive to a sense of self-efficacy.

It is also the case, as Warr clearly acknowledges, that we know much more about how age relates to affective well-being than to other dimensions of psychological well-being on mental health. Hence more research is needed on these dimensions as well as on individual and group differences, and it will be important to determine how age relates to all of these dimensions. I expect this research to refine the conclusions and understandings that Warr has conveyed. It is not likely to alter them fundamentally.

A more important limitation of all of this research, which Warr points to but does not emphasize enough, is that it is almost all cross-sectional in nature, although the conclusions we seek to draw from it are really about change within individuals or cohorts as they age. Warr notes that cohort differences constitute an alternative explanation for age differences in well-being, albeit a not very plausible explanation in the face of the usually curvilinear pattern of the relationships, and I would add the persistence of many of these relationships over a period of not just years, but decades. More troubling, I think, is the possibility of mortality selection effects, not just by exit from the labor force, but by exit from life.

We know that less mentally healthy people are at increased risk of mortality. Does the apparent increase in well-being with age in cross-sectional analyses largely reflect the gradual death or attrition over the life course of less healthy people, who are hence underrepresented in older age groups? Both logically, and on the basis of some analyses we have done of similar age differences in marital satisfaction (Orbuch, House, Mero, & Webster, 1996), I doubt that selection effects account for the phenomena that Warr has so artfully described. But we would be much more confident of these and other inferences if our evidence of variation in well-being by age came from long-term longitudinal data, of the type that the new Health and Retirement Study (HRS) and other longitudinal studies will ultimately yield. Longitudinal data are not a panacea for selection effect or the problem of separating aging, cohort, and time or period effects, but they are an important part of the solution to these problems. Much greater emphasis needs to be given to analyses of existing longitudinal data sets and to the development of new longitudinal data sets such as the HRS.

A second area where Warr's analysis and interpretation converge with ours and a larger literature is the possible explanations of observed cross-sectional increases with age in general or job-related well-being. Warr cogently delineates the major competing explanations and provides a judicious assessment of them. Transitions to better jobs or improvements in conditions of work and life constitute a major explanation of these trends, as we have also observed in the case of marital satisfaction (Orbuch et al., 1996), with psychological shifts in the nature and importance of specific values or comparison standards also being plausible.

After adjustment for any of these explanatory factors or combination of them, however, Warr notes that some age differences in well-being remain, suggesting the potential for additional explanatory mechanisms. One such mechanism that I believe he slights is changes in interpersonal relations and skills. There is reason to believe that individuals, couples, or sets of interacting individuals improve over time in their ability to relate to each other in positive ways. We and others find, for example, that members of older married couples report that they handle actual and potential conflict in ways that are more constructive and promotive of positive relationship bonds. For example, compared to younger married persons, older ones report being less likely to become physically or verbally abusive or hostile in the face of disagreements and more likely to resolve problems constructively. They are probably also less likely to say or do things that they know may antagonize the other. The same may be true in relation to other kin, friends, or coworkers, increasing the quality of interpersonal relations and satisfaction in many specific contexts, and life more generally. Clearly, there are significant individual and perhaps group differences here, but interpersonal relations deserve greater attention as a potential explanation for age-related differences in well-being.

Up to this point, what I have said is largely an extension or refinements of analyses and interpretations that Warr has already covered quite well. Let me now briefly suggest some directions in which I believe research on aging and work, in relation to well-being or otherwise, needs to be extended. Warr's chapter takes at least passing note of all of these but does not develop them to any significant degree.

1. We need to integrate theory and research on age-related variation or change in *psychological* well-being or *mental* health with comparable theory and research on *physical* well-being or health. It is a great paradox that as physical well-being declines with age, though at very different rates in different individuals and groups, psychological well-being is generally stable or improves with age. Somehow, *on average* as age increases, people are doing worse (physically), but feeling better (psychologically). Why this occurs, and how physical and psychological well-being relate to each other over the life course, is a topic ripe for new research.
2. As Warr's discussion of the conditions of work conducive to mental health suggests, we need to think more broadly about the nature and meaning of work in research and theory regarding aging, work, and well-being. Warr correctly observes that retirement from paid work has, again on *average,* no clearly deleterious effects on mental health, and research by David Ekerdt and others has reached similar conclusions regarding physical health. Similarly, Warr notes that voluntarily nonemployed people are *on average* not less mentally healthy than the employed, and the same is true for physical health if we adjust appropriately for health selection effects.

The reason for these findings may be that people at all ages engage in many types of unpaid work, or, as I and my colleagues have termed them in our research, productive activities, including household work, child care, voluntary organizational activities, and informal assistance to family and friends. Among all forms of work and productivity, only paid work and child care decline sharply with age. Failure to consider other activities grossly underrepresents the work or productive activity of many individuals and groups, most notably of women, whose total level of work and productive activity equals or exceeds that of men at all ages, and especially at older ages. The relative well-being of "nonworking" people of all ages, including retired older persons, may in part reflect that most of them are still working, though not for pay, and very likely to be doing amounts and types of work that they have voluntarily chosen and that hence are more likely to be characterized by the conditions of work that Warr suggests are supportive of well-being (cf. Herzog & House, 1991).

When we talk about the actual and potential problems of decreasing labor force participation at older ages, we need to recognize more clearly that the economic and noneconomic aspects of the problem are not necessarily so closely linked as they are in the case of paid work. *For economic reasons,* older people may need to work in the paid labor force, and we may need them to do so. They probably do not need to work in the paid labor force for social or psychological reasons if they and we can derive significant benefits from nonmarket work. As Warr suggests, as individuals, scientists, and a society, we need to understand and assess work or productive activity in all its form and to understand what amounts and types of work by an individual or a population are most promotive of individual and social well-being.

Our own research finds significant variation in the population as to whether they would like to be doing more, less, or about the same amount of paid work as they were doing when interviewed. Older persons are more likely to want to work more, and middle-aged persons to work less. But across the full age range, we observed the greatest physical and psychological well-being in those who are doing as much paid work as they would like to. Warr suggested the impact of part-time work on well-being as an agenda for future research. I would expect that agenda to consider how and why we might achieve a better fit between the amounts and types of work people of all ages wish to do, and what they actually do, both in the paid labor force and outside of it.

This leads to my final wish for broadening our perspective on the problem of aging in work to take a fuller, life course perspective. We live in a society in which many working young and middle-aged people, especially in households with children, increasingly report feeling overworked or overburdened by their combined loads of paid employment, household work, and child care, while many older individuals are being forced out of the labor force against their will and are feeling relatively underutilized. How we might better balance life course distribution of paid and unpaid work, within individual lives and across the total population of our society at a given point in time, is an issue that deserves to be high on our agenda for future research and policy in the areas of aging and work.

REFERENCES

Herzog, A. R., & House, J. S. (1991). Productive activities and aging well. *Generations, 15,* 49–54.

House, J. S., Kessler, R. C., Herzog, A. R., Mero, R. P., Kinney, A. M., & Breslow, M. J. (1992). Social stratification, age, and health. In K. W. Schaie, D. Blazer, & J. S. House (Eds.), *Aging, Health Behaviors and Health Outcomes* (pp. 1–32). Hillsdale, NJ: Erlbaum.

Kessler, R. C., Foster, C., Webster, P. S., & House, J. S. (1992). The relationship between age and depressive symptoms in two national surveys. *Psychology and Aging, 7,* 119–126.

Orbuch, T. L., House, J. S., Mero, R. P., & Webster, P. S. (1996). Marital quality through the life course. *Social Psychology Quarterly, 59,* 162–171.

Work and the Elderly: Crossing the Bounds of Levels and Disciplines

Carmi Schooler

As Warner Schaie noted in the Preface, the overarching goal of this series of Penn State Gerontology Center conferences and books is to "systematically explore the interfaces between social structures and behavior, and particularly to identify the mechanisms through which society influences adult development" (p. ix). The chapters in this volume have not only met this mandate, but have illustrated its importance. All too often, human aging is seen as a strictly biological process that occurs essentially unaffected by the social structural, cultural, and historical circumstances in which it takes place. At the same time, as several of the chapters have made clear, we cannot understand how these environmental conditions affect and are affected by the older individual without taking into account the biological aspects of aging.

In examining the mutual effects of biological and socioenvironmental processes, the chapters in this book have also demonstrated the importance of crossing disciplinary boundaries. Such disciplinary boundary-crossing is complicated by the fact that the different levels of phenomena that the various scientific disciplines deal with force them to adhere to different canons of proof. As I discussed more fully in an earlier volume in this series (Schooler, 1989), the concept of levels implies that phenomena are arranged hierarchically with respect to levels of integration, differentiation, and organizational complexity, with higher levels being more than simple quantitative accretions. They represent, instead, qualitative changes in complexity so that each new level has its own properties and principles. Because the characteristics of both more and less complex phenomena affect intermediate ones, a full understanding of a given level of phenomena (e.g., psychological functioning) requires knowledge both of its subordinate (e.g., neurobiology) and superordinate (e.g., sociology) levels.

Although a variety of biological issues have been considered, much of the discipline-crossing in this volume has been between psychology and social science and among such social sciences as sociology and economics. In this spirit, the introductory chapter by myself, Leslie Caplan, and Gary Oates surveys the general findings in the fields of sociology and psychology relevant to understanding the impact of the workplace on elderly individuals and of elderly individuals on the workplace. In doing this we were able to marshal evidence that although older workers are more likely to react more slowly to novel situations and stimuli than are younger ones, age is generally not a particularly strong determinant of job performance. Underlying this general lack of effect of age on job performance may be older workers' higher levels of involvement and motivation to work. Our review also found numerous instances of macro-to-micro- and micro-to-macro-level influences elucidated in the Aging and Society paradigm developed by the group of scholars centering around Matilda Riley (1994). As Riley makes clear in her comments on our chapter, it is only through the interdisciplinary understanding of the reciprocal causal connections between these different levels of phenomena, as well as of the processes and structures involved in each, that we can grasp what takes place when humans age. The importance of an interdisciplinary approach is also a central theme of William Hoyer's discussion of our chapter. He concludes "that research on the impact of work on older individuals is an area without disciplinary borders" (p. 38). His comments actually represent a full review of the relevant literature on the interactive effects of the aging individual and changing work contexts from the points of view of developmental and cognitive psychology.

Interdisciplinary and cross-level issues are also at the center of the second chapter in this volume—Chikako Usui's discussion of Japanese strategies for older workers. In her chapter, Usui shows how gradual retirement is a principal way of dealing with older workers in Japan and presents an institutional embeddedness explanation for the prevalence of this approach. She argues that although the corporate and government policies that foster such an approach reflect Japanese cultural values, it is the configuration of Japanese institutions that holds these cultural figures in place.

Both Kalleberg and I, in our respective comments on Usui's chapter, raise questions about the historic origins and future of these institutional practices and structures. Although our emphases differ somewhat, each of us is concerned with how more micro-level psychological processes and more macro-level cultural and economic ones have affected the relevant institutions in the past and may change them in the future. Here too, understanding what happens to the elderly requires that we pay attention to the findings of a variety of disciplines that deal with a range of phenomena.

David Ekerdt's chapter on workplace norms for the timing of retirement "is written to support a view of individual retirement behavior as a course of action embedded in the structure of work" (p. 101). In calling attention to how workplace norms about the timing of retirement function as "a mechanism by which work structures convey people out of their work careers" (p. 101), his sociologically oriented chapter runs counter to the economics-based rational choice model that envisions the process of deciding to retire as a calculation of the relative costs of work and leisure.

In his comments on Ekerdt's chapter Mark Hayward raises several sociological questions about Ekerdt's usage of the term "norm." He notes that the survey question on which Ekerdt bases his discussion of norms asks about the "usual" retirement age for those who work with the respondent or have the same kind of job. Hayward suggests that such a definition leaves out two criteria that are often seen as integral to the concept of norms—the feeling of "oughtness" and the application of sanctions to deviants. In his comments on Ekerdt's chapter, Harvey Sterns, in line with the cross-disciplinary approach of the volume, discusses a variety of historical, economic and individual psychological factors that may, in addition to workplace norms, affect the decision to retire.

Farr, Tesluk, and Klein's chapter focuses on the relationship between organizational structures and practices and the older worker. The authors use a systems-theory-based model to integrate a range of findings. The outermost layers of the model are characterized by macro factors, such as organizational design, structure, and strategy, which delimit the organization's technological, work, and personnel practices. These policies and practices are experienced by older workers through their effect on the task requirements, supervisory procedures, and group norms of their immediate work environment. At the core of the model is the older worker who is definitely affected by the organizational system and its changes, but whose personal qualities (e.g., knowledge, skill, personality) interact with the organization's characteristics to affect performance, behaviors, and attitudes.

Gerald Straka's comments on this chapter stress the importance of continuous, and especially self-directed, learning over the work life as a strategic parameter that aids the worker in coping with organizational change. In his comments, Victor Marshall suggests that the systems model is incomplete. At the macro level, he argues for the extension of the model to include consideration of governmental policies and the global socioeconomic system. At a more micro level, he calls for more attention to be paid to the unintended consequences of corporate policies and programs that differentially impact older and younger workers.

Aage Sørensen's chapter blends sociology and economics. In it, he examines the effects on the older worker of employment in three different labor markets: (1) spot labor markets in which workers are hired for a particular job for a particular length of time, (2) job competition markets in which workers stay with a particular firm in a particular job, and (3) promotion systems in which workers are hired by a firm with the expectation that they will spend their careers in that firm and be promoted as they gain skills and experience. Sørensen deduces how the individual's career trajectory and retirement pattern would be differentially affected by working in these different sectors and then details the economic and psychological consequences of such employment for older workers.

In his comments, Thomas Juster provides an economist's perspective on Sørensen's views. He also notes that a move with age from full-time to part-time work is what would be expected on the basis of standard economic analyses of labor decisions and suggests that the reason more workers do not do so may be the absence of part-time market opportunities.

Ann Howard's commentary links Sørensen's theorizing to the findings of an extensive research program on the careers of telephone company managers while also describing some new employment systems that may be emerging with the development of new computer technologies and a worldwide information economy.

Peter Warr's chapter begins with an elaborate conceptualization of the parameters of mental health and a summary of the literature on employment status and mental health, particularly among the elderly. He then goes on to isolate a series of "psychologically desirable" environmental conditions (e.g., opportunity for control, variety, environmental clarity) that may be linked to mental health and examines how the occurrence of various levels of these conditions may specifically affect the mental health of older workers. While doing all of this, Warr remains keenly aware, on the one hand, of biological-level phenomena such as those that can lead to lower levels of cognitive function with age, and, on the other hand, of such possible social and historical influences as cohort effects.

James House's commentary recognizes the impressiveness of Warr's overview and conceptual synthesis of the empirical regularities that have emerged from the study of age, work, and well-being. He does, however, call for a further examination of several questions. One of these is the nature and meaning of work in this area of study. It arises from the findings of Warr and others that retirement from paid work has on average no deleterious effects on mental health. House suggests that the relative mental health of nonemployed people of all ages, including the retired, may reflect the fact that many of them are working, though not for pay, carrying out such productive activities as household work, voluntary organizational activities and informal assistance to family and friends. Retired older persons, in particular, may be doing amounts and types of work they have voluntarily chosen and that may tend to be characterized by those conditions of work that Warr suggests are conducive to well-being.

Other of House's concerns are more historical and sociological. One is that most of the studies on which Warr's conclusions are based are cross-sectional, although the conclusion he draws are really about changes within individuals or cohorts as they age. The second is that racial–ethnic and socioeconomic differences in how work and retirement affect the elderly need more examination. The latter point takes on added significance because House (1977) was one of the pioneers in defining the whole area of research on social structure and personality.

House's concern for how an elderly person's position in the social structure influences the way that his or her psychological functioning is affected by immediate environmental conditions such as the nature of work reflects the complexity of the causal connections between levels of phenomena. It is the acknowledgment of just such complexity that has led to the disciplinary boundary crossing that has marked all of the papers at this meeting. In terms of practical policy, only if we are open to such boundary crossing will we be able to come to an understanding of the impact of work on the elderly that will benefit them. In terms of basic knowledge, it is only through such crossing of disciplinary bounds that our examination of work and the elderly will help us come to an understanding of how different levels of biological, psychological and social phenomena affect each other.

REFERENCES

House, J. S. (1977). The three faces of social psychology. *Sociometry, 40*, 161–177

Schooler, C. (1989). Levels and proofs in cross-disciplinary research. In D. I. Kertzer & K. W. Schaie (Eds.), *Age structuring in comparative perspective.* Hillsdale, NJ: Erlbaum.

Subject Index

Adult education (*see* Education)

Age
  composition
    shifts in, 3
  differences, 7, 9, 35, 40, 260, 267,
      269–270, 272, 279, 285,
      299–300
    in cognitive speed, 8
    in training effectiveness, 7, 9
    in well-being, 299–300
  effects, 7, 8, 11–13, 35, 132, 139,
      153–154, 178, 203, 205,
      264, 306
    in job satisfaction, 11–12
    of women, 11
  limits (Japanese "teinen"), 52–55,
      57, 65, 76–77, 93, 95
  norms, 120–132–133, 140, 197,
      201, 203, 214
  neutrality, 4–5
  and withdrawal behaviors,
      147–149, 153–154
  and work, 146–147
    attitudes, 29, 147–149, 153
    performance, 29, 32–37,
      146–153, 196
Age discrimination (*see*
    Discrimination)
Age Discrimination in Employment

Act of 1967 (ADEA), 4,
    144–145
Age-grading of jobs, 169–172, 218,
    263–364, 268, 270, 272,
    275–277, 280, 284 –286
Age–job (work) performance
    relationship, 144, 149–150,
    152–153, 165, 169, 171, 306
  norms, 165–166, 170, 197, 201,
    203
Age–performance relationship, 144,
    165, 169
Age-related
  attitudes, 10, 146, 153, 178
  behaviors, 3
  changes, 33–36, 38, 216
    in mental capacity, 219
    in productivity, 211
    in work performance, 29, 37, 39
  decline, 6, 8, 10, 133–136,
    139–140, 169, 200, 267
    in late life in memory, 29, 169,
    219
  decrements
    in cognitive functioning, 6–8,
    10, 200, 239
    in tasks, 6
  deficits, 34–35
  differences

Author Index